THE FIRST
INDUSTRIAL SOCIETY

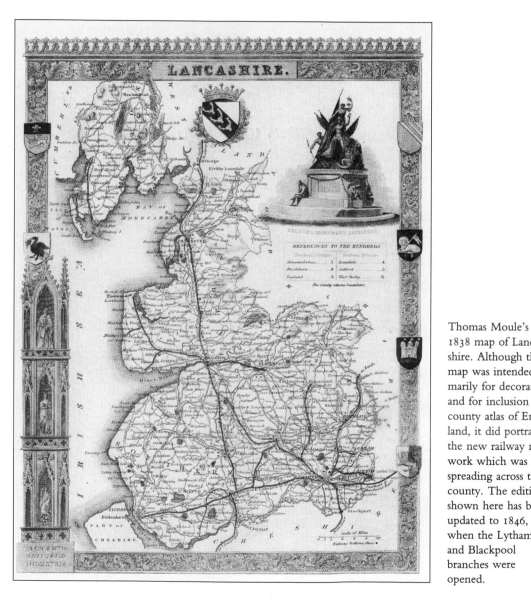

Thomas Moule's 1838 map of Lancashire. Although this map was intended primarily for decoration, and for inclusion in a county atlas of England, it did portray the new railway network which was spreading across the county. The edition shown here has been updated to 1846, when the Lytham and Blackpool branches were opened.

The First
Industrial Society

Lancashire, 1750–1850

CHRIS ASPIN

Carnegie Publishing, 1995

THE FIRST INDUSTRIAL SOCIETY,
LANCASHIRE, 1750–1850

Chris Aspin

First edition published by the
Helmshore Local History Society, 1969

This revised edition published 1995 by
Carnegie Publishing Ltd,
18 Maynard Street, Preston PR2 2AL

Designed and typeset in Monotype Bembo by
Carnegie Publishing
Printed in the UK by The Alden Press, Oxford

British Library Cataloguing-in-Publication Data
Aspin, Chris
  First Industrial Society: Lancashire 1750–1850
  — new edn
  I. Title
  942.7607
  ISBN 1-85936-016-5

Contents

The Triumph of Steam

I. *Mills and Chimneys*

N 1800 a lancashire man in middle life could observe the steam-driven cotton mills of Manchester and look back to the time when every thread in the country, and indeed the world, was spun by hand and when the steam engine was a crude and cumbersome machine used only for pumping water from a few mines. In little more than thirty years a spate of inventions, notably those of Hargreaves, Arkwright and Crompton, had transformed carding and spinning into factory processes to which Watt's rotative engine was increasingly being applied. British history had ceased to be the story of a small ruling class. No one could ignore for long the new merchants and manufacturers or the growing numbers of workers. Towns and villages were expanding, canals were being cut and roads turnpiked to meet the needs of the world's first industrial society. Lancashire, which had seen such astonishing changes, seemed ripe for many more.

The nineteenth century was the age of steam; but though the steam engine sped the growth of cities and became the driving force of industry and transport, its triumph was neither swift nor easy. Handloom weavers resisted angrily; the horse held out on many a canal towpath long after the stage coach had disappeared; and water power was a serious rival in the uplands of East Lancashire until the middle of the century.

The mill engine scored some of its earliest successes in Manchester, but in succumbing to steam the city was soon in danger of being suffocated by smoke. In May 1801, when eleven mill owners were summoned before the court leet for using steam engines which did not burn their own smoke, the steward was reported to have declared that:

> The furnaces of factories worked by steam were of a magnitude that wanted some prompt and effective remedy. The town was in every direction surrounded by them, and numbers were daily erecting in the midst of it. It was the subject of universal complaint, for the houses, the furniture, the persons and the clothing of the inhabitants were all contaminated and the health of thousands impaired by this

offensive and unsalutary nuisance, which if suffered to continue and increase would in a short time render the town unfit for the habitation of man.

In the countryside a steam engine was much more acceptable. Less than four months after the Manchester prosecution, Peel, Yates and Co., calico printers of Church Bank, near Accrington, who had previously used a water wheel, installed a steam engine 'of the greatest power' and were praised by the *Blackburn Mail* for a public-spirited act which 'will call forth the gratitude of many, the works having hithertofore been often stopped by frost and drought.' Many hundreds, the report added, would now have the satisfaction of having their work 'duly progressive without the least interruption.'

The introduction of the power-loom, which began the second great revolution in the textile industries, was marred by outbreaks of unrest,

The 62' diameter water wheel at the Egerton Mill of H. and E. Ashworth in 1848. It produced 150 horse power.

The significance of water power in the industrial development of Lancashire is often forgotten. In the early phases it was the most important power source, and its availability helped to determine when particular industries were located.

particularly during periods of distress. The natural antagonism of the handloom weavers was intensified by periods of acute distress and in 1812 and 1826 steam-driven weaving mills were attacked. The riots of April 1812, during which a cotton mill at Westhoughton was burned down and for which three men and a boy of 14 were executed, perhaps retarded the industrial development of that area. Some have argued that these events checked, for a time, the adoption of power-looms more generally, but others see the slow-down in their adoption as a consequence of the 'crowding out' of investment during the Napoleonic Wars. By April 1826, however, though they were regarded by some manufacturers as 'dangerous articles', power-looms had become sufficiently widespread to provoke a violent uprising by mobs of starving workpeople. Hardly a loom was spared in Blackburn, Accrington, Darwen and Rossendale, and others in Wigan, Bolton and Clitheroe were saved only because the mills were heavily protected. At Chatterton, near Ramsbottom, six rioters were shot by troops guarding a mill, but the looms were broken.

For some years an uneasy atmosphere prevailed and in May 1829, during another trade depression, the firm of Horsfall and Garnett, of Low Moor, Clitheroe, which had threatened to fire on the 1826 rioters with a cannon, were reported to be 'cutting a gulph of considerable width and depth around the outer wall of their premises which will be filled with water from the lodges belonging to their works. This when completed will render the place almost impregnable.' Low Moor's moated mill was certainly exceptional, but it is evidence of the lengths to which manufacturers were willing to go to ensure that steam powered their looms.

In the succeeding years, as improved looms were harnessed to larger and larger steam engines, domestic weaving and the use of water power steadily declined. By the 1870s, the handloom was almost extinct and the water-wheel a comparative rarity. Steam had conquered King Cotton.

The spread of the factory system, not only in textiles, but also in other industries, created an entirely new kind of urban landscape, above which, like dark forests, rose thick clusters of tall mill chimneys. Three at least deserve to be mentioned. In 1842, a chimney 367½ feet high was built at Blinkhorn's chemical works, Bolton, in the space of sixteen weeks, 'a circumstance,' said the *Bolton Chronicle*, 'unparalleled in the history of the World.'

> This splendid work of architecture [the account goes on] has excited the admiration of many engineers and scientific men . . . amongst whom may be named the Government Surveyors of Public Works, and has been pronounced by all, not only the largest, but also the handsomest octagonal chimney in England.

Before the chimney was put into use more than 4,000 people were wound up the inside four at a time in a basket to view the surrounding country from a platform on the top.

A beam engine of the type widely used in the early textile industry in Lancashire (illustration from J. Bourne, *A Treatise on the Steam Engine*, 1872).

By the 1830s most new mills were being powered by steam, although water power was displaced only gradually, particularly in areas such as the valleys of Rossendale.

Two years later work began at Mr Dobb's chemical works in Wallgate, Wigan, on a chimney that was to overtop, if not to outlast, its Bolton rival. Mr Dobb's chimney grew much more slowly than Mr Blinkhorn's, but its foundations were not as good, and when after two years it had reached a height of 435 feet, cracks began to appear near the bottom. The 'Mammoth Chimney', as it had come to be known, was rapidly reduced by a hundred feet or so, and a huge chain was tied around the base, but it was of no avail. In January 1847, 'the whole pile to the very bottom came down with a tremendous crash, blocking up the canal.' No one was injured, but a man who was near the canal bank 'was forced into the water, and from the swelling of the waves, was driven across to the other side.'

If Mr Blinkhorn's chimney could earn universal praise, what must one say of the astonishing structure which ascended 300 feet above India Mill, Darwen, in 1867? A chimney it was (and still is) but into the heart of Lancashire had come the campanile of Venice. The chimney cost £14,000 and the stone on which it stands was one of the largest ever quarried. A special road had to be made from the quarry and thirty-five horses were needed to haul the block to the site.

Besides impressing the visitor with the grandeur of their chimneys, the industrial towns could also enchant them with the unforgettable sight of great mills shining in the darkness with the light of innumerable lamps. Phillips and Lee of Salford lit their factory with gas in 1805 and found that the cost was only £600 a year, compared with £2,000 spent previously on oil and candles. Other manufacturers followed suit and brought a new and unexpected beauty to a district that seemed about

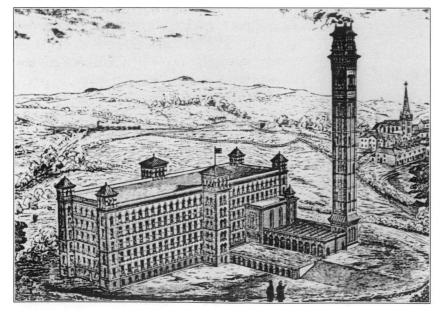

India Mill, Darwen, built 1864–8.

The later periods of mill building produced some extraordinary and daring designs, as professional architects were employed to create buildings which were decorative as well as functional. The breathtaking chimney of India Mill is perhaps the most remarkable architectural achievement of the whole industry.

to be overtaken by ugliness. When Hareholme woollen mill in Rossendale went over to gas, 'this mode of illumination was then so rare and thought so wonderful that visitors from all parts, for miles around, came to witness the unusual sight which it presented when lighted up at night.' And a Swiss traveller wrote from Manchester in 1814: 'It is impossible to describe the magnificent appearance of a mill with 256 windows all alight as though the most brilliant sunshine was streaming through them.'

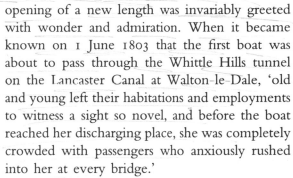

Horse power at work on the Bridgewater Canal in this romanticised engraving printed in Leo Grindon's *Lancashire, Brief Historical and Descriptive Notes* (1882).

The reality was less dramatic and atmospheric, and much more arduous. It is doubtful if whipping a barge-horse would have had much effect—these were slow and ponderous beasts, not racehorses.

2. *Great Days for the Horse*

While mill owners were quick to welcome steam, canal proprietors were content to rely on the horse. The first Lancashire experiment with a steam boat—on the Bridgewater Canal at Worsley in 1799—aroused more antagonism than support. The boat, nicknamed *Bonaparte* and *Owd Boney*, travelled no faster than a horse and the wash from her paddle wheel was seen as a danger to the canal banks. There were few regrets when she sank, though, in fairness, it should be mentioned that the engine was so primitive that moss and horse dung were needed to pack the cylinder. With the sinking of *Owd Boney*, the horse plodded on into a golden age of canals that was to last for forty years.

The early 1800s saw much canal building in Lancashire and the

opening of a new length was invariably greeted with wonder and admiration. When it became known on 1 June 1803 that the first boat was about to pass through the Whittle Hills tunnel on the Lancaster Canal at Walton-le-Dale, 'old and young left their habitations and employments to witness a sight so novel, and before the boat reached her discharging place, she was completely crowded with passengers who anxiously rushed into her at every bridge.'

The completion of the Rochdale Canal in December of the following year was fittingly marked:

The bells at Manchester commenced ringing at half-past two, and the company's passage boat and yacht were greeted from the banks, for a great distance, by an immense concourse of spectators, with many a vociferous cheer of grateful approbations, every person present seeming to feel a high degree of conscious pride and pleasure

at beholding this additional proof of commercial industry, genius and growing prosperity. The two vessels were filled with the gentlemen proprietors and their friends, attended by the band of the Fourth Class Volunteers, who continued to play many loyal and patriotic tunes; each gentleman, together with every servant and workman of the company wore in his hat a blue ribband, with the inscription in gold letters 'Success to the Rochdale Canal'. The gentlemen afterwards repaired to the Bridgewater Arms, where an elegant dinner was prepared for their entertainment. The day was remarkably fine and vast numbers of people lined both sides of the canal.

Towns many miles inland now began to take on the airs of seaports, and Blackburn, watching the advance of the Leeds and Liverpool Canal across East Lancashire, provided itself with a 'commodious stone warehouse . . . a basin so wide that six barges of 40 tons burden each may lie abreast, and three cranes to hoist the goods into the upper rooms.' When the canal was opened in June 1810, giving the town a direct link with Hull, the ceremony was so impressive that the *Blackburn Mail* declared, 'Never since this publication was first started has it been in the power of any editor to record so pleasant a scene.' Some twenty-seven vessels made the inaugural journey from Clayton-le-Moors and there were four bands on board to entertain the passengers. The *Mail's* account goes on:

A rural scene on the outskirts of Liverpool, around 1804. Two horses pull what appears to be a passenger vessel under Chisenhale Street bridge.

The towrope could be as long as 80′ and wore out quickly as it chafed on the bridge stonework. This may be why the vessel is being allowed to pass under the bridge using its own momentum, with a slack rope trailing in the water. (Lancashire Record Office DP 175, reproduced by permission of the County Archivist).

Canals stimulated industrial development in many areas, as here at Blackburn.

The gateway on this photograph leads directly on to the wharf of the Leeds & Liverpool Canal, and coal was still unloaded manually into the early years of this century – not through any particular reluctance to mechanise, but simply because no-one could invent a practical machine to unload canal barges (photograph courtesy of Blackburn Library Local Studies Collection).

When the procession approached near Blackburn, the vessels were much crowded by persons forcing themselves on board under the different bridges. On its arrival at Eanam, we suppose there were not less than 7,000 persons on the water. Multitudes kept pace with the vessels all the way . . . which, when joined to the great number of spectators assembled at Eanam, formed a concourse of at least 25,000 persons, besides the crowds on board the different vessels. Cheers from the water and from the land were constantly exchanged. Such an assemblage of people on such a happy occasion was never remembered in this trading and increasing town by the oldest inhabitant living. The day was very fine.

We are happy to say, no fatal accidents happened. A man on board one of the vessels at Eanam, imprudently thrusting a red-hot poker into the mouth of a small cannon, which was charged with powder and wadding, had his hand most dreadfully shattered. Two children and three men fell into the water during the passage. These were the only accidents worth noting.

For anyone with time to spare, a canal journey at the beginning of the nineteenth century was, as Robert Southey found, a delightful way of travelling. The proprietors of the Lancaster Canal, advertising a trip to the Preston Guild of 1802, fully agreed. 'For safety, economy and comfort,' they announced in the *Lancaster Gazetteer* of 21 August, 'no other mode of conveyance could be so eligible as packet boats; for

No 1827

66

CANAL PACKET BOATS
FROM LIVERPOOL,
TO
Crosby, Southport, Wigan, Manchester,
AND INTERMEDIATE PLACES,
DAILY.

THESE Boats, which possess very superior accommodations, leave the Canal Basin at Liverpool, for Bootle and Crosby, and return to the same place, Four times each day until the 1st of June next; when the extra Boat will, *as usual*, commence plying: from that time until the 1st of October, the communications to and from Liverpool and those places of fashionable resort, will be *Seven times each day*; to and from Southport, Wigan, Manchester, &c. once each day.

Carriages attend the Packets at Scarisbrick to convey Passengers to Southport, where they arrive from Liverpool at 12 o'Clock.

By these Boats Passengers arrive at Liverpool, Manchester, Bolton, Rochdale, Stockport, &c. *without the risk of the Tideway, or the frequent accidents attendant on Steam Boats.*

Arrival & Departure of Packets Daily, during the Summer Months.
(EXCEPT SATURDAY AND SUNDAY.)

Leave LIVERPOOL		Arrive at Bootle Hotel		Arrive at LITHERLAND		Arrive at CROSBY Opposite Hotel		Leave CROSBY Opposite the Hotel		Leave LITHERLAND		Leave Bootle Hotel		Arrive at LIVERPOOL	
	H. M.	H. M.		H. M.		H. M.		H. M.		H. M.		H. M.		H. M.	
Morning at 6	15	7	0	7	20	7	30	Morning 7	45	8	0	8	30	9	15
8	0	8	40	9	0	9	15	9	15	9	30	10	0	10	30
10	0	10	45	11	10	11	30	11	30	11	45	12	10	1	0
Afternoon 1	0	1	45	2	10	2	30	Afternoon 2	30	2	45	3	15	4	0
4	0	4	40	5	5	5	20	5	20	5	30	5	50	6	30
7	0	7	40	8	5	8	20	7	30	7	45	8	15	9	30
8	0	8	40	9	0	—	—	—		9	0	9	30	10	0
SATURDAY.								**SATURDAY.**							
Morning 6	15	7	0	7	20	7	30	Morning 7	45	8	0	8	30	9	15
8	0	8	40	9	0	9	15	9	15	9	30	10	0	10	30
10	0	10	45	11	10	11	30	11	30	11	45	12	10	1	0
Afternoon 1	0	1	45	2	10	2	30	Afternoon 2	30	2	45	3	15	4	0
4	0	4	40	5	5	5	20	7	30	7	45	8	15	8	30
7	0	7	40	8	5	8	20			9	0	9	30	10	0
SUNDAY.								**SUNDAY.**							
Morning 6	15	7	0	7	20	7	30	Morning 7	30	7	45	8	15	9	0
8	0	8	45	9	10	9	30	10	0	10	15	10	40	11	30
9	30	10	15	10	40	11	40	Afternoon 2	30	2	45	3	15	4	0
Afternoon 1	15	1	45	2	10	2	30	6	30	6	45	7	15	7	45
7	0	7	40	8	5	8	20	7	30	7	45	8	15	8	30
8	0	8	40	9	0	9	10	—		9	0	9	30	10	0

FARES.

ONE FAMILY,	To BOOTLE.	LITHERLAND.		To BOOTLE.	LITHERLAND.
4 Weeks	£1 4 0	£1 7 0	One PASSENGER, 1 Year, £7 0 0		£8 0 0
8 do.	2 0 0	2 12 0	Two do. 9 0 0		10 0 0
20 do.	4 10 0	6 0 0	Three do. 10 10 0		10 10 0
The Summer Months, from 1 May to 14 Oct.	6 0 0	8 0 0	Four do. 10 10 0		11 11 0

Subscribers to the LANCASHIRE WITCH to pay one-half additional for the use of the small Boat

MAY, 1827.

An 1827 advertisement for the canal packet service from Liverpool to Manchester and other destinations. There was actually an abortive scheme to build a canal branch from the Leeds & Liverpool to Southport, and a short section was begun just west of Burscough, but as this poster indicates passengers for the fast-growing seaside resort had to disembark at Scarisbrick and complete their journey by carriage.

This poster dates from the year after the final completion of the Leeds & Liverpool, but passenger services on the Lancashire sections had commenced considerably earlier than this (Lancashire Record Office, DP 175, reproduced by permission of the County Archivist).

there the timid might be at ease and the most delicate mind without fear.'

Southey, who travelled on the Bridgewater Canal from Manchester to London Bridge, near Warrington, said that the boats resembled 'the common representation of "Noah's Ark",' except that the roof was flatter for the convenience of passengers. His account goes on:

Within this floating house are two apartments, seats in which are

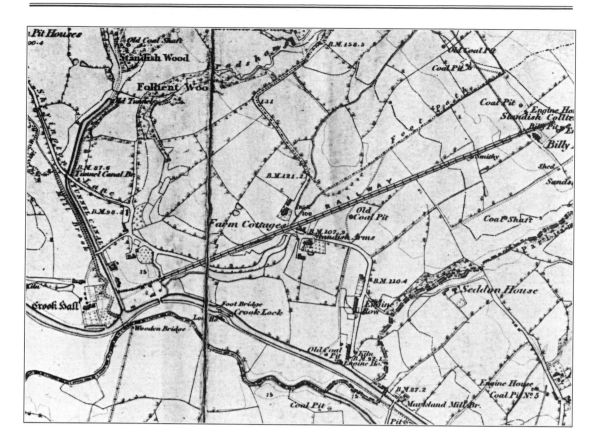

For many years canal and rail complemented each other in many industrial and mining locations, as at Crook on the River Douglas west of Wigan, shown here on the 1st edition Ordnance Survey map of the mid-1840s.

A 'railway' links Standish Colliery to the canal; while a 'tunnel canal' is shown running north under Standish Wood.

Note the large number of 'coal pits' scattered across the district.

hired at different prices, the parlour and the kitchen. Two horses, harnessed one before the other, tow it along at the rate of a league [four miles] an hour; the very pace which it is pleasant to keep up with when walking on the bank. The canal is just wide enough for two boats to pass; sometimes we sprung ashore, sometimes stood up or sat upon the roof, till, to our surprise, we were called down to dinner, and found that as good a meal had been prepared in the back part of the boat while we were going on as would have been supplied at an inn. We joined in a wish that the same kind of travelling were extended everywhere; no time was lost; kitchen and cellar travelling with us; the motion was imperceptible, we would neither be overturned or run away with; if we sunk there was not depth of water to drown us; we could read as conveniently as in a house, or sleep as quietly as in a bed.

The packet boats which plied between Bolton and Manchester also inspired affection. A correspondent of the *Bolton Free Press* remembered them 'tug-tugging away for three hours and a half, per power of a shuffling nag that, splashed up to its knees in mud, paced along the canal side, rudely prompted to its duty by the application of [a] tough hazel twig wielded by a rustic youth whose artless song and whistle proved that he was quite happy in his position.' Travellers from Bolton embarked at the Bull and Wharf and

upon the sounding of the long rusty horn, which was the signal of departure, what a movement of kindred spirits was there; friends shaking hands—lovers exchanging handkerchiefs, and filial and parental affection mingling tears; all deeply impressed with a sense of the hazardous voyage to Manchester. 'Time and tide wait for no man.' No more did Captain Barnes and the packet. The moment is come; dearest friends must part. The horse or horses are yoked, the bold captain proudly seizes the helm; he nothing daunted, gives the signal to move, the lad applies his stick or whip to the horses' posteriors, croaking out at the same time 'Ge-ho, come up' and off we go, ploughing the watery main.

The passengers, a motley group, are not long silent, but soon begin their various time-beguiling chit-chat. In one corner the politician would be loud with matters relating to the State; in another, our Bolton manufacturers would be discussing the nature of yarns and cloth, giving opinion as to the nature of trade, etc; in another part of our vessel some were enjoying themselves with song and sentiment; others were playing at fox and geese; old people talking of their experience and wisdom—young folk laughing at them; here a boy munching an Eccles cake; there a little child blowing a whistle and now and then an occasional roar from our captain would be heard, warning our upstanding passengers to beware of their heads coming in contact with an arch of a bridge.

3. *The Wheels Start to Turn*

The Manchester and Bolton packet boats continued until 1845 when the railway, which did the journey in one seventh of the time, forced them out of business. It was a fate foreshadowed by Southey 40 years earlier after his own voyage in Lancashire:

Excellent as canals are, rail-roads are found to accomplish the same purpose at less expense . . . These roads are always used in the neighbourhood of coal mines and foundries. It has been recommended by speculative men that they should be universally introduced, and a hope held out that at some future time this will be done and all carriages drawn along by the action of steam engines erected at proper distances. If this be at present one of the dreams of philosophy, it is a philosophy by which trade and manufacturers would be benefited and money saved.

In February 1804, only a few months after Southey's remarks were published, Richard Trevithick ran the world's first locomotive at the Penydarren iron works, near Merthyr Tydfil, and four years later tried to fire the imagination of Londoners by offering them shilling rides on a circular railway at Euston Square. Both locomotives came to grief on unsuitable rails and any serious introduction of steam traction seemed likely to remain a 'dream of philosophy' until the Napoleonic wars drove the price of fodder so high that a number of the North Country mine owners saw there were advantages in using on their railways mechanical horses which they could 'feed' cheaply on coal. John Blenkinsop, manager of Middleton Colliery, near Leeds, led the way in 1811 and was quickly followed by Robert Daglish, his opposite number at Orrell Colliery, near Wigan. On both lines the locomotives were driven by a cog wheel which meshed with a toothed rail beside the track. The system was patented by Blenkinsop, who believed the locomotive's smooth wheels could not grip the rails sufficiently when a heavy load was being hauled up an incline. Daglish claimed that his engines—he built three between 1812 and 1816—saved £500 a year and gave good service for 'upwards of 36 years'. From the action of their two upright pistons and the 'hard breathing' noise made by the escape of steam at each stroke the locomotives were nick-named 'walking horses', but they could travel at five or six miles an hour and draw 90 tons on the level.

The introduction of the locomotive into Lancashire coincided with a renewed interest in steam boats. Canal proprietors still regarded them with suspicion, but their ability to operate regular river and coastal services which no sailing ship could undertake was coming to be realised. In June 1815 the 'public curiosity' of Merseyside 'was excited by the arrival of the first steam boat ever seen on our river.' She was the *Elizabeth*, built on the Clyde in 1812 and now bought by a young army officer to begin a ferry service between Liverpool and Runcorn. She was 59 ft long and able to carry about 100 passengers.

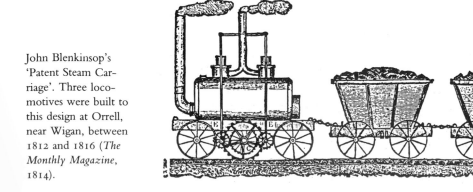

John Blenkinsop's 'Patent Steam Carriage'. Three locomotives were built to this design at Orrell, near Wigan, between 1812 and 1816 (*The Monthly Magazine*, 1814).

At least one canal company, the Ellesmere and Chester, was impressed and in the following year established, in the words of the *Chester Chronicle*, 'an elegant packet, worked by steam, to ply between Ellesmere Port [the termination of the canal] and Liverpool.' Describing the first experimental trip which was made in May, 'in the presence of an immense number of passengers and spectators', the newspaper said:

About half past ten, she [the *Countess of Bridgewater*], set out from Liverpool townside, in the direction opposite to her intended course, to prove her power against the run of the spring tide and adverse wind. Under these very unfavourable circumstances she proceeded nearly a mile with astonishing steadiness and celerity, to the entire satisfaction of every person present. She then commenced her voyage and performed it, without the assistance of a sail in one hour and five minutes: the engines making twenty-five strokes per minute, its general rate being thirty. It is impossible for us to give an adequate idea of the majestic movement of this novel machine, of the elegance of its structure, of the convenience it possesses for passengers: its principal cabin is spacious, elegantly furnished for a large party; there is a handsome private apartment for ladies, in taste and accommodation superior to anything we ever saw on the river. We are informed she is 90ft long, 31ft across from side to side and impelled by a power equivalent to thirty two horses or 180 men.

Before the end of 1816 the ferry boats were being called on to tow sailing ships out of the harbour and in 1817 the *Aetna*, a Liverpool-built boat, began a ferry service between Liverpool and Tranmere. But in

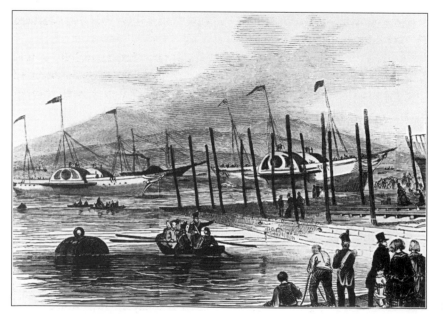

In the eighteenth and early nineteenth centuries Liverpool was still a significant ship-building centre, although eventually the industry dwindled away. This engraving shows the launch of two paddle-steamers in about 1840.

spite of these achievements there were some on Merseyside who preferred horse power to steam power. 'A new packet,' the public were informed in June 1818, 'worked by horses instead of steam and named the *Safety*, sails daily from Liverpool to Runcorn, lands and takes in passengers and luggage at Weston Point and returns to Liverpool with the same tide.' If the vessel's name was intended to hint to travellers that they were taking unnecessary risks by sailing on the newfangled steam boats, the plan failed, and the *Safety*, aboard which the horse plodded in a circle to turn a wheel, was soon withdrawn from service.

Ships using both sails and paddle-wheels were now beginning to undertake longer voyages and the first vessel of this type to cross the Atlantic, the *Savannah*, reached Liverpool in June 1819, 26 days after leaving the American port from which she took her name. By the end of the year steam-assisted ships were leaving Liverpool regularly for Glasgow, Belfast and Dublin; and the Liverpool public were being offered, for 1*s.* 6*d.*, copies of a new comic song *The Adventures of a Steam Packet*, 'as sung by Mr Tayleure of the Theatre on the Benefit Night.'

Further up the Lancashire coast, however, steam boats were unknown until 1822, when the *Duke of Lancaster* began a service between Liverpool and Ulverston via Hest Bank. On her first voyage she called at Bare, now part of Morecambe, and 'being the first steamer that has appeared on this part of the coast, a large number of persons assembled to see such a truly *nouvelle* sight.' At Lancaster in January 1826 a crowd of 6,000 gathered to see the *John o'Gaunt* steam packet, but she was twice grounded on approaching the port. In June 1828 the *St David* reached Preston 'to the gratification of many spectators who were anxious to witness the arrival of the first steam boat that ever entered the Ribble.'

It was intended that the *St David* should take holidaymakers to and from Lytham during the bathing season, but so few people boarded her the next morning that the scheme was abandoned. It was cheaper to go by coach.

4. *Dangerous Coaches*

As the roads of Lancashire were improved, the number of stage coaches grew rapidly, though many years went by before some towns had sight of one. In June 1815, while the inhabitants of Liverpool were watching the first steam boat to sail on the Mersey, the inhabitants of Accrington were hailing the first stage coach to travel between Manchester and Clitheroe. 'Drawn by four gaily bedecked and caparisoned horses,' and

A nostalgic and romanticised view of stage-coaches racing. The reality was reckless and dangerous. A print from Stephen Clarke's *Clitheroe in The Old Coaching Days*, 1897.

An early nineteenth-century engraving of Market Street, Manchester, with the banking house of Cunliffes, Brooks and Co. in the background, and, on the left, a heavily laden stage coach (*Lancashire Illustrated in a Series of Views . . .*, 1829).

followed by hundreds of people the coach was 'greeted with shouts of delight' and the people left their work 'to cheer lustily' as it passed.

Competition on the roads grew keener year by year, but it was not always to the traveller's benefit. The *Liverpool Mercury* of 25 April 1817 declared:

The rate at which the coaches between Liverpool and Manchester are driven ought to be the subject of magisterial investigation. Last week we are assured that one of them arrived from Manchester at

Lowhill, Liverpool, in two hours and a half, averaging about 14 miles in the hour, or twice the speed of the mail.

One is not surprised to read in the same newspaper less than a month later that a man had been awarded £750 damages for injuries received when the Liverpool coach overturned at Prescot.

From all parts of the country came reports of coaches racing one another, often with disastrous results. A Preston man, in a letter to a local newspaper in February 1828, said that the Manchester coaches, their horses flogged all the way from Bolton, were reaching Preston 35 minutes before time. 'If nothing else will answer,' he concluded, '*steam*, I hope, will shortly blow them all up.' The rapid advance of coaching was summarised by the *Preston Chronicle* of 5 June 1830:

> About twenty years ago we had a dozen coaches running in and out of this town daily and even then the country people used to wonder how it happened that there were so many persons 'in the wrong place.' Coaches were then travelling about the rate of *six miles an hour.* and the animals doomed to drag them along were the objects of daily compassion by all those whose sensitive ears were disturbed by the 'cracking of whips and the rattling of wheels.' What must they now think? We have daily in and out of the town except some few that rest on a Sunday, no less than 67 coaches and the approaching bathing season is expected to add fourteen more to that number, making in all 87! And the average rate of running when on the road is little short of *ten miles an hour.*

5. *The Lancashire Witch*

Though stage coaches had reached their zenith, the Preston man who invoked the power of steam to blow them all up was about to see his wish fulfilled. Even as he was penning his letter of protest, a new locomotive designed by Robert Stephenson and far superior to any built previously was taking shape at the Stephenson family works in Newcastle-upon-Tyne. The *Lancashire Witch*, as she was named on joining the Bolton and Leigh Railway later in the year, was the first of a new breed of locomotives, whose speeds, as unexpected as they were gratifying, doomed the stage coach to a quick and total extinction. The tremendous public interest in the new-found power of steam may be judged from the *Bolton Chronicle's* report of the opening of the Bolton and Leigh Railway on 1 August 1828:

> Yesterday having been appointed for the opening of the Bolton to Leigh Railway, a vast concourse of people assembled at an early hour

for the purpose of witnessing this interesting and novel spectacle. In the morning, W. Hulton, Esq., of Hulton, gave an elegant dejeuner at his house to several scientific gentlemen from London, Birmingham, Liverpool, Manchester and various other towns who had come over to be present on the occasion. About a quarter past 12 o'clock the new locomotive constructed by Messrs Stephenson and Co., of New-castle-upon-Tyne, started from Pendlebury Fold, near Hulton Park. Six waggons were attached to the engine completely filled with gentlemen; also a coach of beautiful structure in which we observed Mr and Mrs Hulton and several other ladies and which is intended at some future period to convey passengers on the railway. A number of gentlemen were also upon the roof. Next followed seven other waggons containing ladies and gentlemen and Bolton Old Band. The whole weight attached to the engine could not be less than 40 tons. With this immense weight it proceeded at the rate of seven miles an hour with apparent ease. On the top of each waggon as well as the engine and coach, flags and various colours were flying. The Committee wore green favours in their breasts and the workmen employed by the company had their hats decorated with ribbons. The scene was altogether most lively and animated. When the procession arrived at the stationary engine which is situated a little above the Pike, it halted and the locomotive engine was detached from the coach and waggons and despatched back to one of Mr Hulton's collieries for six waggons laden with coals each containing 2 tons and some of the pieces weighing 12 cwt. Immediately on arrival of the engine with the coals, Mrs Hulton proceeded to perform the ceremony of giving a name to the engine, which after a neat and appropriate speech she called 'The Lancashire Witch'. The amiable Lady then presented a beautiful garland composed of roses and other flowers to one of the engineers who fixed it to the flue belonging to the engine. Several experiments were afterwards made in order to shew the speed at which the engine could travel without any weight being attached to it; and we do not hesitate to say that in one instance it moved at the rate of Twelve miles an hour.

The experiments being finished, the procession was moved down the railway by the stationary engine towards Bolton in the same order in which it was started. When passing under the bridge near Mr Carlile's house, a dense mass of people was standing against a wall under the bridge awaiting the arrival of the procession. From the condensed pressure of the crowd on both sides of the waggons several persons fell and three men were thrown under the wheels of the hindmost waggon, one of whom was severely injured.

The procession then moved on until within a short distance of Bolton, when the waggons and the coach were then separated and the horses were put to each for the purpose of conveying them the remainder of the distance to Bolton, but the populace actually took away the horses and drew the vehicles and their contents to the termination of the railway in Blackhorse Street.

The number of people assembled amounted at least to 40,000; and the windows and roofs of the houses and factories by which the procession passed were crowded with spectators and the cheers of this immense multitude added to the music of our Old Band produced a thrilling and enthusiastic feeling. On the arrival of the procession at the end of the line of road, the band struck up 'God Save the King', the populace being uncovered. When the grand national anthem was concluded the ladies and gentlemen walked in procession headed by the band to the Commercial Inn. Amongst the company assembled on the occasion we noticed several of the clergy and magistrates from the surrounding villages. The weather was extremely favourable and the day will be long remembered in Bolton and the neighbourhood with feeling of the highest and most pleasing gratification.

The locomotive engine, we understand, weighs about 7 tons; its movements are remarkably steady and silent, which elicited from all who saw it the most unqualified testimony and approbation to its construction and operation.

6. Rainhill Shows the Way

The *Lancashire Witch* was the prototype of the *Rocket*, winner of the contest organised at Rainhill in October of the following year by the directors of the Liverpool and Manchester Railway. The 'Grand Mechanical Competition' (to borrow a headline from the *Mechanics' Magazine*) was a glorious moment in the history of steam power. The performance of the locomotives awed and astonished the spectators and left them in no doubt that they had witnessed an event that would change the face and habits of the world.

The *Liverpool Courier* sets the scene on the first day of the contest:

The running ground was on the Manchester side of the Rainhill bridge, at a place called Kenrick's Cross, about ten miles from Liverpool. At this place the rail-road runs on a dead level and formed a fine spot for trying the comparative speeds of the carriages. The Directors had made suitable preparations for this important as well as interesting experiment. For the accommodation of the ladies who might visit the course (to use the language of the turf) a booth was erected on the south side of the rail-road, equidistant from the extremities of the trial ground. Here a band of music was stationed, and amused the company during the day, by playing pleasing and favourite airs. The Directors, each of whom wore a white ribbon in his button hole, arrived on the course shortly after ten o'clock in the forenoon, having come from Huyton in cars drawn by Mr Stephenson's locomotive steam carriage [the *Rocket*], which moved up the inclined plane from thence with considerable velocity. Meanwhile, ladies and gentlemen in great numbers arrived from Liverpool and Warrington, St Helens and Manchester, as well as from the surrounding country, in vehicles of every description. Indeed, all the roads presented scenes similar to those which roads leading to race-courses usually present during the days of sport. The pedestrians were extremely numerous and crowded all the roads which conducted to the race-ground. The spectators lined both sides of the road for the distance of a mile and a half; and although the men employed on the line, amounting to nearly 200, acted as special constables, with orders to keep the crowd off the course, all their efforts to carry their orders into effect were rendered nugatory by the people persisting in walking on the ground. It is impossible to form an estimate of the number of individuals who had congregated to behold the experiment, but there could not, at a moderate calculation, be less than 10,000. Some gentlemen even went so far as to compute them at 15,000.

The public houses in the vicinity were crowded, particularly the Rail-road Tavern at Kenrick's Cross, where the landlady 'very prudently reserved one room for the better class of visitors' who were offered boiled beef and roast mutton at 3s. a portion. Among the better class of visitors may be numbered the 'scientific gentlemen and practical engineers' who, said *The Times*, 'were drawn from all parts of the Kingdom to witness the amazing utility of rail-

The *Novelty*.

The *Sans Pareil*.

The not-too-serious *Cycloped*.

The *Rocket*

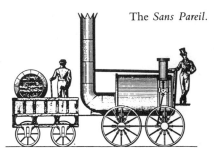

The *Perseverance*.

ways in expediting the communication between distant places.' The locomotives in the competition were the *Rocket* (yellow and black with a white chimney); the *Novelty* (copper and blue), built by Braithwaite and Ericsson of London; the *Sans Pareil* (green, yellow and black) built by Timothy Hackworth, of Darlington; and the *Perseverance* (red wheels) built by Timothy Burstall, of Leith. There was also the *Cycloped*, built by T. S. Brandreth, of Liverpool, and powered by two horses walking on an endless moving belt. Neither the *Cycloped* nor the *Perseverance*, which gave a belated and feeble performance, was taken very seriously.

Soon the locomotives were 'surprising and even startling the unscientific beholders by the amazing velocity with which they moved along the rails.' During the afternoon, the *Rocket* reached 24 m.p.h., 'shooting past the spectators and dropping red hot cinders as it proceeded.' The *Novelty* was even more impressive and according to the *Courier*, 'was universally allowed to exhibit in appearance and compactness the *beau-ideal* of a locomotive engine.' The account goes on:

> Its performance, whilst exercising without a load was most astonishing, passing over a space of 2¾ miles in seven minutes and a quarter, including a stoppage. With this delay its speed was about 23 miles an hour. While running, the progress was upwards of 28 miles an hour. The velocity at which it moved surprised and amazed every beholder. It seemed, indeed, to fly, presenting one of the most sublime spectacles of human ingenuity and human daring the world ever beheld. It actually made one giddy to look at it, and filled thousands with lively fears for the safety of the individuals who were on it, and who seemed not to run along the earth, but to fly, as it were, on 'the wings of the wind'. It was a most sublime sight—a sight, indeed, which the individuals who beheld it will not soon forget.

As the trials continued the locomotives performed even greater miracles. On the fifth day, the *Novelty* achieved what the *Courier* described as the 'inconceivable' speed of 35 miles an hour while hauling 45 passengers. One of them was the correspondent of the *Mechanics' Magazine*, who wrote: 'We can say that we never enjoyed anything in the way of travelling more . . . though the velocity was such that we could scarcely distinguish objects as we passed them.'

The *Novelty* seemed certain to win the £500 prize when it was beset by mechanical difficulties and had to withdraw from the contest. The *Rocket* was declared the winner, though the *Novelty* gained what the *Liverpool Albion* called 'the grand prize of public opinion' and the support of 'nine tenths of the engineers and scientific men' who watched the trials.

After Rainhill, the future of locomotives was assured and the country looked eagerly to Lancashire to see what feats they would accomplish next. There was not long to wait. Within a few weeks of the contest, the *Rocket*, after 'considerable alteration, which greatly increased its powers,' drew a 20-ton load at 18–20 miles an hour and then a 42-ton load at 14 miles an hour. These were performances, said the *Liverpool Times*, 'which exceeded the warmest anticipations of the friends of locomotive carriages.'

Next it was the turn of the *Sans Pareil* which, on 1 December 1829, in just three and a half minutes, puffed its way to the top of a 1-in-30, three-quarter mile incline on the Bolton and Leigh Railway, normally worked by a stationary engine. The achievement, said the *Bolton Chronicle*, fully exceeded the expectations of its designer, Timothy Hackworth, who declared that he had 'never contemplated the idea of these engines running up an inclined plane.'

After its triumphant ascent, the *Sans Pareil* rather disgraced itself. It went on to Chequerbent, 'where Mrs Hulton and a few friends were waiting to have a ride as far as Bolton.' When they had gone about half way, a boiler plug was 'blown out with great violence . . . and the party and the engine were completely enveloped in one dense cloud of steam.'

7. *Thirty-Five Miles an Hour!*

Speeds of more than 20 miles an hour evoked a variety of sensations in the breasts of the first railway travellers. In November 1829 Thomas Creevey (1768–1834) the Whig politician and diarist, took a five-mile ride on the Liverpool and Manchester line in a carriage hauled by the *Rocket*. It was 'a *lark* of the highest order,' he wrote to a friend on the same day, but added, 'the quicket motion is to me *frightful*: it is really flying and it is impossible to divest myself of the notion of instant death to all upon the least accident happening. It gave me a headache which has not left me yet.'

The young actress Fanny Kemble, who accompanied George Stephenson on a trip from Liverpool in August of the following year, was captivated by the adventure and dashed off a delightful account:

> We were introduced to the little engine which was to drag us along the rails. She (for they make these curious little fire-horses all mares) consisted of a boiler, a stove, a small platform, a bench and behind the bench a barrel containing enough water to prevent her from being thirsty for fifteen miles,—the whole machine not bigger than a common fire engine. She goes upon two wheels, which are her feet, and are moved by bright steel legs called pistons: these are propelled by steam, and in proportion as more steam is applied to

The Railway Office, Liverpool, one of a series of engravings by R. Ackermann published soon after the opening of the Liverpool and Manchester Railway. Note the absence of platforms and the fact that passengers have to cross the tracks to reach the trains. Note also the sequence of three turntables or 'traverses', a useful device for reducing manoeuvres when locomotives were few and small.

the upper extremities (the hip-joints, I suppose) of these pistons, the faster they move the wheels: and when it is desirable to diminish the speed, the steam, which unless suffered to escape would burst the boiler, evaporates through a safety valve into the air. The reins, bit and bridle of this wonderful beast is a small steel handle, which applies or withdraws the steam from its legs or pistons, so that a child might manage it. The coals which are its oats, were under the bench, and there was a small glass tube affixed to the boiler, with water in it, which indicated by its fullness or emptiness when the creature wants water, which is immediately conveyed to it from its reservoirs. There is a chimney to the stove, but as they burn coke there is none of the dreadful black smoke which accompanies the progress of a steam vessel. This snorting little animal which I felt rather inclined to pat, was then harnessed to our carriage, and Mr Stephenson having taken me on the bench of the engine with him, we started at about ten miles an hour. The steam-horse being ill adapted for going up and down hill, the road was kept at a certain level and sometimes appeared to sink below the surface of the earth and sometimes to rise above it. Almost at starting it was cut through the solid rock, which formed a wall on either side of it, about sixty feet high. You can't imagine how strange it seemed to be journeying on thus, without any visible cause of progress other than the magical machine, with its flying white breath and rhythmical, unvarying pace, between these rocky walls, which are already clothed with moss and ferns and grasses; and when I reflected that these great masses of stone had been cut asunder to allow our passage thus far below the surface of the earth, I felt as if no fairy tale was ever half so wonderful as what I saw. Bridges were thrown from side to side across the tops of these cliffs, and people looking down upon us from them seemed like pigmies standing in the sky. We were to go only fifteen miles, that distance being sufficient to show the speed of the engine and to take us on to the most beautiful and wonderful object on the road. After proceeding through this rocky defile, we presently found ourselves raised upon embankments of ten or twelve feet high; we then came to a moss or swamp of considerable extent, on which no human foot could tread without sinking, and yet it bore the road which bore us. This had been the great stumbling block in the minds of the committee of the House of Commons; but Mr Stephenson had succeeded in overcoming it. A foundation of hurdles, or, as he called it, basket-work, was thrown over the morass, and the interstices were filled with moss and other elastic matter. Upon this the clay and soil were laid down, and the road *does* float, for we passed over it at the rate of five and twenty miles an hour, and saw the stagnant swamp water trembling on the surface of the soil on either side of us.

On the return journey,

the engine was set off at its utmost speed, thirty-five miles an hour, swifter than a bird flies (for they tried the experiment with a snipe). You cannot conceive what the sensation of cutting the air was; the motion is as smooth as possible, too. I could either have read or written; and as it was I stood up, with my bonnet off, 'drank the air before me.' The wind which was strong, or perhaps the force of our own thrusting against it, absolutely weighed my eyelids down. When I closed my eyes this sensation of flying was quite delightful, and strange beyond description: yet, strange as it was, I had perfect sense of security, and not the slightest fear. At one time, to exhibit the power of the engine, having met another steam engine which was unsupplied with water, Mr Stephenson caused it to be fastened in front of ours; moreover a waggon laden with timber was also chained to us, and thus propelling the idle steam-engine, and dragging the loaded waggon which was beside it, and our own carriage full of people behind, this brave little she-dragon of ours flew on. Farther on she met three carts which, being fastened in front of her she pushed on before her without the slightest delay or difficulty; when I add that this pretty little creature can run with equal facility either backwards or forwards, I believe I have given you an account of all her capabilities.

Fanny Kemble's description gives some idea of the magnitude of Stephenson's task in building the line over 31 miles of obstacle-filled country. It was an undertaking that probably no other engineer of the day could have carried through; yet Stephenson found time to concern himself with other railways while the work was going forward. He was mainly responsible for the Bolton and Leigh line and at the invitation of William Hulton, spent some time at Hulton Park. There, to widen his education, the man who has been called the father of railways often joined Hulton's sons when they took lessons from a visiting teacher during the school holidays.

8. *The Railway Age Begins*

Railways, in the modern sense of the word, began with the opening of the Liverpool and Manchester line by the Prime Minister, the Duke of Wellington, on 15 September 1830. It was perhaps the most remarkable day in Lancashire's history. Half a million people watched the procession; William Huskisson, MP for Liverpool, was killed by the *Rocket*; the distinguished guests were pelted by a mob and the Duke departed hastily from Manchester when the superintendent of police refused to guarantee his safety. The journey also inspired Tennyson, who was among the passengers and who believed the wheels ran in grooves, to pen the celebrated line: 'Let the great world spin for ever down the ringing grooves of change'—an expression of the belief in progress that was beginning to capture the imagination of many Englishmen at that time.

In the week before the opening Liverpool was 'crowded to overflowing and carriages stood in the streets at night for want of room in the stable yards.' The railway, said the *Liverpool Courier*, formed a general topic of conversation with all classes of the community and 'so intensely were the lower orders absorbed in the anticipations of the day, that if by common consent a holiday had not been talked of, few, very few, would have had sufficient resolution to pursue the toils of the day whilst the novel spectacle was exhibiting.' By early morning on the 15th 'vehicles of every description and crowds of gay and happy pedestrians' were heading for points of vantage. The heights above the Spekeland cutting

> were crowded with a dense body of individuals, all striving to obtain a glimpse of the preparations that were in progress in the deep chasm below, which were rendered increasingly interesting as the different carriages came in view of the spectators. Along the entire line, as far as the eye could reach, the heights and slopes on each side of the road, were thronged with individuals all in their holiday suits and gayest attire . . . The sports of the turf, with all their

An engraving of the 'steam engine manufactory and iron works, Bolton' from *Lancashire Illustrated*, 1829.

The works were owned by Rothwell, Hick & Co., and produced a wide range of industrial machinery as well as steam engines.

A large locomotive boiler is being moved around the site by a horse-drawn waggon.

allurements, afford no record of anything like a similar congregation of spectators.

As the 752 guests—'an assemblage of rank, wealth, beauty and fashion'—began to take their places in the 32 carriages, 'every elevation and building around was converted into an observatory, from which many an eager eye was bent; and female hearts seemed to have forgotten their timidity in anxious expectation, enlivening the house tops with their fair and smiling faces.'

One of the guests, the Rev. Edward Stanley, later Bishop of Norwich, described the scene as 'a compound of the Lord Mayor's show and Epsom races.'

It was like the jubilee of the Jews, when all grievances were forgotten; enmities and heart-burnings evaporated like smoke, and the very Quakers, throwing aside their gravity, looked as gay as larks, and joined in the general joyousness.

The excitement in Manchester was no less intense and as early as nine o'clock 'hundreds of persons were observed wending their way towards the Railroad.' *Wheeler's Manchester Chronicle* goes on:

As the morning advanced the streets in the Western part of the town became crowded by foot passengers, gentlemen on horse-back and parties in carriages and gigs. Towards twelve o'clock at least one hundred thousand persons had assembled within immediate view from the Company's warehouses, the whole of the elevated land in the vicinity being covered by men, women and children all anxious to obtain a sight of some part of the Railway . . . Numbers of individuals were elevated on the roofs of buildings, others had ventured to stand on the tops of water-tubs which had been covered

The celebrated skew bridge at Railhill was one of the many engineering marvels on the Liverpool and Manchester Railway. The novelty of 'watching the trains go by' is suggested by the spectators assembled on the bridge.

The Moorish Arch at Edge Hill, Liverpool was an attempt to disguise the stationary steam engines which operated the incline down to Lime Street station, opened in 1836. The cables of the incline can be seen in the foreground, while on the right a locomotive is being turned on the turntable.

for the purpose, and several elegantly-dressed ladies, at the risk of despoiling their flounces and furbelows had the temerity to look out from the top of a building in Water-street, part of the roof of which was stripped off in a trice for their special accommodation. On the whole line from Ordsall-lane to Eccles the assemblage was proportionably numerous, the fields adjoining the Railway and the various bridges being densely crowded with spectators.

For the Duke of Wellington and the principal guests, the company provided 'a costly and splendid car' 32 feet long and 8 feet wide and carrying 'a lofty canopy of crimson cloth' which rested on eight carved and gilt pillars. Ornamental gilt balustrades, 'handsome scrolls' and two ducal coronets which could be raised above the canopy added to the splendour. Inside a 'rich crimson covered ottoman' provided seats for 30 people and 'the whole,' said the *Courier* 'had a magnificent and imposing effect in the Grecian style of architecture.'

The Duke's carriage, two smaller ones of a similar design and an open car carrying a band were attached to the *Northumbrian*, and on the other set of lines were seven trains in the following order: *Phoenix* (five carriages), *North Star* (five carriages), *Rocket* (three carriages), *Dart* (four carriages), *Comet* (four carriages), *Arrow* (four carriages) and *Meteor* (four carriages).

At twenty minutes to eleven a signal gun was fired and 'the splendid cavalcade' moved off watched by 'myriads of spectators who looked down with rapture from both sides of the stupendous cutting.' The *Courier* reporter was also enraptured and he goes on:

> The procession must have been the grandest ever beheld, whether we consider the triumph of mechanical art which it exhibited, the engines moving 'like things of life', or the brilliant display of rank and talent, beauty and fashion which it contained. Then the splendour of the cars; the brilliance of the coaches and carriages; the neat elegance of the humbler vehicles in the form of open cars; the gay appearance of the variegated flags which fluttered in the breeze; the beauty of the engines, the men and boys who worked them dressed in the new blue livery of the company, faced with red, the words 'fireman' with the name of the machine to which they were attached appearing on their caps in red letters on a blue cloth ground; above all, the beauty, the variety and the extent of the cortege must have presented a most enchanting spectacle as it rolled majestically onwards.

After 'rushing' at 24 miles an hour through the Olive Mount cutting, the trains reached the open country, where 'vehicles of every description stood in the fields on both sides, and thousands of spectators still lined the margins of the road.' Grandstands had been specially built at several places, and below the Sankey Viaduct 'the fields were filled by thousands, who cheered us as we passed over the stupendous edifice. Carriages filled the narrow lanes, and vessels in the water had been detained in order that their crews might gaze up at the gorgeous pageant passing far above their mastheads.' Among the throng was a reporter of the *Preston Chronicle*, who said of the Duke's train, 'The movement was like that of a magnificent fairy temple, impelled by an unseen agency of a magic spell, filling the mind of the beholder with wonder and delight that cannot be expressed.'

One of the travellers was Fanny Kemble, who wrote of the journey:

> Enormous masses of densely packed people lined the road, shouting and waving hats as we flew by them. What with the sight and sound of these cheering multitudes and the tremendous velocity with which we were borne past them, my spirits rose to the true champagne height and I never enjoyed anything so much as the first hour of our progress.

Stanley was equally delighted. 'No words,' he wrote,

> can convey an adequate notion of the magnificence (I cannot use a smaller word) of our progress. At first it was comparatively slow; but soon we felt that we were indeed GOING, and then it was that every person to whom the conveyance was new, must have been sensible that the adaption of locomotive power was establishing a fresh era in the state of society; the final results of which it is impossible to contemplate.

At Parkside, the procession stopped to enable the engines to take on a fresh supply of water, but as the passengers walked about 'congratulating each other on the truly delightful treat they were enjoying . . . a murmur and an agitation betokened something alarming.' William Huskisson, MP for Liverpool, a former President of the Board of Trade, and a prominent advocate of the railway, had gone to shake hands with the Duke of Wellington when the *Rocket* came up quickly on the line on which he stood. Huskisson was told to stand clear, but he became confused, hesitated and then tried to reach the Duke's carriage. He was too late. The engine struck him and crushed his left leg.

As the dying man was placed in the musicians' car and taken at full speed by the *Northumbrian* to Eccles, deep gloom replaced the gaiety and shortly afterwards a thunderstorm added to the discomfort. While the *Northumbrian* went to Manchester to bring back any surgeons who might be among the crowd, the travellers at Parkside debated whether they should go on or return to Liverpool. The Duke wished to return, but when the Boroughreeve of Manchester warned him that the disappointed mass might react in an ugly way, he decided to continue. The *Phoenix*, the *North Star* and their carriages were joined together and were also linked by a chain to the Duke's train, which was towed to Eccles, where the *Northumbrian* was waiting. Deprived of their carriage, the bandsmen were left to return to Liverpool as best they could. 'I saw them,' said Stanley, 'picking their way homewards through the mud and mire.'

It was now half past one, but despite the long delay and the thunderstorm, huge throngs waited by the line. The monotonous surface of Chat Moss, said the *Courier*, 'was cheeringly broken up by villagers and whole families, with their store of provisions, some seated on benches, other round turf fires.'

The last six miles of the journey were made through what the *Courier* described as 'an avenue of living beings.' But now the cheers became increasingly interspersed with shouts of abuse and cries of 'No Corn Laws'. The vast crowd, said Fanny Kemble

> was the lowest order of artisans and mechanics, among whom great distress and a dangerous spirit of discontent with the Government prevailed. Groans and hisses greeted the carriage, full of influential personages, in which the Duke of Wellington sat. High above the grim and grimy crowd of scowling faces a loom had been erected, at which sat a tattered, starved-looking weaver, evidently set there as a *representative man*, to protest against the triumphs of machinery and the gain and glory which the wealthy Liverpool and Manchester men were likely to derive from it. The contrast between our departure from Liverpool and our arrival at Manchester was one of the most striking things I ever witnessed.

On reaching the three miles of cutting leading into Manchester the engine drivers were alarmed to see the track completely covered with people through which the trains moved 'as a stagecoach may sometimes be seen driving through a flock of sheep on a turnpike road. The carriages had to force their way through masses of the lower orders, including women and children, who, notwithstanding the presence and exertions of the police, danced across the road to the great terror of those in the procession who had the means of witnessing such daring and frightful experiments repeated.' Robert Stephenson, who was on the *Phoenix*, slackened speed, but as an eye-witness observed:

> Caution had its disadvantages; for the more reckless of the multitude caught hold of the carriages and climbed up their sides whilst they

The deep narrow cutting at Olive Mount, Wavertree, was excavated in solid rock and was one of the wonders of the age. Later widening of line has greatly reduced its impact, but something of the impression it gave can be appreciated by the present-day descent from Edge Hill to Lime Street Station.

were slowly rolling along. To complete the confusion, the political animosities of the mob broke out in acts of insults and violence and brickbats were aimed at the state carriages. Eventually the trains reached Manchester without accident or loss of life, but only to find the station occupied by another mob.

Taking on water at Parkside, the station where Mr Huskisson fell: the very basic passenger facilities shown in this view were typical of those on most early railways. The artist has greatly exaggerated the gauge of the track.

The long tunnel from Edge Hill to Wapping, under the densely-built city, gave access to Liverpool docks and was the world's first railway tunnel. Here, at the Wapping end, can be seen manual shunting of a wagon on the 'traverses' which crossed the running lines.

Some of the passengers fought their way to the company's warehouses, where a meal was waiting, but the Duke refused to leave his carriage and for more than an hour and a half 'kept the rioters in good humour by shaking hands with their women and children'. The situation, however, was rapidly getting out of hand. 'Numbers of highly-respectable gentlemen, whilst walking on the railway, were attacked by the mob, who threw lumps of clay, stones and other missiles,' and when the chief of the Manchester police learned that several thousand people were preparing to advance to the bridge near which the carriages were standing, he said that if the Duke did not leave immediately he would not answer for the consequences. At half past four, to the great relief of the police and company officials, the Duke's train and one other wormed their way out of Manchester.[*]

This sudden retreat upset the arrangements for the return of the six trains remaining. Three locomotives which had gone to Eccles for water were on the same line and in front of the Duke's train and since all but one crossover between the termini had been removed to ensure extra safety during the day, they had to go to Huyton before they could return to their original track. At twenty past five and in a heavy downpour the three engines and twenty-four carriages at Manchester were formed into one train, which worked its way through the throng and reached Eccles without mishap. Here it stopped while enquiries were made about Huskisson, but on restarting some of the coupling broke and strong ropes had to be sent for. At Parkside the train was met by the three other engines. Two were attached, but as it was now dark, the other, the *Comet*, was sent on in front and the crew were given instructions to signal any obstacles by swinging a lighted tar rope. The ascent at Rainhill proved too much for the train and all the men had to get out and walk up the incline. A little farther on, the pilot engine ran into a wheelbarrow which had been maliciously placed on the line and it was not until ten o'clock that the passengers alighted at Liverpool.

Only a few drunken fellows were there to cheer us, wrote the *Courier* reporter at the end of what he described as 'one of the most melancholy and disastrous journeys every performed.'

A month after the opening of the line, the *Manchester Chronicle* reported:

---

[*] On his return the Duke stopped at Eccles, where he and Lord Wilton found considerable confusion at the vicarage and could get nothing to eat. The two noblemen 'went to forage for something and found a leg of mutton in the larder. There was a very large old-fashioned kitchen with an immense fireplace and spit. The Duke turned the spit, cooked the mutton and no doubt was equal to the occasion.'—See Constance Pitcairn, *The Fife Pitcairns* (1905), p. 280. The author was the daughter of Canon Pitcairn, vicar of Eccles from 1861 to 1892.

The viaduct over the Sankey Canal and its valley, near St Helens, was another of the many remarkable engineering feats on the Liverpool and Manchester Railway. It was the first railway viaduct in the world.

No fewer than 14 stage coaches which travelled daily between this town and Liverpool have been withdrawn from the road, although the coach fares have been materially reduced . . . There are 12 daily coaches still upon the road, but it is not expected that the proprietors of these will long be able to compete with the railroad shareholders.

The merchants and manufacturers, who had promoted the railway because of the high cost and low speed of canal traffic, were soon reaping the benefits of their enterprise. In pre-railway days goods were often carried across the Atlantic more quickly than between the two cities. How different things were now, and with what satisfaction the directors must have read reports such as the following, which appeared in the *Manchester Chronicle* in January 1831:

Until very lately the arrivals at the Manchester station consisted of single engines, with from six to eight vehicles attached; but on Wednesday last a train came from Liverpool in 'linked' continuity, which in extent and tonnage surpassed those of every previous occasion. There were four engines, five coaches and passengers, and eighteen waggons containing upwards of 60 tons of goods! Friday, however, was the crowning affair. *Four* journeys were accomplished each way, *one* of which was performed by a connected train of three engines and twenty-four waggons, which brought to this town between 80 and 90 tons of goods!!

9. *Early Days*

Few regulations governed the running of trains during the early days of the Liverpool and Manchester Railway. Even the rule of road was sometimes waived, for when the company ran excursions to Newton Bridge soon after the opening, 'there were two trains, one on each line, and for the amusement of passengers, they arranged the speeds so as to pass each other frequently.' As Newton was the only station between the two cities, travellers on the ordinary trains were able to go to any point on the track and by waving an umbrella or handkerchief signal the engine driver to stop. There were also unscheduled halts for refreshments. At Eccles villagers waited for the trains with Eccles cakes, and public houses beside the line did a brisk business by sending out trays of drinks and cigars. On Chat Moss passengers were allowed to go to a public house to 'get a quiet glass and lunch' while the guard waited patiently for their return. It was soon obvious that these stage coach habits were unsuitable for a railway and, in March 1831, the directors announced that they were determined to prevent the supplying of liquor on the line and that in future there would be only sixteen stopping places. Moreover, only second-class trains would use them and passengers were asked to have their money ready to pay the guard.

The first rail travellers never knew quite what to expect once a tune played on a bugle had signalled the train to start. 'There have been occasions,' said a writer in 1832, 'when the railway was so slippery that there

Early Lancashire railways, 1828–1840		
1828	Bolton – Leigh	7¾ miles
1830	Liverpool – Manchester	32 miles
1831	Leigh – Kenyon Junction (L.M.R.)	2¾ miles
1831	Warrington – Newton le Willows	4½ miles
1832	Parkside (L.M.R.) – Wigan	7 miles
1833	St Helens – Runcorn Gap (Widnes)	8 miles
1836	Edge Hill – Liverpool Lime Street	1½ miles
1838	Salford – Bolton	11 miles
1838	Preston – Wigan	18 miles
1839	Manchester – Littleborough	15½ miles
1840	Manchester – Stockport	5½ miles
1840	Lancaster – Preston	20 miles
1840	Preston – Fleetwood	21¾ miles
1840	Preston – Longridge	6¾ miles

was no adhesion of the wheels to the rails and the passengers were obliged to alight and assist in pushing the carriage up the incline.' The engine drivers and firemen also had to contend with bad weather and smoke—there were no enclosed cabs—and an uncertain signalling system. Edward Entwistle, the first man to drive the *Rocket*—he made from two to four trips a day between Liverpool and Manchester—broke down under the strain after two and a half years and went to work on a coastal steamer. Sharing the engine crews' miseries were the third-class passengers, who were herded like cattle—and sometimes with cattle—in open waggons. 'When the train stops and starts,' said one early traveller, 'the jolting and bumping causes the greatest confusion amongst the passengers. The unwary and the intoxicated are sometimes thrown out on to the line.' Some idea of the discomforts endured in the first trains may be gained from the following account of a journey from Manchester to Leeds:

> The third-class carriages were big boxes, without seats and neck high. Children and people of small stature were monarchs of all they surveyed, and that was limited to the contents of the big box and the sky overhead. There were holes at the bottom of the box to let off rain water unabsorbed by the people's clothing, open umbrellas being an unendurable nuisance. Having thus passed through various tunnels pouring down floods of dirty water and behind a steam engine belching forth volumes of black smoke and showers of hot ashes, these heroic passengers, after an hour and three quarters in purgatory, safely arrived at their destination, but so wet, bedraggled and begrimed that they had first to recognise the anxious friends who met them, for their friends knew not them who had been metamorphised from whites to blacks during their exciting and perilous journey.

Overleaf (pp. 34–5). Riding on the railway. Four trains, each with different classes of passenger or freight. The very close resemblance between the first-class carriages (top) and contemporary road coaches is immediately apparent—they were, in effect, mail-type coaches on rails. Second- and third-class passengers rode in open wagons, exposed to the elements and—as observers often comment—not unlike the trucks in which cattle were transported.

One reads with some surprise a railway guide of 1838, which actually recommended travellers to take a place 'outside', in other words, on the carriage roof. 'You will want,' said the writer, 'an extra greatcoat and a pair of gauze spectacles to keep the dust and smoke out of your eyes.' Thus equipped the adventurer would see in comfort all the 'bustle and excitement' at the station and enjoy the journey ten times more than the 'inside' passengers, who were likely to be rocked to sleep by the 'gentle and composing' motion of the train.

Though the practice of carrying passengers on carriage roofs was soon abandoned, railways continued for many years to astonish their patrons. The Manchester and Bolton company decided to run its trains on the right, 'a circumstance,' said the *Manchester Guardian*, 'which caused some alarm' to one of the passengers at the opening in May 1838. 'After the train had gone half a mile he put his head out of a carriage window and called loudly to the guard, asking him if the train was on the right line.'

Drawn by J. Shaw, Liverpool.

Drawn by J. Shaw, Liverpool.

MARQUES OF STAFFORD RAILWAY COMPANY   MANCHESTER   LIVERPOOL   THE ASSURER   MANCHESTER   ROYAL MAIL

Aquat.ᵗᵉᵈ by S.G.Hughes

◦ outside Passengers.

Aquat.ᵗᵉᵈ by S.G.Hughes

◦h Cattle.

In March of the following year the directors of the Liverpool and Manchester Railway were surprised to learn that an 'unauthorised' locomotive had been running on their line. This was the *Bridgewater*, the first locomotive built by James Nasmyth, whose foundry at Patricroft adjoined the track. Nasmyth set out for a trial run after making arrangements with a very junior official who saw nothing unusual in the proceedings, but a more senior member of staff met the locomotive at Parkside and ordered the inventor to return to his works. In a letter of apology Nasmyth pointed out that while on trial the locomotive 'fell in with a disabled train and returned with it to Manchester' and added in a postscript: 'The engine took several trains of coal &c., and was made as useful as possible to the company.'

The rules and regulations of the Manchester, Bolton and Bury Railway Company, published in 1841, conjure up some delightful pictures of early railway practice.

Liverpool and Manchester
RAIL-WAY.

TIME OF DEPARTURE
BOTH
From Liverpool & Manchester.

FIRST CLASS, Fare 5s.	SECOND CLASS, Fare 3s. 6d.
Seven o'Clock Morning.	Eight o'Clock Morning.
Ten „ Do.	Half-past Two Afternoon.
One „ Afternoon.	
Half-past Four Do.	

⁎ For the convenience of Merchants and others, the First Class evening train of Carriages does not leave Manchester on Tuesdays and Saturdays until Half-past Five o'Clock.

The journey is usually accomplished by the First Class Carriages under two hours.

In addition to the above trains it is intended shortly to add three or four more departures daily.

The Company have commenced carrying GOODS of all kinds on the Rail-way.

January, 1831.

If it be required to warn an engineman or guard to stop a train [says Rule III] then the signal made for this purpose in the day time must be, to wave a red flag or a hat UP AND DOWN (up to the height of the head and then to the ground).

Rule XX, drawn up especially for use 'during fog or thick weather', instructed the engine driver, on stopping a passenger train in a station 'to send someone [his fireman, if necessary] to run back 400 yards behind the train, or so far as may be necessary to warn any coming engine, in order to prevent its running against the other.' The athletic fireman was also responsible for opening all the gates when an engine had to travel along the line at night.

A retired Preston engine driver, looking back to the 1850s, recalled:

Alongside the line at Scorton was a big field celebrated for its mushrooms and many times a train was stopped while the driver, fireman, guard and even passengers alighted to gather the edible. An extra spurt afterwards made up for lost time.

There were some odd scenes in stations, too.

The locomotives were not remarkable either for speed or power and in starting his train, especially with an extra coach or two, the driver had usually to request the services of the whole station staff,

A Liverpool and Manchester Railway poster of 1831.

The rather uncertain and vague indication of times and length of journey shows that the principles of strict timetabling had still not been adopted.

stationmaster included, to push at the side in order to give the engine a start.

This method indicated a resourcefulness lacking on 25 June 1840, when the Lancaster and Preston Junction Railway was opened. On that occasion, the engine attached to the eleven carriages containing 200 guests and 'Mr Harrison's band of music' was unable to pull away from Lancaster station and another had to be sent for to help.

A curious incident occurred in 1846 when a passenger train travelling from Preston to Fleetwood ran through a covey of partridges near Kirkham. One was caught in the cinderbox and soon afterwards, to quote the *Preston Guardian*,

> a savoury odour arose from the fowl undergoing the process of roasting under the bars of the engine fire. Arrived at Kirkham, the fireman stepped down to see how the partridge was getting on, and finding that it was cooked on one side only, he turned it over. On arrival at Poulton, he again inspected the prize and found it perfectly cooked. At Fleetwood, the engine driver and foreman sat down to a 'sumptuous repast' consisting of the partridge roasted in its feathers and without the least bruising, and which they declared was really delicious.

When a train arrived at Blackpool late one evening in August 1851, the people waiting on the platform 'were amused to see an ass emerge from a second-class carriage. We mean,' explained the *Preston Pilot*, 'a veritable four-legged ass, fully caparisoned with saddle and bridle. The animal appeared to belong to some gentleman on the train.'

Lancashire railway companies opened their new lines with understandable pride and were unstinting in the pains they took to make the ceremonies memorable and delightful. Into Rawtenstall on 25 September 1846 steamed a train which could hardly have failed to inspire the 'loud and long-continued cheering' with which it was greeted. Drawing 30 carriages—sky blue and bearing the East Lancashire Company's coat of arms—were two sturdy engines, their dark green boilers and polished brass domes and chimneys 'adorned with British Ensigns and Union Jacks.' In an open carriage was a military band, which enlivened the journey from Manchester with popular airs, though it had to compete against the sound of the church bells and 'the cheers of countless spectators who thronged the line on either side.' The 400 guests were entertained in the weaving shed of a new cotton mill, 'where they found the tables laid with a splendid collation, champagne being in the greatest abundance.'

The Ulverston and Lancaster Railway, with its huge iron viaducts over the Kent and the Leven, was opened in August 1857, with a trip along the line and a 'sumptuous banquet' for the 300 guests amid the ruins of Furness Abbey. The toastmaster was brought specially from London.

10. *The Navvies*

Railways, which are the most impressive reminders of nineteenth-century industrial Lancashire, are a monument to those extraordinary men, the British navvies. With picks and shovels, wheelbarrows and gunpowder, they changed the landscape and, in little more than two decades, completed a network of lines which required little extension. One feels they would have had no qualms about undertaking George Stephenson's scheme of 1837 for building a line across Morecambe Bay, though it is anyone's guess how they would have regarded the proposal put forward two years later by a Mr Buttle for a railway from the Lancashire coast to the Isle of Man.

Hard working, hard drinking, fond of a fight, but immensely loyal, the navvies were both feared and admired. The *Bolton Chronicle* said of them:

> The strongest and most distinguished . . . are collected principally from the hills in Lancashire and Yorkshre and are men of the finest physical stamina in the country. In strength and energy they have not been exceeded by any in the United Kingdom and equalled by none on the continent . . . On average they are stated not to last beyond their fortieth year; but with fair treatment they would last in health and vigour until their term of three score.

The men who built the Manchester and Bolton Railway terrorised the villages along the line, 'knocking down parish constables as if they were ninepins' and threatening to pull down the Farnworth 'dungeon' if any of their colleagues were imprisoned in it. Soldiers from Bolton barracks were called on frequently to restore the peace.

Most of the many fights in which the navvies became involved were caused by an intense antipathy between the English and the Irish. In May 1838 Irish navvies working on the Preston to Wigan line at Farington picked a quarrel with the workers at a local cotton mill. The outcome was a pitched battle in which one man was shot dead and 40 others were wounded. Guns, pikes, forks and clubs were among the weapons used.

There was more trouble in October of the same year when Irish navvies were taken on by contractors building the Lancaster to Preston line. Though the Irishmen were paid 9d. a day less than the 2s. 6d. received by English labourers, the Englishmen decided to enforce a 'closed shop'. First the Irish were chased from their lodging houses and then a gang of 200 English navvies assembled at Hampson Green, near Lancaster, and armed with bludgeons 'proceeded along the whole line, beating every Irishman who came in their way.' Some of the Irish swam a river to escape attack.

Hostilities between the two races continued for years. In May 1846

Navvies at work on the construction of the entrance to the tunnel of the Liverpool and Manchester Railway, Edge Hill, Liverpool. The tunnel was built not because of any geographical or technical requirement but because of the objection of various Liverpool interests to the idea of a railway cutting through the centre of the town (from *Lancashire Illustrated*, 1829).

Ackermann's engraving of the completed tunnel entrance. The tall chimney belongs to the adjacent engine house, where a stationary steam engine hauled wagons and carriages up from Wapping on a cable incline.

a dispute over wages paid to the English and Irish making the line through Ramsbottom led to a riot in which 2,000 became involved. 'Many men on both sides,' says a report, 'were severely beaten and a number of the Irish were driven from their houses by the English.' Two policemen were repeatedly struck when they tried to intervene. In November the navvies working between Bury and Heywood went to a beer house on pay day and before long a dispute between the English and the Irish turned into a fight. 'In a short time, they broke nearly all the windows as well as tables, chairs, pots, forms and everything they came on.' When the police arrested two of the ringleaders 'the excavators, upwards of twenty in number, immediately forgot their quarrel' and freed the men after attacking the police 'with spades, clubs and other weapons.'

A month earlier the navvies at Hapton, near Burnley, with engaging enterprise, had discomfited a group of treacherous foremen in a manner that must have delighted all who heard about it. The *Blackburn Standard* of 16 September reported:

> On Saturday and Sunday last, considerable excitement prevailed in Burnley in consequence of some of the overlookers or 'gaffers' on the East Lancashire Railway having defrauded their workpeople of their wages. It appears that on Saturday afternoon the 'gaffers' received the amount of the wages from Mr Hattersley, the contractor, and sent it away by their wives, intending to follow as early as convenient. The 'navvies' however, 'smelt a rat' and securing the delinquents kept guard over them in a room at the Angel Inn during Saturday night and Sunday. In consequence of the crowds of persons attracted to the place on Sunday the 'navvies' determined to have an exhibition and parties were admitted inside the room to see the 'wild beasts' at the charge of one halfpenny each, except 'when feeding' when the charge was a penny. The police, however, soon interfered and the prisoners were removed to the Court House after offering considerable resistance.

When a navvy on the Blackburn and Preston Railway died in February 1846 his comrades, who had supported him during his five weeks' illness, collected £7 11s. for his funeral. Fifty of them wearing white smocks and stockings attended the burial service at Blackburn, after which 'the sexton was spared all further trouble, for the mourners provided themselves with spades and threw the last coverings on the deceased themselves.' A balance of £3 15s. left after all expenses were paid was sent for the relief of the sick. After reporting that the navvies building the Sough Tunnel near Darwen had raised £16 for the widow of a colleague killed at his work, the *Blackburn Standard* observed on 28 October 1846, 'This shows pretty fairly that railway men have hearts as well as other folks, though their manners are not quite so finished as might be desired.'

11. *The Clifton Blockade*

A dispute between the Lancashire and Yorkshire and the East Lancashire Railway companies in 1849 led to what the newspapers called 'a most extraordinary and unprecedented scene' at Clifton Junction. The companies could not agree on a method of collecting tolls for passengers carried in East Lancashire trains over the Lancashire and Yorkshire line from the junction to Manchester. The Lancashire and Yorkshire demanded that all trains should stop at Clifton while the passengers were counted but the East Lancashire refused, contending that the returns it submitted were sufficient and alleging that the move had been made out of spite because the companies had begun to compete for the Bradford traffic.

When their ultimatum was ignored, the Lancashire and Yorkshire managers decided to block the line and on Monday 12 March, just before the first through train was due, their workmen laid 'an immense balk of timber' across the points and drove down two long, heavy crowbars to hold it firmly in position. A train of six carriages was then backed up to the balk to strengthen the blockade, and, it was hoped, to carry the East Lancashire passengers to Manchester. When the East Lancashire train arrived, Lancashire and Yorkshire ticket collectors boarded the carriages but only to find that all the tickets had been given up at the previous station. The invasion, however,

was the signal for retaliatory measures by the East Lancashire party, who had till now walked in silence on either side of their own line, as servants of the other company had done on theirs; the police meantime, looking on at both from the window of the railway station house. The first act of the East Lancashire Company's servants

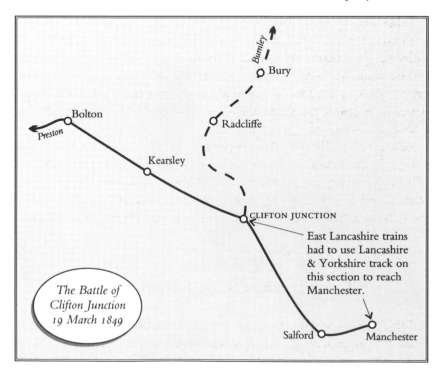

Bury

Bolton

Preston

Radcliffe

Kearsley

CLIFTON JUNCTION

East Lancashire trains had to use Lancashire & Yorkshire track on this section to reach Manchester.

The Battle of Clifton Junction 19 March 1849

Salford   Manchester

was to remove the balk of timber, and this they did without hindrance; and the next to run forward their train and attempt to force before them the Lancashire and Yorkshire's blockading train. This, however, the others appeared to have anticipated; and having put on the brakes and brought up another engine, they were able to maintain their ground.

Not to be outdone, the East Lancashire officials ran a train of stone-filled wagons across the junction on the up line, thus preventing all traffic between Manchester and Bolton. Scheduled trains now began to build up behind the blockade and soon eight were 'extended side by side for more than half a mile.' Many of the passengers got out to remonstrate with the railway officials and one group sent to Pendleton for a post-chaise, threatening to bring action for detention. After more than an hour, the Lancashire and Yorkshire blockading train was withdrawn and the East Lancashire travellers were allowed to complete one of the oddest journeys in railway history.

In June of the following year the East Lancashire Company became involved in a dispute with the Bolton, Blackburn, Clitheroe and West Yorkshire Company over running rights through Blackburn tunnel and station, and blockaded the line at Daisyfield for two days. More than two hundred navvies, several engines and a heavy train of stone wagons were brought in and might have blocked the line indefinitely had not the Lancashire and Yorkshire Company, seizing the opportunity to be revenged for their defeat at Clifton Junction, threatened retaliation at Salford.

An artist's vivid impression of the violent confrontation at Clifton Junction on 12 March 1849.

12. *Across the Oceans*

At the beginning of 1830 the *Liverpool Times*, commenting on the smoke from steamboats, declared:

> During the last ten years the nuisance has gone on increasing until it has become almost intolerable, and if nothing is done to check it, it will increase every year until the atmosphere of Liverpool will become as much defiled as that of Birmingham, Manchester or any other manufacturing town in the Kingdom.

But once steam had become waterborne there was no possibility of checking its advance and by August 1833 the praises of Liverpool steamboats were being sung even in Manchester. 'The power of steam in promoting the facility of intercourse between distant countries daily develops itself and is truly wonderful,' said the *Manchester Guardian* in a reference to the introduction by the St George Steam Packet Company of a service between Liverpool and the Rhine towns via Cork, Plymouth, London and Rotterdam.

Five years later, on 5 July 1838, 40,000 people lined the Mersey to

A section of Ackermann's 'aerial view' of the Liverpool waterfront in 1849, showing a paddle steamer towing a sailing ship downstream and part of the dock system, with the Customs House behind and the parish church of St Nicholas to the left.

watch the *Royal William*, a 175 ft paddle steamer, leave Liverpool for New York to establish a steamship link between the two ports. A cabin fare in the 270 horsepower vessel was 35 guineas, which included 'wines and all stores'.

The *Royal William* reached New York on 24 July, after a passage of 18 days 23 hours, and though much of the voyage was made in the face of stormy weather she 'behaved nobly' and 'floated over the mountain wave like a perfect duck.' After remaining in New York for ten days 'to allow travellers to visit the splendid scenery of the Hudson River and the celebrated Falls of Niagara,' the *Royal William* returned to Liverpool in 14 days 19 hours. Crowds of spectators lined the sea wall from George's Pier to the Clarence Dock as she steamed up the New Channel with all her colours flying. 'When in Bootle Bay,' said the *Liverpool Mercury*, 'she threw up blue lights and fired guns. She soon afterwards passed the Clarence and the Prince's Piers amidst loud cheering and cast anchor off George's Pier where the passengers landed.'

The *Royal William* was followed in 1840 by the *Britannia*, the first Cunard liner and the first steamship to establish a regular service across the Atlantic. She sailed from Liverpool on 4 July, and reached Halifax, Nova Scotia, on the 17th. On the following day she was given a tumultuous welcome at Boston. The *Britannia*, 207 feet long and with accommodation for 115 passengers and a cow to provide fresh milk, made 40 crossings and in June 1847 won the first Atlantic steamship race, beating the United States vessel *Washington* by two days. Charles Dickens sailed in her in 1842 and wrote at some length of

The Prince's Dock, Liverpool, begun in 1815 and completed in 1821. Bath Street runs to the left of the dock.

During the early nineteenth century the system of docks at Liverpool underwent a major expansion, and the transformation of the waterfront was well under way by 1830.

what proved to be a painful experience. The famous vessel failed entirely to impress him:

> Before descending into the bowels of the ship, we had passed from the deck into a long and narrow apartment, not unlike a gigantic hearse with windows in the sides; having at the upper end a melancholy stove at which three or four chilly stewards were warming

The *Great Britain* on her trials in 1852.

A forest of masts lines the Mersey in this early view from Toxteth. The long low building in the middle distance may be a rope walk, several of which are marked on Swire's map of Liverpool of 1824.

their hands; while on either side extending down its whole dreary length was a long, long table over which a rack fixed to the low roof and full of drinking glasses and cruet stands hinted dismally at rolling seas and heavy weather.

The rolling seas duly appeared and were fully described; and one suspects that Dickens was secretly delighted with the *Britannia* for the excellent copy she provided for his *American Notes*.

Another historic occasion on the Mersey in 1840 was the visit of the first screw propeller ship, the *Archimedes*, which had been built at London in the previous year. 'The natural spirit of emulation was manifested by the commanders of several of our river steamers,' said the *Liverpool Times* of 10 June, 'but the stranger beat two of the swiftest craft—the mail tender *Redwing* and one of the Egremont new iron boats, both exceedingly quick sailers.'

The *Archimedes* greatly influenced the engineer I. K. Brunel, who was building the 322 ft iron steamer the *Great Britain* at Bristol. He had intended to fit paddle wheels, but decided on a screw propeller after a cruise in the *Archimedes*. The *Great Britain*, the first screw steamer and the first built of iron to cross the Atlantic, sailed from Liverpool to New York on 26 July 1845.

The *Great Britain* also prompted the invention of the steam hammer. In 1839, when it was still planned to use paddle wheels, no hammer powerful enough to forge the paddle shaft could be found and James Nasymth, whose engineering works at Patricroft was internationally famous, was asked to help. 'In little more than half an hour of receiving the request,' he wrote in his autobiography, '. . . I had the whole contrivance in all its details before me in a page of my Sketch Book.' Brunel's decision to fit the *Great Britain* with a screw propeller and the onset of the trade recession of 1840–41 delayed the introduction of the steam hammer, but thereafter it became one of the most valuable machine tools of the nineteenth century.

When Leonard Horner, the factories inspector, visited the Patricroft works in 1846, his friend Nasymth showed him an immense steam hammer built 'to forge the great iron beams for steam vessels.' The hammer weighed six tons, 'but so completely under control is this vast power that he told me that he could place an egg in a wine glass under it and he could let the hammer fall with such gentleness that it would be no more than breaking the egg like the tap of a teaspoon.'

On 22 September 1846 the *Great Britain* was stranded in Dundrum Bay, Ireland. Eleven months went by before she was refloated, but the way in which she withstood a heavy pounding did much to hasten the introduction of iron ships. After being rebuilt, the *Great Britain* made one trip to New York in 1852 and then began a service to Australia, when the discovery of the gold fields brought a tremendous demand for passages. She sailed from Liverpool with 600 passengers on 21 August 1852, and reached Melbourne on 10 November. The fare was seventy guineas.

13. *The Horse's Last Stand*

Steam conquered the oceans of the world long before it had conquered the inland waterways of Lancashire. The fear that the wash from the paddle boats would seriously damage canal banks persisted and it was not until the last quarter of the nineteenth century that the horse was seriously challenged.

The horse might not have been able to keep pace with the locomotive, but its steady four miles an hour could be increased to a gallop. In July 1833 a fast service between Preston and Kendal was introduced on the Lancaster Canal by the *Water Witch*, a narrow boat drawn by two horses which were changed every four miles. The *Water Witch* reached speeds of ten miles an hour on level stretches. Her helmsman signalled instructions to the driver, who was mounted on the second horse, by sounding a dog whistle and a trumpet.

The first steamboat on the Mersey and Irwell Navigation, the *Jack Sharp*, was no faster than the company's swift packets which continued to run following her introduction in 1845. The packets were towed at a fast trot and sometimes at a gallop by 'three or four high-class horses with red-jacketed jockeys, the leader with a horn to warn all others to give way, and on May Day all decorated with ribbons and small bells.'

The *Jack Sharp*, a 12 horsepower, 66 ft paddle boat, which carried 120 passengers, first visited Manchester at the beginning of June 1838, and made a number of experimental trips from the New Bailey steps.

> The novelty of a *steam packet* at Manchester [said the *Manchester Chronicle*, of 9 June] has attracted multitudes of our townsmen and women this week down to the banks of the Irwell. On Monday morning last the proprietors of the Mersey and Irwell Navigation started the new steam packet . . . and she has been plying throughout the week to and from Barton, Daveyhulme, etc., with cargoes of pleasure parties glad of such an interesting opportunity to enjoy their holiday season . . . She moves very smoothly and pleasantly without so much vibration as is generally observable in steam vessels, at the rate of *seven* or *nearly eight* miles an hour.

'Many country people,' observed the *Manchester Guardian*, 'embarked for a short trip, apparently in order to tell their astonished relatives and friends, on their return home, something more of the wonders of steam.'

When Queen Victoria and Prince Albert visited Worsley in 1851 they travelled from Patricroft on the Bridgewater Canal and were drawn, not by 'the wonders of steam,' but by horse power. The Queen wrote in her diary:

> We walked through a covered and prettily ornamented corridor to the boat which was waiting on the Canal. It was a very elegant barge, to which a rope was fastened, drawn by four horses . . . Half was entirely covered in; the other half had an awning over it. The boat glided along in a most noiseless and dreamlike manner, amidst the cheers of the people who lined the sides of the canal, and passed under the beautifully decorated bridges belonging to the villages connected with the vast coal-pits belonging to Lord Ellesmere.

The Queen does not mention, however, that one of the horses, frightened by the cheering of the crowds, fell into the canal, nor that the tow-top broke, causing a further delay.

Another attempt to introduce a steamboat on the canal—it used an endless chain to provide a form of caterpillar traction—failed after extensive experiments in 1859; and steam's eventual triumph, aided by an epidemic which killed many horses, was rather squalid.

On the Leeds and Liverpool Canal experiments with steam power began in 1845, and in 1852 the Ince Hall Coal & Cannel Company proposed the use of steam tugs for Liverpool coal traffic. In 1858 the Leeds and Liverpool Canal Steam Tug Company was set up, with this aim, and began to operate four vessels, each of which could tow six laden boats. Despite initial optimism the company failed, and although steam power was introduced on the Yorkshire stretch in 1866 it was not until 1878 that regular steam haulage began in Lancashire. There had been other problems, notably that the boats damaged the banks with their wash, although their use increased scour of the river beds and reduced the need for dredging.*

The Bridgewater Canal, which had so delighted Southey and Queen Victoria, was by 1884 the subject of a strong complaint. A Stretford correspondent of the *Eccles and Patricroft Journal* protested on 20 June about the dense smoke of the steam tugs and 'their harsh unnecessary whistling.' Moreover, several people were suffering from 'Canal Throat', an infection peculiar to people living near the canal and one 'which is no doubt caused by the foul emanations given off by its horribly filthy water.'

---

* Mike Clarke, *The Leeds & Liverpool Canal, A History and Guide* (Carnegie, 1990).

2

New Disciplines

1. *The Great Upheaval*

HE great technical advances of the Industrial Revolution were not accompanied by any comparable improvements in human relationships. Some men of humble birth were enabled to make fortunes with a rapidity previously undreamed of, although others who were the pioneers and innovators of technological change and advance died in poverty and obscurity, while rivals reaped the financial rewards of their genius. In society as a whole, however, the headlong pursuit of wealth dragged many thousands into misery and degradation. Government, badly informed and often misled about the state of the manufacturing districts, reacted to the people's unrest with exaggerated alarm and too often introduced measures that added fuel to the fire beneath the Lancashire cauldron, which for more than half a century simmered, and from time to time boiled over, with the bitter passions of class hatred.

The decline into wretchedness of large numbers of once-prosperous handloom weavers, the barbarities of the factory system and the horrifying conditions of the new industrial slums cast their long dark shadows over the age. But other, brighter, changes were taking place. Among the mills and mean streets rose Sunday schools, co-operative stores and mechanics' institutions; and Lancashire men, once notorious for their brutishness, became the best-informed and most politically-conscious in the land. Among them were reformers who challenged the belief that poverty for all but a priviliged minority was inevitable and incurable and whose courage and resolve helped to change the course of British history. At the same time, the doctrine that property had its duties as well as rights was accepted by a growing number of the middle class, so that the mass of Lancashire people, after watching the exploitation of invention with resentment, fear and despair, began to share in the prosperity of a new era and to enjoy a freedom that no previous generation had known.

Just how completely they were affected by the industrial society in

which they learned to live may be illustrated from the experiences of two eminent men, one of whom visited Lancashire before the great upheaval; and the other after. When John Wesley passed through Rossendale in 1747 and 1748, he preached on the first occasion to 'a large congregation of wild men' and met on the second 'a mob savage as wild beasts, who, undeterred by the authorities, proceed to every extremity of persecution short of murder.' In 1864, when Mr Gladstone opened a public park at Farnworth, he told an orderly and attentive audience of between 50,000 and 80,000 working people: 'It is not too much to say that a moral transformation has passed over the district. Go now through the length and breadth of England and where is the man, whatever be his ignorance or prejudice, who will speak of the Lancashire population as degraded?'

The story of that transformation is the subject of the following pages.

Galvanised by the great inventions and the enthusiasm of the men who rushed forward to exploit them, the cotton industry in the last quarter of the eighteenth century expanded amazingly until it eclipsed all others and was the wonder of the world. The mercurial success of entrepreneurs like Sir Richard Arkwright, the barber-turned-cotton spinner, and the Oswaldtwistle yeoman Robert ('Parlsey') Peel, inspired men from all classes to seek their fortunes in Lancashire so that by 1795 a farmer was able to tell the agriculturist John Holt:

Mule spinning, 1835. The architecture of the cotton industry was already assuming its familiar form, with extensive use of cast iron to allow wide roof spans and large floor spaces for increasingly sizeable machinery.

The cotton factories on Union Street, Manchester from *Lancashire Illustrated*, 1829. The canal-side location of these mills is very typical of the early phases of the industry—the canals brought the constant supplies of coal necessary to feed the steam engines which power the mills.

Never enquire about the cultivation of the land or its produce within ten or twelve miles of Manchester; the people know nothing about it. Speak of spinning jennies and mules and carding machines and they will talk for days with you.

The new machines increased the output of yarn prodigiously, bringing prosperity not only to those who owned and worked them, but also to handloom weavers long starved of supplies. 'Any young man who was industrious and careful might from his savings as a weaver lay by sufficient to set him up as a manufacturer,' said William Radcliffe, the Stockport inventor, who advanced in just this way.

For large numbers, however, the booming cotton industry offered more mundane opportunities. Holt noted:

The yeomen and the labourer are both tempted from the plough—all competition is precluded. Who will work for 1s. or 2s. a day at a ditch when he can get 3s. 6d. or 5s. a day in a cotton works and be drunk four days out of seven?

This blissful life was soon interrupted as the vulnerability of an industry which imported all its raw material and exported much of its yarn and finished cloth was painfully exposed by the wars with France and America. The cotton industry now began its long history of unpredictable and often violent fluctuations, which stimulated fierce competition among the rapidly expanding ranks of spinners, manufac-

Engraved by T. E. Nicholson.

The spinning jenny. By allowing the output of yarn to be vastly increased, the spinning jenny was instrumental in transforming the cotton industry in the late eighteenth and early nineteenth centuries. This, in turn, brought about the 'golden age' of the handloom weavers since the mechanisation of weaving was less well advanced.

turers and calico printers, and hardened the enterprise of many into a ruthlessness which was quickly matched by the hostility of their work-people. Bad harvests at the turn of the century added to the economic tribulations brought by the war, and the years 1799–1801 were long remembered in Lancashire as 'The Barley Times', from the fact that few people were able to pay the high price of corn. In April 1800 the Oldham diarist William Rowbottom noted that 'scores of poor wretches' were wandering about plucking nettles, docks and water cresses as a substitute for potatoes and that nettles were sold at Oldham for 2d. a pound. In the countryside around his home at Great Harwood, the nine-year-old John Mercer, who was to become one of the country's greatest chemists, 'went up and down seeking docks, which my mother boiled for us to make a meal.' William Yates, of Bury, Robert Peel's partner, wrote in March 1801, 'My heart bled to see so many children not more than half fed,' and he feared there would be a revolution if food prices remained so high.

The Peace of Amiens exactly a year later replaced poverty with a sudden but short-lived prosperity. Oldham mule spinners were soon earning 30s. a week, a sum which Rowbottom considered 'beyond all imagination', and in May the *Blackburn Mail* described what proved to be the pinnacle of the handloom weavers' prosperity:

> There was never known so great an activity in the manufacture of Blackburn calicoes as at present, the orders for the same being immense. It is also extraordinary that many weavers at this time are able, singly, to earn from forty-five to fifty shillings per week: and numbers of boys and girls of twelve years of age can earn a guinea a week at the loom also.

About the same time, Robert Southey visited a Manchester cotton factory where other boys and girls were at work. Here, too, business was brisk. 'There is no idleness among us,' said the manager. 'The wheels never stand still.'

> I was looking while he spoke [said Southey] at the unnatural dexterity with which the fingers of these little creatures were playing in the machinery, half giddy myself with the noise and the endless motion: and when he told me there was no rest in these walls, day or night, I thought that if Dante had peopled one of his hells with children, here was a scene worthy to have supplied him with new images of torment.

Unlike Crompton's hand-driven mule, Arkwright's power driven spinning frame with which factories such as this were filled, required no skill to operate and young children, many recruited from the workhouses of the large cities, were easily drilled to be machine minders.

2. *Men of Spirit*

Most Lancashire men, however, were not so easily persuaded to ex-change their resolute independence for the discipline of mill life. Great numbers preferred the privations of handloom weaving and among the comparatively well-paid spinners, there were many who, for at least the first twenty years of the nineteenth century, were highly irregular in their attendance. A House of Lords committee was told in 1818 that spinners frequently stayed off work without notice and then sent for their wages at the end of the week. One of the largest Manchester firms, McConnel and Kennedy, replaced spinners who were absent two or three hours after starting time on Mondays on the usually correct assumption that the men had left. Turnover of adult labour at the mill was 20 a week, or 100 per cent a year. The traveller Richard Ayton met a boisterous group of these men when he visited Poulton-le-Sands (now part of Morecambe), in the spring of 1813. Their 'honest and heedless vulgarity' and their love of strong ale deeply impressed him.

> It is no unusual thing for a man, who, by a course of severe industry and abstinence, had collected a stock of cash, to retire altogether from his home and live for a fortnight at a public house; during the whole of which time his only concern is never to allow himself to get sober. When he has expended all his money, he will return to his employment and toil away resolutely and cheerfully; but his industry benefits anybody but himself; for as soon as he has money enough in his pocket to last through such a debauch as he thinks

worthy of his pains, he quarters himself again at the public house, again to drink himself a bankrupt. I have been informed by a proprietor of a manufactory that several of his most skilful hands were men who spent their time in these alternations of drunkenness and industry—fellows who would not quit their drink while they had a sixpence left, and who would only work that they might return to drink again.

Ayton goes on to describe the character of Lancashire working-class people and his account shows that while they had advanced considerably from the state of savagery in which Wesley found them nearly seventy years earlier, they had not undergone the moral transformation that was to impress Mr Gladstone fifty years later.

I have observed [says Ayton] that in the manners and deportment of the people of the lower orders in Lancashire, there is at all times something peculiar and very far from prepossessing. A stranger would unquestionably pronounce them to be rude, coarse and insolent; though I have heard it said in their defence, that this external roughness is only a kind of way that they have, and that on more familiar acquaintance with them if it be not found to wear away, it cannot be traced to any ill disposition. They have certainly less of that common politeness, that common courtesy, which forms one of the distinctions between men and bears, than any people that ever fell under my observation. Their manners to strangers, whether their equals or their betters, are of the same rude, untempered kind that they indulge in among themselves; they have no best or second-best forms of behaviour for particular occasions or particular company, but appear invariably, whatever the season, under the same rough and every-day guise. But with this total want of any degree of polish, they are remarkably quick and intelligent; and indeed their rudeness is quite distinct in character from that gross boorishness and rusticity, which we may notice among the inhabitants of less populous counties, and which are the result of mere ignorance and inexperience. They are blunt and abrupt in their manners, but obviously rather from self-complacency and a high opinion of their own importance, than from any want of familiarity with the formalities of social life . . . In Cornwall and Devonshire, and in all parts of Wales through which I have travelled, I found that a shilling would always procure me a service and a bow with it: but whatever it might purchase in Lancashire, it would certainly not bribe to civility. The people here are fully aware of the importance of their labour, and take their reward as a matter of simple right, looking upon any expression of thanks as an unworthy sign of inferiority and dependence.

The great manufacturing system is without a doubt the first cause of all the distinctions I have noticed; this collects the people in crowds together, and putting more money into their pockets than is necessary to their support, furnishes them with means and opportunities of dissipation that persons of their rank and character in life must not be expected to resist. Much vice and profligacy necessarily prevail among them; but while their morals are corrupted, the powers of their minds are called forth: they become lawless and unprincipled, but quick, cunning and intelligent. The public houses are the great schools of the county, in which, under the presidency of ale, the manners, habits and opinions of the people are fashioned as soon as each can swallow his draught, and earn an extra shilling to purchase it. In such seminaries they learn to laugh at all moral restraint, and certainly acquire no sound principles or useful knowledge; but by a constant exercise of reason or quarrelling, or bantering among themselves, they gain an unusual shrewdness and great readiness and volubility of expression. A Lancashire man of the class I am describing piques himself upon his powers of repartée, and not without reason. In the company at Poulton, I heard frequent bursts of humour, which a more chastened taste might have repressed in better society, but which nevertheless had so much of the real essence in their composition that I ventured to be much entertained by them.

3. *Political Citizens*

'The great manufacturing system' also had another effect. 'Operative workmen being thrown together in great numbers,' said Richard Guest, 'had their faculties sharpened and improved by constant communication.' As a result

> conversation wandered over a variety of topics not before essayed; questions of Peace and War which interested them importantly inasmuch as they might produce a rise or fall of wages, became highly interesting and thus brought them into the vast field of politics and discussions on the character of their government and the men who composed it. They took a greater interest in the defeats and victories of their country's armies, and from being only a few degrees above their cattle in the scale of intellect, they became political citizens.

When working men, and in particular the handloom weavers, began to strengthen their associations, the government took alarm and in 1799 and 1800 passed the Combination Acts, which outlawed trade unionism and indirectly put enormous power into the hands of the master. But despite this setback the weavers were confident that the government would protect them from exploitation by legalising minimum wage rates. It was a vain hope. The rigid attitude of the government was summed up by the magistrates of Salford Hundred in 1799 when they warned that opposition to the Combination Act would be vigorously suppressed:

> It required little experience to know, that at all times, the Price of Labour ought and must be free and unshackled. It is governed by a greater or less demand, which depends on Circumstances beyond the Control of Masters or Servants.

In 1808, a year of distress and rising food prices, the weavers intensified their campaign for a minimum wage. 'The hand of Oppression has again snatched from you a considerable portion of the miserable Wages former Reductions had left you,' said a handbill issued by the Bolton Weavers' Committee in January, but it added, 'A wise and just Legislature will e'er long relieve your grievances.' On 19 May, however, a Bill to regulate wages was withdrawn, even though it was stated that many weavers could earn only between 6s. and 10s. a week by working 18 hours a day on six days out of seven. Sir Robert Peel, who was among a number of employers who had earlier supported the Bill, now published an address in the Lancashire papers, arguing that the regulation of wages would drive trade out of the country. The starving weavers were unconvinced and showed their discontent at two huge meetings in Manchester. 'Loud indeed were the murmurs of the poor wretches, but not the least indication was there of a riot,' said *The Times* of the meeting on 25 May, which was attended by more than 10,000 people. Troops were called when the crowd refused to disperse and they killed one man and wounded several others. Strikes for a 33⅓ per cent increase in wages followed, notably at Wigan and Rochdale, where the woollen weavers seized the shuttles of all who refused to support them. Two unguarded bags of shuttles fell into the hands of the constables and were locked away in the House of Correction. When the constables refused to return the shuttles, the strikers broke into the prison and burned it to the ground. The weavers gained some increase in pay, but only for a month or so.

The first Sir Robert Peel (1750–1830); an engraving by H. Robinson from the portrait by Sir Thomas Lawrence.

Peel, calico printer and founder of the modern Bury, was one of the first manufacturers to sit in the House of Commons. His son, Sir Robert, the second baronet, was the first prime minister from a commercial family.

The Old Market Place, Deansgate, Bolton, from *Lancashire Illustrated*, 1829. The very varied architecture is characteristic of most Lancashire towns at this time. Half-timbered buildings, pointed gables, an irregular building line and roughly cobbled streets were invariably found, but almost without exception such scenes were swept away by the improving zeal and ambitious re-developments of the Victorian period.

'Oh misery and wretchedness, when will ye cease to torment the industrious artisan?' asked the Bolton cotton weavers, appealing in February 1811 for a public meeting to consider their distress. There seemed no prospect of better times and three months later a petition for help from the Manchester district with 40,000 signatures and another from Bolton with 7,000 were presented to the Commons. Faith in 'a wise and just legislature' had been steadily eroded by a spirit of parliamentary reform and when the petitions were dismissed the little confidence in the Government that remained was entirely swept away. In the following year the weavers tried to enforce two ancient acts which empowered magistrates to regulate wages, but though there was support from the authorities at Bolton, the government acted at once to repeal what the Home Secretary, Lord Sidmouth, described as 'the pernicious statutes'.

The antipathy between the government and the people and between the masters and their workers was further intensified in 1812 by a wave of food and Luddite riots during April. Dear food, widespread un-employment, alarm at the growing use of power looms, the mischief of unscrupulous informers and above all the feeling that no one cared about their wretchedness, drove the more volatile to violence. Just how numerous and well organised the secret committees of workpeople were or how serious a threat to law and order they presented is not easily determined. The Lancashire magistrates and the Home Office certainly feared a general uprising and though the reports from their spies were usually exaggerated and often fictitious, there can be no doubt that in some areas the malcontents made active preparations for rebellion. Francis Raynes, an army captain, who served in the troubled areas, said:

> The Luddites attained a military system of operation and held their meetings upon commons and moors for the purpose of drilling etc., and posted their sentinels to give the alarm. Signals were made by the firing of a gun and not unfrequently by rockets and blue lights. Their muster rolls were regularly called over, not by names, but by numbers; each man answering his own number. In the neighbourhood of Ashton-under-Lyne, on a Sunday, during divine service, they were seen drawn up as a regular batallion.

In the Worsley district, however, Luddism lasted for only a few months and its brief history is recorded in the notebook of Thomas Bury, manager of the Bridgewater Collieries. Bury lists the Luddites' names, the dates on which each man was 'twisted in', the houses where the ceremonies took place and, finally, a record of their confessions. The Luddite oath, which Bury quotes, obviously was not taken very seriously. No one, so far as is known, used his best endeavour to punish by death those who disclosed the secrets, nor was anyone's name and character 'blotted out of existence, never to be remembered any more, but with contempt and abhorrence.'

The disturbances of 1812 began with food riots at Manchester, Oldham, Ashton-under-Lyne and Bolton, but the Oldham mob, which included many miners, went on to Middleton and forming with a local contingent a force several thousands strong, attacked the power loom factory of Daniel Burton and Sons. After warning the attackers, who bombarded the factory with volleys of stones, Mr Burton and his men opened fire, killing five and wounding eighteen. Determined on revenge, the rioters met on the following day and were joined by between one hundred and two hundred men armed with muskets and colliers' picks, who marched into the village in procession. 'At the head of this armed banditti,' said the *Leeds Mercury*, 'a Man of Straw was carried representing the renowned General Ludd, whose standard bearer waved a sort of red flag.' Soldiers arrived too late to save Mr Burton's house from being ransacked and burned down, but in a battle that followed they killed five more rioters and wounded many others.

Four days later, the power loom factory of Rowe and Dunscough at Westhoughton was burned down by a mob, which had been largely organised and provoked into action by an informer in the pay of the local magistrates. In the succeeding weeks 71 companies of infantry,

27 troops of horse guards and dragoons, together with several thousand special constables, were on duty in Lancashire and following the trials later in the year, eight of the rioters were hanged.

4. *Fresh Hostilities*

A man who received a portion of meat when an ox was roasted at Swinton to celebrate the Battle of Waterloo, recalled in later life: 'I had tasted neither beef nor mutton for two years.' But the peace of 1815 signalled the beginning of fresh hostilities in the manufacturing districts. The Corn Law of that year kept up the price of food at the very time when thousands of demobilised soldiers and sailors flooded the labour market and when large government contracts for textiles were ended. Competition increased, with the result that wages were lowered and the hours of toil were extended. Lancashire, once a stronghold of Toryism, in a decade had become the most radical county in the land, but though hatred of the government was intense, it did not explode into the revolution that the authorities feared. Indeed, the next move by the people was to stage the world's first hunger march. The Blanketeers who set out from Manchester on 10 March 1817, were concerned only to present petitions to the Prince Regent in London, but they were regarded with consternation by the authorities. Troops surrounded the hustings of the 'send-off' meeting in St Peter's Field and the organisers were arrested. A large band of marchers had set out, however, but before they reached Stockport, 167 had been taken prisoner. A few hundred reached Ashbourne in Derbyshire and several struggled on to Loughborough; but only one man is known to have arrived in London. He was Abel Couldwell, of Stalybridge, who handed in his petition on 18 March.

An improvement in trade which began at the end of 1817 and continued during the following year brought no benefit to the weavers, many of whom now had to contend with the greed of callous masters. Throughout the cotton districts manufacturers used the excuse of foreign competition to keep down wages, which were raised to subsistence level only by considerable supplements from parish relief. The spinners also came into conflict with their employers who, having reduced wages by 20–25 per cent when trade was bad in 1816, refused to increase them again when business revived two years later. Both the spinners and the weavers went on strike, but after eight weeks the spinners had to admit total defeat and the weavers, while gaining some small but short-lived advances, were crushed as an organised body when their leaders were imprisoned for conspiracy.

The plea for minimum wage rates for weavers was again heard in Lancashire, but this time it was the manufacturers who led the campaign for government action. James Hutchinson, a Bury employer, writing to Lord Sidmouth in 1819 on behalf of thirty-five firms which favoured a minimum wage scale, complained that low wages were caused by the 'numbers of people of little capital and less feeling who, having obtained credit, embark on business and attempt to realise a profit by underselling their more respectable competitors.' Thomas Ainsworth of Bolton, who had been in the cotton trade for forty years, said it had become 'a trade of oppression, demi-swindling and deception. A master cannot live by the honest pursuit of trade, nor can a weaver by hard labour.' Calico printers supported the manufacturers, but the government remained inflexible.

But 1819 was above all the year of the Peterloo Massacre. On 16 August some 60,000 working people with their bands and banners marched in an orderly way to St Peter's Field, Manchester, for a reform meeting at which the popular orator Henry Hunt was to speak. The proceedings had hardly begun when the local Yeomanry, composed mainly of manufacturers, merchants, publicans and shopkeepers, made a cavalry charge into the defenceless and densely-packed crowd, killing eleven and wounding more than 400 as they struck out wildly with their sabres. The action was ostensibly to prevent a disturbance—none

A contemporary cartoon of the Peterloo Massacre, entitled 'Manchester Heroes'. 'Peterloo' was by no means the only violent and bloody confrontation in the years from 1805 onwards, but more than any other it captured the popular imagination—and not just in Lancashire— becoming part of the 'heritage' of the labour and democratic movements.

was ever threatened—but in effect it was the most vicious attack in the class war by men whose political rancour 'approached absolute insanity.'

> In ten minutes [wrote Samuel Bamford, the Middleton reformer] the field was an open and almost deserted space. The hustings remained with a few broken and hewed flag staves erect and a torn or gashed banner or two drooping; whilst over the whole field were strewed caps, bonnets, hats, shawls and shoes and other parts of male and female dress, trampled, torn and bloody. The Yeomanry had dismounted—some were easing their horses' girths, other adjusting their accoutrements and some were wiping their sabres.

Peterloo was a turning point in British history. The working classes gained much middle-class sympathy—Shelley wrote *The Masque of Anarchy* on hearing the news—and though the government passed the notorious Six Acts in an attempt to end all agitation, it came increasingly to the view that blind repression would never succeed.

The reform movement profoundly affected the people of Lancashire. Francis Place wrote in 1819:

> In spite of the demoralising influence of many of our laws and the operation of the poor laws, it has impressed the morals and manners and elevated the character of the working men. I speak from observation made on thousands of them, and I hold up this fact as enough of itself to satisfy any man not wholly ignorant of human nature as a very portentous circumstance.
>
> Strangers to Lancashire towns were hooted and pelted with stones and 'Lancashire brute' was a common and appropriate appellation. Until very lately it would have been very dangerous to have assembled 500 of them on any occasion. Bakers and butchers would at least have been plundered. Now 100,000 people may be collected together and no riot ensue, and why? Why, but for the fact stated, that the people have an object, the pursuit of which gives them an importance in their own eyes, elevates them in their own opinion, and thus it is that the very individuals who would have been the leaders of the riot are the keepers of the peace. In every place as reform has advanced, drunkenness has retreated and you may assume that any cause which can operate so powerfully as to produce such a change is capable of producing almost anything.

5. 'Alas, Poor Weaver'

In January 1820 William Varley of Higham, near Burnley, expressed the feelings of a great army of workers when he wrote in his diary:

> Alas, poor weaver, thy fond hopes of better days always proves abortive; distress and scorn is thy true companions; thy haggard and meagre looks plainly indicate thy hard usage, slavery which knows no bounds.

Varley was then earning 15 to 16s. a week, or half the amount he had drawn when times were good, but within six years his wages had been halved again.

The decline of the handloom weavers is a sad and harrowing story. Where in the whole history of Lancashire is there anything comparable? That so many men and women existed and were exploited for so long in conditions of extreme misery and destitution and still retained a measure of independence and dignity was little short of miraculous. As the 1834 Select Committee on handloom Weavers' Petitions observed:

> . . . the sufferings of that large and valuable body have for years continued to an extent and intensity scarcely to be credited or conceived and have been borne with a degree of patience un-exampled.

There were several classes of weaver. Most worked at home; some independently, others for manufacturers or large firms. In 1816 Hor-rocks, Miller and Co., who ran four mills in Preston, employed 'a whole countryside of weavers,' 7,000 in all, and about the same time Peel Yates and Co., of Bury, who were calico printers as well as spinners, 'had some thousands of handloom weavers in Darwen, Padi-ham, Bacup and Burnley and also put out work through agents in many parts of Lancashire.' The weavers worked in cellars, in lean-to loomshops and in attics. Many town weavers spent their working days in cellars, but this phenomenon has now been recognised in the rural areas as well. In North East Lancashire, where coarse cottons were woven, and in the Rochdale area with its woollen weaving, upper-storey loomshops were common, and this may well have been true of the silk areas, too. In the countryside there were many specially built ground-floor loomshops, often as lean-to buildings attached to farm-houses. Many country weavers rented small farms which added greatly to their distress when they were called upon to pay poor rates in times of depression.

Another group worked in loom shops and factories, but whatever their status, the weavers saw their standard of living decline outrageously.

Part of Dob Wheel Mill near Rochdale, which dates from around 1800, was probably a loomshop. Although many individual handloom weavers' cottages survive in mid-Lancashire, there are now relatively few examples of purpose-built loomshops of this type (photograph Royal Commission on the Historical Monuments of England).

A few who wove fine cloths were able to earn reasonable wages, but the rest sank into wretchedness, and until industry was widely established, they had little else to which they could turn. There were few vacancies in the mills, even for those who were prepared to give up their independence. Horrocks, Miller and Co. employed ten times more weavers than factory workers; in 1816, 73 per cent were under the age of eighteen. Hundreds saw emigration as their only escape, but many set themselves up as manufacturers and by joining in the price-cutting war, added to the general distress.

'Weavers and mechanics are daily springing up into manufacturers, commencing business with their accumulated savings,' an Oldham magistrate observed in 1822, and five years later, during one of the worst periods in the cotton trade's history, an army officer reported, 'A very great evil about Blackburn and Burnley is the number of weavers, who, owing to the facility of obtaining credit and County Bank paper, have become small manufacturers.' Many of these men failed, but among the successful was Thomas Haworth of Radcliffe, who began in business in a cottage in about 1825. Haworth bought yarn and sent it to be dyed and sized. He made warps on a round warping mill and these he distributed with weft and patterns to the weavers. Haworth frequently walked to Bury with a warp on his shoulder and from time to time he set out on horseback to sell cloth to drapers in Preston, Kendal and Penrith. He also travelled with a cart to outlying districts with supplies of warp and weft and to collect woven cloth.

Elkanah Armitage, one of the greatest of the cotton lords, began business in a room over a stable at Swinton, and another former weaver,

David Whitehead of Rawtenstall, described in his autobiography how he and his two brothers, after accumulating a stock of weft in 1815, bought some warps and began to manufacture:

> I got a few weavers in the neighbourhood of Balladenbrook. I got my mother, who lived at Newchurch, to weave for us and a few weavers more at Newchurch. I took in pieces at my mother's house and made them up there ready for the market. My mother was one of the best weavers I had and when I had any cloths more difficult than the rest, I gave them to her to weave. And what is worth remarking, when she was sixty years old [in 1820] she wove six pieces per week for which I paid her 2s. 6d. per piece.

After ten years' successful trading, Whitehead built a large steam driven spinning and weaving factory, but within a few months of opening it he experienced the wrath of a desperate mob of handloom weavers, who regarded the power-loom as one of the chief causes of their misery. All 96 of Whitehead's looms were smashed.

6. The 1826 Riots

To understand the power-loom riots of 1826 one must consider the appalling state into which the handloom weavers had been thrown by the severe trade depression of that year. By February 1,500 of the 6,000 looms in Bolton were idle and another 1,500 on half work. On the 27th of the month the weavers of the town issued a statement in which they compared current wages and prices with those of 35 years earlier.

	1792	1826
Wages, 60 reed	3/- a yard	3½d. a yard
Best bread	1½d. a lb.	2d.
Butter	7d.	1s.
Cheese	4d.	7d.
Butcher's meat	4d.	7d.

A good workman, who formerly earned from six shillings to eight shillings a day, cannot now earn six shillings a week by labouring sixteen hours a day. Many manufacturers have put weavers on half work—say three shillings a week and with that miserable pittance we have to meet the wants of our hungry and naked families. And how, it will naturally be asked, is this accomplished? We answer: a solitary meal each day of oatmeal and water is absolutely more than a man with a family of small children is able to obtain. With

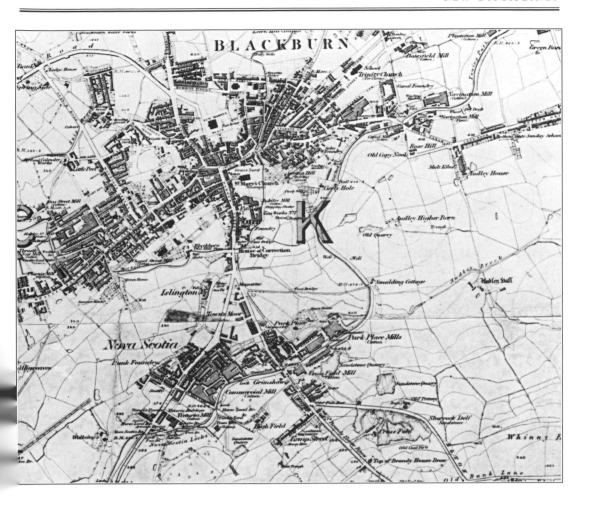

A section of the 1st edition Ordnance Survey map of Blackburn. The expansion of industry along the canal is immediately apparent in the Nova Scotia and Eanam areas, which were at this stage distinct communities separate from the old market town. The map dates from the early 1840s: by 1870 almost all the area shown had been built over.

this wretched allowance, is it possible that we can much longer exist? . . . From the unexampled pressure under which we have laboured for so many years we have not had the means of renewing our apparel, our bedding and other conveniences of life; consequently we are at this inclement season of the year without sufficient clothing and obliged to sleep on straw with scarcely a rag to cover us.

Statistics collected from Blackburn, Witton, Ramsgreave, Rishton, Lower Darwen and part of Oswaldtwistle in March showed that of the 10,686 weavers 6,412 were out of work and 1,467 were working half-time.

A number of appeals for help sent to the Home Secretary describe the plight of thousands in the countryside. At Lower Darwen, only four of the 377 families (2,238 persons) were 'not directly dependent on the labour of the loom.'

The occupiers of land are with very few exceptions tenants at rack tents of small farms, the rents of which they raise partly by the sale of milk and butter to the cottagers and partly by the weaving of calicoes. Three of the four families not immediately concerned in the trade live upon small farms of their own; the remaining one is the tenant of a farm of between 200–300 acres . . . The trade consists, with the exception of a small spinning concern in which 20 men and 80 children are employed, wholly of weaving of calicoes on the handloom . . . For six weeks [the petition was written on 1 May] not one in four has been enabled to get work upon any terms . . . Extreme deprivation and absolute want has become almost general.

A petition from four townships in the Burnley area showed that there was almost one loom for every two inhabitants. The figures were:

	Inhabitants	Looms
Laund Booth	400	219
Goldshaw	769	387
Barley with Whiteley	737	345
Roughlee	1009	429
Total	2916	1380

The petitioners of Colne Chapelry said 17,000 people there were almost wholly employed in handloom weaving and pointed out that:

This district is divided into small farms, each of which, on average, may keep three or four milch cows, and the principal part of the farmers depend upon weaving for the support of their families, the labour on the farms being done during their intervals of leisure.

One village in this district was Barrowford, where, said a correspondent of the *Blackburn Mail* in March 1826, two thirds of the weavers were unemployed and half of those in work were earning only 1s. 3d. a week. Three manufacturers had withdrawn from the trade. The principal butcher killed only two sheep a week and other butchers had been driven out of business. Three publicans who used to brew four packs of malt a week were unable to sell one pack a month. Another publican at Downham told the correspondent 'that he had not one penny to pay to the Excise at the last sitting.'

At Higham, Varley wrote in his diary:

There are a great many people who are poorly . . . and well they may be, what with hard work and mean food: but there are many without work: what must become of them? They must lie down and die for anything I know: for if they would beg, I know of none who will give anything, and if they rob or plunder, they have soldiers at Burnley ready to give them their last supper.

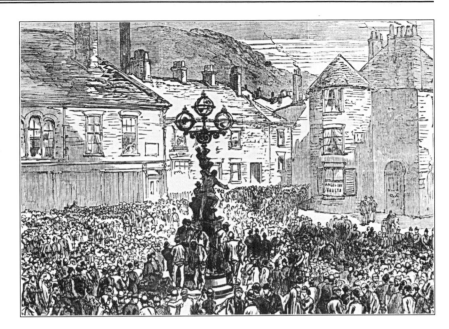

Rioters in Darwen town centre, an engraving from the *Illustrated London News*. Darwen, previously a small village, was fast growing as a mining, textiles and engineering town. As elsewhere, the older architectural heritage would soon be gone, although even today the ghost of the old village is detectable in the street pattern of the town centre.

Varley constantly denounced the manufacturers. To him they were 'inhuman and relentless', 'omniverous', 'satanic' and 'base fiends', who would rather pay to maintain soldiers at Burnley than raise wages to prevent 'poor vassals' dying at their looms.

In April, the Weavers Union Society of Blackburn wrote to the Home Secretary 'in the unadorned language of British mechanics':

> Within the last eleven years we have experienced rapid reductions in the prices of labour: and often there was not the least reason, until at this time we cannot procure more than one or two meals a day. Our dwellings are totally destitute of every necessary comfort. Every article of value has disappeared, either to satisfy the cravings of hunger or to appease the claims of relentless creditors; our homes where plenty and contentment once resided, are now become the abodes of penury and wretchedness. This, however, is only a faint picture of the situation of those fully employed. No adequate idea can be formed of the sufferings of those who are unemployed, of whom there are upwards of 7,000 in this town and neighbourhood. Were a humane man, Sir, to visit the dwellings of four-fifths of the weavers and see the miserable pittance, which sixteen hours of labour can procure, divided between the parents and the starving little ones, he would sicken at the sight and blush for the patience of humanity.

On 24 April rioting began in East Lancashire and continued for three days. Twenty-one mills were attacked and more than 1,000 power looms destroyed. Many of the rioters who marched on the first day

from Clayton-le-Moors through Accrington to Blackburn 'were farmed with pikes. There were two armed with guns, some with hammers, others with iron balance balls with wood handles driven into them, some with hatchets and picks. There were about sixty pikemen.' Thomas Duckworth, a 16-year-old Haslingden handloom weaver, who rose early that day to turn the grindstone on which the rioters sharpened their pikes, recalled in later life:

> Cotton weaving got to starvation work in 1826. I don't think anyone could make above 9s. a week, work as hard as they could. Food was dear—salt 4d. a pound, broken sugar 8d., lump sugar 1s. But working people didn't use much sugar. They had porridge and milk. I have had porridge twenty-one times a week . . . All farmers had loom shops and they fancied the power-loom was going to starve them to death.
>
> That morning we set off to the loom-breaking. When we had got on the road we saw horse soldiers coming towards us. There was a stop then. The soldiers came forward, their drawn swords glittering in the air. The people opened out to let the soldiers get through. Some threw their pikes over the dyke and some didn't. When the soldiers had come into the midst of the people, the officers called out, 'Halt!' All expected that the soldiers were going to charge, but the officers made a speech to the mob and told them what the consequences would be if they persisted in what they

Higher Grange Lane Factory, Accrington, the first factory attacked during the riots of April 1826. The factory was pulled down early in this century (photograph Accrington Library Local Studies Collection).

were going to do. Some of the old fellows from the mob spoke. They said, 'What are we to do? We're starving. Are we to starve to death?' The soldiers were fully equipped with haversacks and they emptied their sandwiches among the crowd. Then the soldiers left and there was another meeting. Were the power-looms to be broken or not? Yes, it was decided, they must be broken at all costs.

Hunger and despair drove these men and women to desperate acts, which were accomplished with a fearlessness that astonished all who witnessed them. On 26 April, an army officer wrote to the Home Secretary:

As Haslingden yesterday, notwithstanding the vicinity of a troop of cavalry, a mill [at Helmshore] was attacked and the machinery destroyed . . . Col. Kearney went to Haslingden this morning to endeavour to see something of the state of things and as early as seven o'clock the population were in movement to the number of almost 3,000 and successfully destroyed the power-looms of three mills. Having been applied to most earnestly by the proprietors of two other mills for protection, the colonel got together a picquet of 15 dragoons of the Bays with 20 men of the 60th Rifle Corps, when the Riot Act was read by a magistrate and every means used to prevail upon the mob to desist, but without effect and the military were consequently placed in a position to defend a mill at Chatterton, belonging to Mr Aitken, when they were immediately assailed with volleys of stone, which placed the colonel in the necessity of ordering them to fire. Several of the mob were killed [the actual figure was six] and it is to be feared from the incessant firing, which was kept up for more than a quarter of an hour, that a considerable number must have been wounded. Between 500 and 600 shots were fired. The populace then dispersed gradually, but with the avowed intention of returning with an overbearing force. They were supplied mostly with bludgeons, clubs, etc., but no arms were observed. The obstinacy and determination of the rioters was most extraordinary and such as I could not have credited had I not witnessed it myself.

Whitehead describes how the disturbances were ended—not by soldiers' bullets, but by a simple act of terrorism. The magistrates swore in a large number of special constables, who went 'in the dead of night' and arrested about twenty ringleaders. The prisoners were sent immediately to Lancaster Castle, so that in the morning

The inhabitants were all in amazement, one telling another that such and such had been fetched out of bed . . . This method of arresting them and taking them away at once completely put a stop to the breaking of power looms . . . The rioters were so frightened that a-many durst not go to bed in their own houses. Some left the country; others hid themselves for weeks, some in one place, some in another, some in coal pits—some, who few, if any, would have thought would have been guilty of such a crime.

7. *Starving to Death*

Following the riots, a number of manufacturers agreed to pay standard prices for weaving. The Bolton employers admitted that theirs was a 'starvation' list, but by August it was being disregarded by a number of men who were paying 30 per cent below the agreed amount. In an address to the manufacturers the weavers complained that 'a few unprincipled wretches' seemed fully determined to lower wages so long as there was a single shilling to deduct.

> The weavers are absolutely famishing; their houses in many instances are bereft of every particle of furniture; straw and shavings with the miserable rags which they are obliged to wear during the day time to cover their nakedness constitute the principal part of their bedding at night.
>
> It would be folly in us to expect that you continue to pay your present rate of wages unless others are compelled to do the same. We know that your stocks of cloth are accumulating beyond all precedent and that buyers do not even deign to call at your warehouse while the *grinders* are selling as quickly as they can produce, and their workmen receiving part of their wages out of the poor rates.

The manufacturers appealed to William Huskisson, President of the Board of Trade, to introduce legislation for a minimum wage. They enclosed the weavers' statement, which they fully supported. Some men, they said, by reducing wages far below the list agreed to, had monopolised trade 'to the exclusion of the respectable and humane manufacturers.' Huskisson replied that theirs was 'a vain and hazardous attempt to interpose the authority of the law between the labourer and his employer in regulating the demand for labour and the price to be paid for it.'

In the months that followed the weavers' distress, if anything, grew worse. A Haslingden correspondent of the *Blackburn Mail* reported in November 1826 that but for the work of the local ladies' relief committee, 'a great majority of the unemployed must literally perish from extreme want,' and the following month the *Liverpool Courier* gave this account of the district that included the nascent Southport.

A handloom weaver at work, one of a very small number of surviving illustrations of the subject, from the *Book of Trades*, 12th edition (1824).

It used to be assumed that the introduction of the power loom quickly ended the days of the handloom weaver, but remarkably large numbers continued the trade until the middle of the century and beyond, although they suffered increasingly poor earnings and living conditions.

The parish of North Meols contains about four thousand inhabitants, and a very considerable part of the people depend upon weaving for their daily bread: their business is now at the lowest ebb; many weavers cannot obtain work and those who do cannot provide for their families even by working hard for fifteen or sixteen hours a day. The distress which prevails there is very great, and as many of the sufferers are almost naked it would be a great kindness if old clothing or bedding or the means of procuring these necessities could be obtained for them.

In February of the following year, the *Liverpool Commercial Chronicle* described the state of the weaving districts:

The cotton weavers who reside principally in the neighbourhood of Bolton, Chorley, Wigan, Blackburn, Haslingden, Padiham, Burnley, Colne and Todmorden are by far the most wretched body in this part of the country. The number of cotton weavers in the places above-mentioned must exceed 60,000 and probably is near 100,000 and the utmost sum they can earn per week, on a fair average, working diligently from six till eight, allowing out of that time an hour and a half for meals, is only four shillings, even if the loom be their own; but if they have to hire the loom, they pay tenpence a week for it, and they must also buy shuttles etc., and keep the loom in repair. Great numbers cannot earn two shillings and sixpence, three shillings or three shillings and sixpence per week, but a very few good hands working at the best kind of work at Blackburn have earned eight shillings a week. I heard of a very active young man, and a good workman, who, by beginning at four o'clock in the morning and working till ten and eleven at night, earned last week the large sum of eight shillings and ninepence.

The colliery owner William Hulton, giving evidence to the 1827 Select Committee on Emigration, spoke of cases of distress, which 'I could not have conceived to exist in a civilised country.' It was 'almost incredible,' he said, to see the difference between the comfortable state of the miners in Hulton and the misery of the handloom weavers, who lived 'over the hedge' in the adjoining township of Westhoughton. There, half the 5,000 inhabitants were 'totally destitute of bedding and nearly so of clothes' and six per cent were in a state of famine.

Mrs Hulton and myself in visiting the poor, were asked by a person almost starving to go into a house. We there found on one side of the fire a very old man apparently dying; on the other side a young man about eighteen with a child on his knee whose mother had just died; and evidently both the young man and the child were suffering from want; of course, our object was to relieve them, and we were going away from the house when the woman said, 'Sir, you have not seen all'. We went upstairs, and, under some rags we found another young man, the widower; and on turning down the rags, which he was unable to move himself, we found another man who was dying and who did die in the course of the day. I have no doubt that the family were actually starving at the time.

In another case of extreme distress there were a widow and three

'Winding and weaving in the old days', a retrospective impression from Shaw's *Manchester Old and New*, published later in the 19th century.

This view, a 'compilation' from older engravings and paintings, tries to capture the crowded conditions and air of decay which were generally associated with the trade. But was it really like this? A vase of flowers on the windowsill and a bird in a cage hint at attempts to 'improve' the image—and certainly to sentimentalise it.

children who had not tasted the meal and water, which is the only thing almost they eat there for eight and forty hours.

I found a young man of sixteen in such a state of exhaustion that I was obliged to send a cart to bring him home and he is now under my care and we have hardly been able to maintain him in life. We found many families who had not made a meal in twenty four hours.

In the popular view handloom weaving, until its final extinction, remained a heart-breaking trade, and the commonly held belief is that the trade was more or less dead throughout Lancashire before 1850. Recent research using parish registers and census returns, however, has established that handloom weaving was much more resilient and adaptable than was once believed, and that it survived far longer. Certainly, it eventually died out and, since history is rarely written by the losers, its long and tenacious resistance was often ignored. And handloom weaving was unglamorous and unexciting to those thrilled by the onward march of technological progress, so it was perceived as inevitably doomed and, like the dinosaur, a failure.

But the work which has shown the unexpected tenacity and longevity of the trade has also thrown new light upon why the handloom weavers kept going. The shock stories of distress and misery were unquestionably based on true circumstances, but they often relate particularly to times of economic depression when all trade was bad. The handloom weavers could enjoy better times, and better wages. Many adapted their craft, learning to weave highly specialised textiles which could not be manufactured on the new but unsubtle and crude mechanical looms, or for which the market was limited—which meant that it was not worth investing in new specialised machinery. These were often high-value textiles, which meant that volume might be lower but income was not necessarily reduced.

And underpinning considerations such as these were other factors, often less tangible. Handloom weaving gave the opportunity for family working at home, and the advantages and social pleasures which that afforded are not to be discounted. It gave the possibility of combining weaving with other work, or with farming and smallholding. It allowed flexibility of timetables and working hours, and it enabled supervision of young children and babies while the mother worked.

At the other end of the process, many masters were—contrary to the popular image—conservative and unattracted by new technology and techniques. Many were seriously under-capitalised and lacked the opportunity to make changes in their methods. Not everybody could become a great mill-owning capitalist—by definition, indeed, most people could not—and many masters never even tried. So the eventual

Songs sung in 1853 during a Haslingden cotton mill strike for more pay.

The Haslingden Strike.

Air...................."Uncle Ned."

You may see of a truth that the people are not dead,
    Though 'tis said that they died long ago ;
But we've risen from our sleep, a holiday to keep,
    Determined to work under price no more.

Chorus.—So we've put by the reed-hook and the comb,
        And hung up the shuttle on the loom ;
    And we'll never be content till we get the 10 per cent,
        In spite of their "let well alone."

Old Ned wants a rest for we're sure that he's tir'd,
    And as he cannot speak for himself,
We'll put in a word that is certain to be heard,
    And place his crank-grinding music on the shelf.

Chorus.—So we've put by the reed-hook and the comb,
        And hung up the shuttle on the loom ;
    And we'll never be content till we get the 10 per cent,
        In spite of their "let well alone."

The fields they are green, and fragrant are the flowers,
    And the birds sweetly warble their notes ;
These things we'll enjoy while we hold our holiday,—
    'Twill be pleasanter than unweaving floats.

Chorus.—So we've put by the reed-hook and the comb,
        And hung up the shuttle on the loom ;
    And we'll never be content till we get the 10 per cent,
        In spite of their "let well alone."

We have spirit, tho' we're poor, we have pride although a mob
    We wish for the honour of our town ;
Yet we'll wander far and wide, whatever may betide,
    Aye! egad too, before we'll knuckle down.

Chorus.—So we've put by the reed-hook and the comb,
        And hung up the shuttle on the loom ;
    And we'll never be content till we get the 10 per cent
        In spite of their "let well alone."

THE TEN PER CENT QUESTION.

AIR.—"Oh! Susannah."

You lasses all of Haslingden, and lads to give consent,
To achieve a glorious object, namely, the Ten Per Cent,
When trade was bad in 48, and with hunger you was spent,
That was the time you was reduced in wages Ten Per Cent.

CHORUS.

    So now we'll try to make their hearts relent,
        And never rest until we've gained the advance of Ten
        Cent.

When trade was bad in 47, the food was very high,
And mothers had to learn again, the art of cookery,
For instead of flour we'd yellow meal, not so pleasant to the
    eye,
*Steam Engines superceded were by American bean pie.

    So now we'll try to make their hearts relent,
        And never rest until we've gained the advance of Ten
        Per Cent.

We ask now trade is good again, that employers should relent
And give us back, without delay, the advance of Ten Per
    Cent,
We know they can afford it, then why should they resent,
We only ask for justice, when we ask for Ten Per Cent.

    So now we'll try to make their hearts relent,
        And never rest until we've gained the advance of Ten
        Per Cent.

In days gone by our Town, though less, was more alive,
But now it's sad and gloomy like some monastic hive ;
If you wish to know the reason why,—this answer I have
    sent,
It is because our wages are too low by Ten Per Cent.

    So now we'll try to make their hearts relent,
        And never rest until we've gained the advance of Ten
        Per Cent.

triumph of the machine should not blind us to the fact that it was a long-lasting struggle, and that the handloom survived with remarkable persistence well after 1850. There were over 1,500 handloom weavers in the Leigh area as late as 1871, and even 1,250 in Oldham.

But poverty, misery and distress undoubtedly went hand-in-hand with the long fight for survival. The wretchedness and squalor of the weavers' lives had become a byword by the 1830s, and when the newspapers recorded conditions they often dismissed them in a few lines of statistics.

Conditions in May 1829 were as bad as those of 1826–27. Troops were stationed in all the manufacturing towns and rumours circulated of new plots to destroy the power-loom factories. In Burnley, some 2,760 people were existing on an income, exclusive of parochial relief, of 1s. 1½d. a week and there were 801 workers in the town whose weekly wage did not exceed 2s. 4½d. At Colne, 1,940 people, a third of the population, had an income of twopence a day; another 801 had threepence a day. A survey made in 1833 of thirty-five small towns and villages in north Lancashire showed that 49,294 people in 8,362 families dependent on handloom weaving had an average income of 1s. 3½d. a week for food and clothing. The investigation at Crompton was made by Joshua Milne, a local spinner and manufacturer, who found that many of the people he interviewed were so undernourished that they were unfit for work. Shocked by what he saw, he organised a public subscription and distributed blankets and clothing to the fustian weavers and their dependants. Milne told the 1833 Select Committee on Manufacturers Commerce and Shipping that many weavers would have been glad of factory employment not only for themselves, but also for their children. In many of the remote areas, however, handloom weaving was the only work available.

Probably the best description of the weaving districts of the east Lancashire uplands is that written by William Howitt in his *Rural Life of England*, published in 1838:

> Everywhere extend wild, naked hills, in many places totally un-reclaimed, in others enclosed, but exhibiting all the signs of neglected spiritless husbandry; with stunted fences or stone walls; and fields sodden with wet from want of drainage, and consequently overgrown with rushes. Over these naked and desolate hills are scattered to their very tops, in all directions, the habitations of a swarming population of weavers. The houses are as free from any attempt at beauty or ornament as possible. Without, where they have gardens, these gardens are as miserable and neglected as the fields; within they are squalid and comfortless. In some of these swarming villages; ay and in some of the cottages of the manufacturing towns, too, you can scarcely see a window with a whole pane of glass. In one

house in the outskirts of Blackburn, and that, too, an alehouse, we counted in a window of sixty panes forty-eight broken ones, and this window was in a pretty uniform character with its fellows; both in that house and the neighbouring ones. It is not possible to conceive a more melancholy contrast than that which the filth, the poverty and forlornness of these weavers' and spinners' dwellings form to the neatness, comfort and loveliness of the peasantry in many other parts of the kingdom. Any man who has once been through this district might again recognise the locality if he were taken thither blindfold, by the very smell of oatcake which floats about the villages and the sound of the shuttles with their eternal 'latitat, latitat'. I ranged wide from the bleak hills in the neighbourhood of Padiham, Belthorn, Guide and such places, and the numbers and aspect of the population filled me with astonishment. Through the long miserable streets of these villages children were as thick as motes in the sun. The boys and men, with their hair shorn off, as with a pair of

wool shears, close to their heads, and yet left hanging long over their eyes till it gave them a most villianous and hangman look. What makes these rough heads more conspicuous is their being so frequently red, a testimony of Nature to the ancient prevalence of the Dane on these hills. The men are beside long and bony; the women often of stalwart and masculine figure, and of a hardness of feature which give them no claims to be ranked amongst the most dangerous of the 'Lancashire Witches'. Everywhere the rudeness of the rising generation is wonderful. Everywhere the state of mingled ignorance and insolence meets you; everywhere a troop of lads is at your heels with the clatter of their wooden clogs, crying, 'Fellee, gie's a hawpenny.' In Ribchester our chaise was pursued by swarms of these wooden-shod lads like swarms of flies and were only beaten off for a moment to close in upon you again, and their sisters showed equally the extravagance of rudeness in which they were suffered to grow up, by running out of the houses as we passed and poking mops and brushes at the horses' heads. No one attempted to restrain or rebuke them; yet no one of the adult population offered you the least insult; and if you asked the way, gave you the most ready directions, and if you went into their houses, treated

For many emigration was the only way out . . . a characteristically heartbreaking mid-Victorian view, the young man's face raised in farewell ('the leaving of Liverpool'?) but also in hope of a new dawn, the young woman with the baby at her breast. But while the likes of these were leaving Lancashire, tens of thousands of Irish thought that immigration, not emigration, was the only salvation from their plight.

you with perfect civility and showed an affection for these little brats that was honourable to their hearts and wanted only directing by a better intelligence. The uncouthness of these poor people is not that of evil disposition, but of pressing poverty and continued neglect. As is generally the case, in the poorest houses were the largest families. Ten and eleven children in one small dirty hovel was no uncommon sight, actually covering the very floor till there scarce seemed room to sit down; and amid this crowd the mother was generally busy washing or baking oatcakes; and the father making the place resound with the 'latitat, latitat' of the shuttle. One did not wonder that the poor creatures are glad to turn out the whole troop of children to play on the hills, the elder girls lugging the babies along with them. The wildness into which some of these children, in the more solitarty parts of the country grow is, I imagine, not to be surpassed in any of the back settlement of America.

It would be wrong to suppose that the weavers' children led lives as carefree as Howitt's account might suggest. Child labour was as much a part of cottage industry as of the factory system, and its abuses, though rarely recorded, were equally appalling. Joseph Livesey, the temperance advocate, who was born in 1794, describes in his autobiography how 'as soon as I was able I was put to weaving' in the cellar in a house at Walton-le-Dale where his grandfather and uncle had three looms.

For seven years I worked in the corner of that damp cellar, really unfit for any human being to work in. From the day it was plastered to the day I left it, the mortar was soft, the water remaining in the walls. And to make matters worse, the Ribble and Darwen sometimes overflowed their banks and inundated this and cellars adjoining. It has often been the subject of surprise how I escaped with my life, sitting all the long day close to the damp wall, and I can only suppose that this was counteracted in a great measure by the incessant action of almost every muscle in the body required in weaving.

In January 1830 a Royton handloom weaver was arrested for cruelty to two boys and two girls he employed. After getting up at five, six and at the latest seven o'clock, the children were compelled to work at their looms until midnight and sometimes until one and two o'clock the next morning. When their master was dissatisfied with their work, he beat them with a knotted rope. The children were never allowed to go out of the house and their only food was porridge and occasionally potatoes. They were reduced to one meal a day if their master considered they were not working hard enough.

Children and young people who wove in their own homes were more to be commiserated with than most operatives in large factories, a witness told a parliamentary committee in 1843.

I have frequently seen them at work in their cold, dark, damp cellars without any fire or means of ventilation, and the atmosphere, on entering the room was literally foetid with the breath of the inmates. They are at liberty to work what hours they please; but many of them work from very early in the morning till late at night to make the smallest pittance. I have frequently been told by young boys in this trade that they work from five in the morning till twelve at night for many days without intermission.

Like the mill workers, the handloom weavers were fined for faulty or alleged faulty workmanship. Peter Holland in his *Recollections of 'Old' Swinton* tells of the 'tyrannical' Giles Gee of Kearsley, a putter-out who measured the weavers' pieces with a thirty eight inch 'yardstick' and who fined them a shilling for every hole he discovered in their cloth. On one occasion a weaver, who was found to have two small holes in his piece, complained that the fine was unreasonably large. 'It's a shilling a hole, big or small,' said Gee, whereupon the weaver took out his knife and made the two small holes into a large one. 'I have spoiled your cloth,' he observed, 'but I have saved a shilling.'

The system of 'baiting and fining' in cotton mills was insignificant when compared with 'the terrible robberies' committed on the Lancashire silk weavers, said a writer in 1840.

A putter-out who goes to Leigh twice every week to take in weavers' work, says that he takes in abatements £15 each day at least. And he says the weavers call him the best putter-out in the district. On being asked why he took so much of the weavers' money from them, his answer was that, 'I must either do it or go weaving myself . . . then others would do the same to me.'

The Rossendale historian Thomas Newbigging, in a reference to the handloom weavers who lived on the bleak moorland between Bacup and Todmorden, quotes an 'old dame' who recounted the days 'when,' as Newbigging put it, 'there was plenty of law, but a sad lack of justice dealt out to the workers.'

Yei, it wur hard wark for poor folk i' those days. We geet sixpence a cut for weyving and in a whool week, working long hours, we couldna get through moore nor about nine or ten cuts—for they were twenty yards long apiece. That would mak five shillings a week at moast; and when we had finished 'em we had to carry 'em on our backs two or three miles to th' taker-in. I con remember my owd mon once takin his cuts in, and he had tramped through th' weet and snow on a cowd winter's mornin, and when he had gettin his cuts passed by th' taker-in, he axed him if he would gie him a penny to buy a penny moufin to eat as he wur goin back home. But th' taker-in said to him: 'Eh, mon! If I wur to gie thee a penny it would be gieing thee o th' profit 'at our maisters get fro' a cut! [whereas at the time they were probably making a clear guinea by each of them]. They're nearly working at a loss now by every cut yo weyving. No, it'll never do to gie thee pennies i' that reckless way, Jone.' It wur hard wark i' thoose days, I con tell thi to get porritch and skim milk twice a day, wi' happen a bit o' bacon on Sundays. Once I had to go fro' near to Stoodley Pike across Langfield Moor wi' my cuts. It wur a raw cowd mornin, very early, before it wur gradely leet. An' when I geet to th' taker-in—eh' an' they wur hard uns wur thoose takers-in!—he says 'Hillo! are you here so soon, Betty? Warn't you fley'd o' meetin' th' deil this morning as you coom across Langfield Moor?' I said, 'Nowt o' th' soart. I wur noan feart o' meetin th' deil up o' th' moor, for I knew th' hangments weel that I'd find th' deil when I geet here!'

The old dame's sentiments find an echo in the verses of Joseph Hodgson, the Blackburn handloom weaver.

> *Ye weavers of Blackburn, come hear to my song*
> *When I sing of tyrants I seldom do wrong;*
> *For if they transport me to Canada's wild shore,*
> *I then shall have freedom when I have sailed o'er;*
> *Free from slavery,*
> *Fetters and knavery,*
> *Never tormented with tyrants again!*

Wherever one looks, it is impossible to find a single cheerful event with which to relieve the story of the weavers' woe. After listening for many hours to fearful evidence, a member of the 1834 Select Committee asked John Makin, a Bolton manufacturer: 'Do you recollect an instance of any handloom weaver having by prudence contrived to save a sum of money and to build a house or invest it in any other way?' Makin replied that he did indeed know of a street of fine houses built by weavers, 'but it was under very extraordinary circumstances.' The money was borrowed, relations helped and the weavers 'happened to have families that were very industrious, labouring from four o'clock in the morning till 10 at night and who denied themselves the comforts and luxuries of life.' One man had not tasted strong drink or butter or sugar for ten years, but even with such frugality the weavers could not maintain the houses with the income from their looms alone.

A Heywood man of 83, looking back over his life in 1840, was filled with gloom by what he saw.

When I was a boy of fifteen [in 1772] I wove upon a handloom;

Occupation	Men	Women	Children
Weekly earnings in Manchester trades, 1832 (selected examples)			
Spinners	20s.–25s.	10s.–15s.	
Piecers			4s. 6d.–7s.
Scavengers			1s. 7d.–2s.7d.
Cardroom hands	14s. 5d.–17s.	9s.–9s. 5d.	6s.–7s.
Nankeen hand weavers			
fancy	9s.–15s.		
best	10s.–13s.		
Check hand weavers			
fancy	7s.–7s. 5d.		
common			6s.–7s.
Cambric hand weavers	6s.–6s. 5d.	6s.–6s. 5d.	6s.–6s. 5d.
Non-textile:			
Porters	14s.–15s.		
Shoemakers	15s.–16s.		
Carpenters	10s.		
Bricklayers' labourers	12s.		

(after J. G. Timmins, *The Last Shift* (1993), Table 6.1)

my mother carded cotten by hand and spun on the hand-wheel. We managed to get a good living by working eight hours a day. The weft I wove was eight hanks to the pound and I could get more at this time than two weavers can get now in Heywood, taking into account the price of provisions. With few exceptions matters have been getting worse from that day to this.

As the industrial stagnation of the first three years of the new decade overwhelmed handloom weavers and mill workers alike, bringing distress as severe as that of 1826–27, few would have disagreed with his assertion.

In October 1840 the *Bolton Chronicle* reported that the value of hand machinery in the Rochdale woollen trade had fallen so greatly that a poor man had sold four pairs of broad looms and two spinning jennies for thirty shillings to pay his rent. A few years before 'they would have been sold for as many pounds.' In September of the following year Mr Sharman Crawford, MP for Rochdale, told the Commons that 136 people in the town were living on 6d. a week, 200 on 10d., 500 on 1s. 6d. and 1,500 on 1s. 10d. Five-sixths of these people had hardly any blankets and 85 had none. There were 46 families with no covering at all.

Mount Pleasant Street West, Preston, photographed in the early 1950s shortly before these cottages were demolished.

The cellars were originally used by handloom weavers. There were hundreds of dwellings of this sort in nineteenth-century Preston. Today only three survive in the whole town.

By November 1841 conditions in Bolton were 'scarcely possible to conceive.' Living in a cellar in Higher Bridge Street, was a weaver, his wife and four children. The weaver's weekly budget was:

Income after paying for hire of loom		3s. 6d.
Rent	1s. 0d.	
Coal	10d.	
Candles	3d.	
Total Outlay		2s. 1d.
Remaining		1s. 5d.

In addition he received a shilling for each of two children of his wife's previous marriage, making a total of 3s. 5d. for food and clothing. A correspondent of the *Bolton Free Press* described a visit to the cellar:

There is a pair of bedsteads and a scanty bed, with an old sheet and cover, but neither table, chair nor stool. The wife told us that she had no chemise to wear, neither had three of the children [girls], but the other, a boy, had a shirt on. On my asking why she laid out so much for coals, while they had so little for food, she replied 'that on account of the cellar being very damp, they were obliged to keep up a fire, if possible, or they would be 'shivered' to death.' There was not a mouthful of anything eatable in the house, and she said their only food was water gruel and that only twice a day. Indeed, it is hardly possible to conceive how they manage to get that when we consider that two meals a day for six persons will make eighty four meals a week, to be provided for out of 3s. 5d.!!!—about one halfpenny a meal!

In December 1841 the Statistical Committee of the Anti-Corn Law League collected information from 1,003 poor families in Bolton. They found that 5,305 persons were living on 1s. 2d. to 1s. 2½d. a week; that more than half the 1,553 beds were filled with chaff; that some 53 families were without beds; that 452 people were sleeping on the floor; and that there was one blanket for every ten persons. In Accrington the Committee learned that many families had been existing for months on a shilling a head per week and a Manchester clergyman listed 2,000 people in the city who had no bed to go to and 8,666 living on 1s. 2½d. a week.

The Committee also calculated that a handloom weaver who wove a mile of cloth forty inches wide received thirty three shillings.

> For this sum his feet travel (with the treddles) through a space of nine hundred miles; his hand in picking the shuttle travels through the space of 2,160 miles. In addition to all this, the weavers are known to walk ten miles to and from the warehouse in fetching and taking back their work. The calculation is based on a common fabric, a 28-reed jaconet, 10 picks to a quarter inch, the price of weaving being 4½d. for twenty yards.

Joseph Livesey, in the second number of his anti-Corn Law newspaper *The Struggle*, told the story of a poor woman who paid a visit to her relations in Preston at the end of 1841.

> She went to nine houses, and none of them could afford her a meal's meat: the last place she called at was in Albert Street, where the man pawned his shirt for 6d. with which four pennyworth of bread, one pennyworth of butter and one pennyworth of tea were purchased for the party.

Five months later, he noted in the same paper that every day 'immense quantities of goods' were taken for sale in Preston town centre.

> Crowds of people are in attendance, and two or three auctioneers are frequently employed. Much of the furniture, if it can be so called, consists of poor people's 'traps' distrained for rent; while no small portion belongs to persons who are preparing to leave the country.

By the middle of 1842 thousands of Lancashire people had been reduced to utter wretchedness and despair. Dr P. M. McDouall, the Ramsbottom Chartist, told the Select Committee on Payment of Wages that he had seen as many as five hundred handloom weavers and factory workers begging through the villages around Blackburn, Clitheroe and Bury. 'They said they had not been in a bed for the last five months and had to sleep on wood shavings or anywhere that shelter was afforded.' And the *Liverpool Mercury* said of East Lancashire:

> This part of the country is in a terrible state for hundreds and thousands have neither work nor meat. They are daily begging in the streets of Haslingden, twenty and thirty together, crying for bread. Meetings are held every Sunday on the neighbouring hills attended by thousands of poor, hungry, haggard people, wishing for any change, even though it should be death.

W. Cooke Taylor, who made a tour of the Lancashire manufacturing districts in the summer of 1842, found at Burnley 'groups of idlers . . . their faces haggard with famine and their eyes rolling with that fierce and uneasy expression which I have often noticed in maniacs.' At Colne:

> I visited eighty three dwellings selected at hazard. They were destitute of furniture, save old boxes for tables and stools, or even large stones for chairs; the beds were composed of straw and shavings, sometimes with torn pieces of carpet or packing canvas for a covering, and sometimes without any kind of covering whatever. The food was oatmeal and water for breakfast, flour and water with a little skimmed milk for dinner; oatmeal and water again for a third supply for those who went through the form of eating three meals a day. I was informed in fifteen families that their children went without the 'blue milk', or milk from which the cream had been taken, on alternate days. I was an eye witness to children appeasing the craving of the stomach by the refuse of decayed vegetables in the root market. I saw a woman in the very last stage of extenuation suckling an infant which could scarcely draw a single drop of nourishment from her exhausted breast. I inquired the child's age? Fifteen months. Why was it not weaned? Another mouth would be added to the number of those for whom the present supply of oatmeal was insufficient. I was told that there had been several instances of death by sheer starvation.

But wherever Cooke Taylor went he found that 'the extreme of wretchedness' was combined with 'a high tone of moral dignity, a marked sense of propriety, a decency, cleanliness and order.' And he concluded: 'I have often seen and heard of abject distress, but noble distress was worth coming hundreds of miles to witness and thousands of miles if the visitor could bring relief.'

8. *The Factory System*

If the first half of the nineteenth century left the handloom weavers dispirited and on the verge of extinction, it left most factory workers with a sense of achievement and the prospects of better times to come. The worst abuses of the factory system had disappeared, and what was equally important, working hours and conditions were regulated by law and enforced by paid inspectors. (Few MPs, and even fewer working people, even as late as 1830, would have foreseen Parliament embarking on such extraordinary legislation.) Leonard Horner, the Factories Inspector, wrote in his report for June 1853:

> I have again and again heard those who knew the state of the children in factories prior to 1833 and contrast it with what it is now, bless the members of the legislature by whose individual

Children in a mule spinning room, *c.*1835, from F. Trollope, *Life and Adventures of Michael Armstrong* (1840).

exertions the merciful curtailment of the long weary working day was brought about. Nor do they confine themselves to the state of the children; they speak of the happy change produced by the general operation of the law upon the condition moral and physical of the whole factory population.

A Blackburn mill worker spoke for a great many of his class in 1849, when he said of the Ten Hours Act, which had come into force in the previous year:

> It is only now that operatives can enjoy gardens and other advantages they have gained by the Act. Formerly they could not take a walk in the mill yard, but were locked inside the mill from five in the morning till nine at night. For 38 years of my life I was so closely immured in the factory that I never saw a field of corn cut by the hand of the husbandman. I had no opportunity of witnessing such a sight except on Sunday and that was the day the harvestman rested from his labour.

In February of the same year, the Rev. J. R. Stephens, the Ashton-under-Lyne Nonconformist minister and factory reformer, also looked back over the years.

> It will be difficult [he wrote in the *Ashton Chronicle*] for the reader of history to realise that here, in this England of ours, men were made to work, and did work, in hot and stifling rooms, fifteen and even seventeen hours out of every twenty-four. Still more difficult will it be for him to comprehend that women of all ages, and children not as yet come to any reckoned age at all, worked nearly as long as their fathers and their husbands; that whilst health sunk, strength failed and death ultimately hurried all away, the only gain the worker had was the barest bread from day to day, and even this had to be doled out to him from the parish purse. Most certainly will that which is now considered as our glory form material for sad moralities under the more appropriate title of 'England's folly in the nineteenth century.'

It is certainly difficult, a century later, to realise how bad life was in a great many Lancashire mills. Stephens was not exaggerating and if he failed to mention the masters who showed an interest in their workpeople's welfare, it was doubtless because they represented such a tiny percentage of their class. Even when one bears in mind the fact that long hours were worked by most people before the Industrial Revolution and that severe corporal punishment of erring children was advocated by the leading educationalists of the early nineteenth century; even when one agrees that discipline was essential in factories; and even when one makes allowances for ill-educated mill masters who were so dazzled by unaccustomed riches that they became blind to the hardships endured by their workers, one still finds great difficulty in comprehending the barbarities that were so widespread in Lancashire.

Of all the many statements made by Lancashire workers about their experiences of the early factory system, there is only one that is entirely enthusiastic, and this loses much of its rapture when it is considered in its proper context. The long eulogist was Kitty Wilkinson the pioneer (in Liverpool) of British public bath-houses, who went to work at Low Mill at Caton, near Lancaster, in 1798, when she was twelve. The mill was unusual in having a library and an 'airing ground', and the apprentice house according to Kitty was 'a heaven on earth, where we were brought up in ignorance of evil, and where Mr Norton, the manager, was a father to all.' *Chambers' Miscellany*, of 1845, which told the story, said the hours of work 'were not long and were precisely fixed,' but in 1823, the mill worked twelve and a half hours a day with only a quarter of an hour for breakfast and three quarters of an hour for dinner. To appreciate the young girl's feelings, one must consider the conditions under which many of her contemporaries laboured. By contrast, Caton was indeed 'a heaven on earth'.

Joseph Livesey, the Preston temperance reformer, who was born in 1794, spent his childhood in Walton-le-Dale, where the apprentices from Penwortham Factory attended church on Sundays. They were, he wrote in his magazine, *The Moral Reformer*, 'poor, squalid, deformed beings, the most pitiful objects I think I have ever beheld. They were apprenticed to a system to which nothing but West Indian slavery can bear any analogy.' In his autobiography he added that many of the children—they were said to have been obtained from the Foundling Hospital in London—were crooked-legged through having to stop the machinery by placing their knees against it.

Robert Southey, who visited a Manchester cotton mill at the beginning of the nineteenth century, was told by the manager:

> Manufacturers are favourable to population. The poor are not afraid of having a family here. The parishes therefore have always plenty to apprentice, and we take them as fast as they can supply us.

One group of children, with only an hour and a half for meals, worked from five in the morning until six in the evening when they were replaced by another group who worked throughout the night. ('It is a common tradition in Lancashire that the beds *never got cold!*' John Fielden, the factory reformer, wrote later of apprentices like these.) Southey said of the Manchester workers:

> They are deprived in childhood of all instruction and all enjoyment; of the sports in which childhood instinctively indulges, of fresh air by day and natural sleep by night. Their health, physical and moral, is alike destroyed, and they die of diseases induced by unremitting

task work, by confinement in the impure atmosphere of crowded rooms, by the particles of metallic or vegetable dust which they are continually inhaling; or they live to grow up without comfort and without hope, without religion and without shame, and bring forth slaves like themselves to tread in the same path of misery.

Not far away at Pendleton many apprentices employed by William Douglas (1746–1810) became lame from standing for fourteen or more hours each day. Local people spoke of 'The Cripples Factory' and 'The White Slave Mill' long after 'Black' Douglas was dead. Another infamous mill was at Backbarrow, a remote hamlet near the southern tip of Windermere. The life led by the 150 children, who were recruited from London and Liverpool workhouses, was described to a Commons Committee in 1816. The apprentices rose at 4.30 and began work in the cotton mill at 5. They had a half-hour break for breakfast and another from 12 to 12.30 for dinner. From then until 8 o'clock the children, who were aged from seven to eleven, worked without rest and were given no refreshment apart from an afternoon drink, which they took while tending the machines. Sometimes the mill worked until 9 o'clock and even later. And for all this time the children had to stand: there were no seats in the mill. From 6 a.m. to mid-day on Sundays was spent in cleaning the machinery. The apprentice master said he inspected the dormitory every night because a number of children were always missing. Some ran away and some fell asleep exhausted on the mill floor. Young workers were 'very frequently' injured by the machinery and several became deformed. 'There were two or three that were very crooked,' he said. When one mill owner went bankrupt, he had the apprentices taken in carts to the edge of Morecambe Bay and turned adrift to beg their way to their former parishes, but following complaints by a number of gentlemen at Lancaster they were eventually returned to the mill and resumed work for a new proprietor. The Commons committee had before it a letter from the minister of Finsthwaite Chapel, to which the children were sent on Sundays. 'During the service they behave with great propriety and they appear to be neat and clean,' he wrote and then added in a postscript, 'I beg leave to state that out of 150 children there have been only six deaths in the last seven years; and three of these came to the place in a very sickly state and one was drowned by accident.'

9. *Fourteen Hours A Day*

The Lancashire apprentices were not alone in their misfortune. Mill life for most children was abominable, as Robert Dale Owen found in 1815, when he accompanied his father Robert Owen on a tour of the chief textile factories to gather information about child labour. In his autobiography, *Threading My Way*, he wrote:

> The facts we collected seemed to me terrible almost beyond belief. Not in exceptional cases, but as a rule we found children of ten years old worked regularly fourteen hours a day, with a half-an-hour's interval for the mid-day meal, which was eaten in the factory. In the fine yarn cotton mills they were subjected to this labour in a temperature usually exceeding seventy five degrees; and in all the cotton factories they breathed an atmosphere more or less injurious to the lungs because of the dust and minute cotton fibres that pervaded it.
>
> In some cases we found that greed had impelled the mill owners to still greater extremes of inhumanity, utterly disgraceful indeed to a civilised nation. Their mills were run fifteen and in exceptional cases sixteen hours a day with a single set of hands; and they had no scruple to employ children of both sexes from the age of eight and we actually found a considerable number under that age.
>
> Such a system could not be maintained without corporal punishment. Most of the overseers openly carried stout leather thongs and we frequently saw even the youngest children severely beaten.
>
> We sought out the surgeons who were in the habit of attending these children, noting the names and the facts to which they testified. Their stories haunted my dreams. In some large factories from one-fourth to one-fifth of the children were cripples or otherwise deformed, or permanently injured by excessive toil, sometimes by

Factory life as portrayed by Robert Cruikshank in 1832. Cartoons such as this, depicting the evils of the factory system, played an important part in the campaign of persuasion and propaganda which resulted in the passing of successive Factory Acts.

NOTICE!

On the 1st of January, 1872, the following alterations in hours of WORK and MEAL TIMES will take place :--

45 minutes will be allowed for Breakfast.

The Works will Open at 6 a.m. and Close at 6 p.m. on every working day except Saturday, when the Works will close at Half-past 12 as usual.   To state in full detail :--

The Bell will ring on Monday, Tuesday, Wednesday, Thursday and Friday, as follows :--

In   at   6-0   a.m.
Out at   8-0   „   for Breakfast.
In   at   8-45   „
Out at   12-30   p.m.   for Dinner.
In   at   1-30   „
Out at   6-0   „

The Bell will ring on Saturday :--

In   at   6-0   a.m.
Out at   8-0   „   for Breakfast.
In   at   8-45   „
Out at   12-30.

57 hours will constitute 6 days.
9½   „   „   „   1 day.

The Gates will be closed immediately the Bell stops ringing, and all late-time will be strictly deducted.

No preparations for Meals will be allowed in working hours. Every person must be ready for work when the Bell stops ringing IN, and must not prepare to leave before the Bell commences ringing OUT.

BROAD OAK PRINT WORKS.   **F. W. Grafton & Co.**

J. EDWARDS, MACHINE PRINTER, 11, ABBEY-ST., ACCRINGTON.

An 1871 poster from Accrington advertising meal times and hours of work. The regulation of hours, the defining of meal times, and the giving of formal notice of changes all represented—by the standards of the time—major improvements upon the situation forty years before.

brutal abuse. The younger children seldom held out more than three or four years without severe illness, often ending in death.

When we expressed surprise that parents should voluntarily condemn their sons and daughters to slavery so intolerable, the explanation seemed to be that many of the fathers were out of work themselves and so were, in a measure, driven to the sacrifice for lack of bread; while others imbruted by intemperance, saw with indifference the abuse of the infant faculties, compared with which the infanticide of China may almost be termed humane.

There is ample evidence to support Owen's statement. William Hall, who was sent to work in a Preston cotton mill at the age of seven, wrote in 1826:

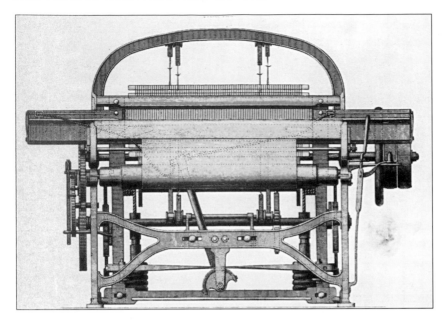

The front view of a
cast-iron power loom
of about 1830, from
Baines, *History of the
Cotton Manufacture*
(1835).

A Stockport power
loom weaving factory
in about 1830: an en-
graving from Ure,
*The Philosophy of
Manufactures* (1835).

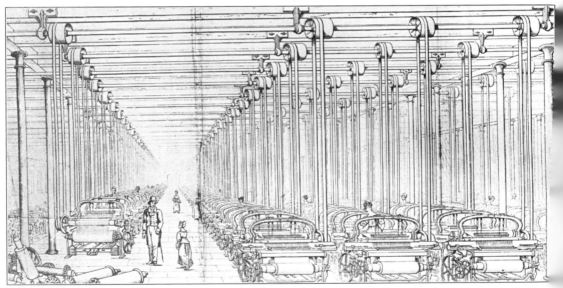

I had to rise early and work late; and to endure heavy infliction
for very trifling faults. My orders were never to sit down during
the hours of actual work . . . I have been knocked down without
warning and brutally kicked when prostrate and dare not com-
plain . . . Once I was fifteen minutes late: for this offence I was
beaten, kicked and scourged a length of time that would appear
incredible were I to name its duration. My whole frame was covered
with weals and contusions. I could hardly stand when my tormentor
gave over, but was instantly driven to my work. I lost my appetite

for food that day and for weeks afterwards I felt the effect of that merciless correction.

For another slight offence, Hall had to stand for some time with his neck trapped between a heavy window frame and the sill. Later he took a job at Hoghton Bottoms, between Blackburn and Preston. There

> I was almost daily the silent witness of extreme suffering amongst the children, whose general appearance bespoke every species of wretchedness . . . I saw a sickly, diseased-looking boy under eight years of age fixed upon a box and forced [for half an hour] to stand erect, his right hand elevated as nearly perpendicular as possible, and forced to hold a weight, which I think rather exceeded than fell short of seven pounds, in the palm of his hand. If the feeble creature bent the arm, the overlooker gave him severe blows with a strap.

A correspondent of the *Preston Chronicle* wrote in April 1846:

> So far back as 1804, to my own knowledge, some of the mills in the Wigan neighbourhood ran from five o'clock in the morning in the winter season until nine o'clock at night: and at times a goodly number of children from eight to ten years of age were employed in them, who, after nightfall, had to be kept awake by the energetic powers of the overseer's strap.

In March 1827, the Manchester firm of Thackery and Russell was fined £20 for employing a six-year-old girl from a quarter to five in the morning to a quarter past ten at night. She and other children were allowed half an hour for breakfast and an hour for dinner, but 'took their tea by snatches as the work went on.' A witness said he had frequently seen children at the mill nod over their work as if scarcely able to keep on their feet. The girl earned 1s. 6d. a week as a scavenger in the spinning room, but was taken away from the mill when her health began to fail. The firm defended the case, arguing that scavenging was not an occupation covered by the Factory Acts.

At meetings held to protest against working conditions, Lancashire men often described their early days in the mills. The following accounts are typical of many:

> Fifty three years ago, when I was six years of age, I was taken to the factory—dragged from my bed at five o'clock in the morning with the rising of the sun and kept at it until the sun had gone down.—*A Preston operative in 1844.*

> Before I was seven, I was placed in a mill and at that time the strap and rope were used, and we were belaboured with them twice

a day at least. We thought ourselves lucky if we escaped with less than three knocks a day.—*A Bolton overlooker in 1845.*

The rising generation enjoy many advantages over those who were brought up in the mill when I was a lad. Then they were sent to the factory when only seven or eight and had to work and eat like horses—first a bite and sup, then piece up, next to clean under and so on continuously.—*A Bolton operative in 1851.*

A Rossendale father was so incensed at the long hours his children were compelled to work that he went to the mill and threw a bed on the workroom floor, telling them in the hearing of the master, 'Theigher, tha con go to bed straight away when tha wark's done; and tha'll be theur ready i' t' morn.'

Another Rossendale man, Moses Heap (1824–1913), wrote in his autobiography:

I do not know at what age I began to go to the mill, but I do remember being carried on father's back at five years of age to work . . . I often think of the dark and dreary times we had in those days with twelve hours work each day . . . Even as I grew older the nights of Winter seemed dreadfully long.

At the mill where Heap worked a lifesize effigy made of cotton was carried on a man's back to frighten the young children and so keep them awake.

Children who lived at a distance from their work had extra tribulations. The Haslingden historian, Major David Halstead, set down this story told to him by a factory operative:

When I was a boy, my younger brother, who was then under six years of age, and I worked at Pinch Dickey's mill at Edenfield. We lived in Haslingden and had to make the journey of about four miles every morning and reach the mill by six o'clock, winter and summer, wet or fine. Sometimes we had to fight our way through snowdrifts during a winter blizzard, and my younger brother often dropped from fatigue and exposure. Then I had to carry him on my back and at the end of the journey we were both dead beat before commencing work. Imagine our condition during the long day, soaking wet or half frozen: and when work was

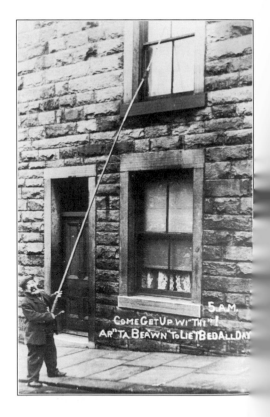

A knocker-up (Burnley Library Local Studies Collection).

The knocker-up— often an elderly man who had had to give up more arduous work—was the textile workers' alarm clock. His job was a vital one, although it eventually became (perhaps because of the *double entendre* of the name) an ingredient of music-hall 'stage Lancashire'.

finished the long journey home through the snow and mud—and no lamplights. A hurried meal and off to bed, sometimes having to be carried up asleep—shirt, stockings and every patch of clothing drying before the fire—and to be awakened again for another agonising day before we had obtained half the sleep we required. Before I reached my 21st birthday I felt like an old man and have been denied good health because of the hardships of my early youth.

A surgeon told a public meeting in Bury in 1846 that some of the children who worked as piecers in the mills walked 24 miles a day. He often called on the factory workers and had seen children return home and immediately fall asleep on the floor before they had time to eat a meal.

For a family too poor to afford a clock or the services of a 'knocker-up'—a man who woke the workers by rattling on their bedroom windows with a long pole—getting to the mill on time was a daily worry, and there are several accounts on record of children arriving long before starting time. A Manchester correspondent of the *Lancashire and Yorkshire Co-operator* wrote in April 1832 that when he and a friend were returning home from a public dinner at two in the morning they saw a girl aged about seven shivering with cold by the gates of a factory:

> Such a sight at such an hour excited our curiosity and we enquired why she was sitting there. She replied that she was waiting for the factory gates to open and very innocently enquired how much it wanted to six o'clock. 'Four hours, child,' was our reply. The poor little creature was astonished, but told us that she had been beaten for not being in time the morning before, and that she could not sleep and her mother had no clock and she was afraid of being late again.

Rowland Destroisier, the self-taught Manchester workman, who became a mill book-keeper and a celebrated lecturer on social and political subjects, told the 1833 Factory Commission:

> I have seen children, who have been too early called, sitting together in the ash-pit of the fire of our boilers, placing their bare feet in the warm ashes and sleeping with their heads on one another's shoulders until the bell rang, at which time they were expected to go to work. On those occasions, I have observed mischievous lads snatch up the hot cinders as they fell from the fire and throw them on those who were sleeping.

Recent opinion has tended to correct the view that very large numbers of children were sent to work at the earliest possible age. Child labour was, entirely properly, a subject of the gravest concern to early and mid-nineteenth-century reformers, and their powerful and harrowing accounts have led later generations to suppose that child labour was well-nigh universal. That it was not, and that many children—even in the mill towns of Lancashire—did not labour in this way is now becoming apparent.

10. *A Depressing Report*

As early as 1802, Parliament, largely at the instigation of the first Sir Robert Peel, had passed an Act 'for the preservation of the health and morals of apprentices and others employed in cotton and other mills.' It laid down that no apprentice was to work more than twelve hours a day, excluding meal times, and that every apprentice was to be taught reading, writing and arithmetic during some part of the working day. Another provision was the appointment in all the manufacturing districts of two visitors—a JP and a clergyman of the Established Church—who were required to report 'from time to time' to the quarter sessions on the state of the mills and the apprentices. This Act, as we have seen, was widely ignored, as was the Factory Act of 1819, which forbade the employment in cotton mills of children under nine and restricted the working hours of those aged between nine and sixteen to twelve hours daily. In 1823, however, the Home Office called for reports on the working of the Acts and visitors were hurriedly appointed to tour the factories. Their reports, some of which were not received until the following year, vary considerably. Despite considerable hostility in some quarters—Rochdale workpeople were taught to consider them as 'persons decidedly inimicable to their private interests'—several visitors carried out their duties conscientiously, but others, who showed no great keenness for an unpaid task which involved them in considerable travelling, appear to have made only superficial investigations. The 1823–24 reports, however, are important in giving the first official description of factory conditions. What emerges is a depressing picture relieved only by the accounts of two or three well-conducted mills.

The visitors for the Lower Division of Blackburn Hundred said they had not met with a single instance in which all the requirements of the Factory Acts had been complied with. Children under nine were found in all but four of the twenty-two mills in the district, though the visitors pointed out that most of them were 'engaged, paid and discharged by the spinners, without the interference of the masters, who seldom make any inquiry as to their age.' The children at one mill refused to give their ages; at another they claimed not to know how old they were; and at a third one boy said his mother had told him to say he was nine, though he admitted he was younger. Half the mills were found to be dirty or very dirty and only three were clean and well ventilated. Only one mill, that of Lund and Foster, at Wensley Fold, near Blackburn, had a day school, but three masters sent their factory children to Sunday schools. Most mills worked 72 hours a week, usually 12½ hours from Monday to Friday and nine and a half hours on Saturday, but time lost because of accidents or repairs to the steam engine was made up at the rate of half an hour a day. A mill in Haslingden Grane worked only 70 hours, but two at Chipping worked 78. Neither of the Chipping mills followed the usual practice of allowing half an hour for breakfast and an hour for dinner. At Mr Bond's factory, which employed 36 people, no regular time was allowed for breakfasts. 'Such as can be spared,' said the visitors, 'are allowed to go to their breakfasts and the remainder have their breakfasts brought to them. Half an hour is allowed for dinner in the winter and a longer time in summer.' The 74 workers at Middleton, Routh and Co.'s factory had their breakfasts brought to them and the machinery was not allowed to stop while they ate. They had 50 minutes for dinner. When the visitors went to Mr James Livesey's mill at Hoghton Bottoms, they were told that the usual meal breaks were observed, 'but being in the neighbourhood about dinner time, we noticed the time which elapsed between the ringing of the dinner bell and the work bell, and it did not exceed thirty-five minutes.' At only one mill, at Holden Wood, near Haslingden, were the workpeople given a half hour break for tea in the afternoon. A novel method of time keeping was used by Banister Eccles and Co., of Blackburn. The firm used an 'engine clock', an instrument affixed to and worked by the steam engine.

> The steam engine is calculated to make, at its regular speed, twenty three strokes in a minute, but in consequence of a greater quantity of machinery being connected with it than there ought to be, the engine is not able to make more than twenty strokes in a minute . . . Thus the workpeople are confined to an hour extra every day, and are only paid for doing the work which is accomplished in the usual hours in other factories.

In their attitude towards meal breaks, the mill owners in the Blackburn Lower Division were far more generous than many of their colleagues. Not one of the 60 mills in Royton, Oldham, Chadderton and Crompton stopped for breakfast and only three out of twenty-seven did so in the Bolton area. At Richard Constantine's mill at Halliwell, 'the engine never stops for breakfast or dinner and the workmen get the meal promiscuously.'

The visitors for Leyland Hundred found all but one mill 'very defective in cleanliness and ventilation' and their opposite numbers at Winwick apologised for a report they had been obliged to base on 'equivocation and deceit.' They came across 'many little ones said to be nine, who were not more than seven or eight.'

The Wigan area visitors had a particularly unhappy tour. In Wigan itself they found three mills in 'a most abominable and filthy state' and with insufficient air; and the 'filth and wretchedness' of John Jones's mill at Blackrod earned their 'decided disapprobation.' The ceiling in the top room had not been brushed for eighteen months and the cotton and dust hung down in foot lengths. There was a hole at one end of the ceiling from which the wind blew the cotton and dirt over the room. Of Taylor and Urcher's mill at Horwich, the visitors wrote:

> On entering we were nearly suffocated with the heat and a most intolerable stench; and on inspecting the interior (though it was with difficulty we did so) we found the whole building in a truly disgraceful state. The rooms were exceedingly low and crowded with workmen. The ceilings were literally covered with cotton and dust, and from the small number of windows in each room, we cannot conceive it possible for the children or the workmen to have sufficient air or to enjoy good health.

At Messrs Isherwoods' mill at Bedford, in Leigh parish, 'the cotton which floated around the rooms made respiration extremely difficult and our lungs were much oppressed by it,' and at the mill of Messrs Ormerod in Westleigh, the rooms, none of which was ventilated or had a window that opened, were heated to 'not much under eighty degrees. The smells arising from the rancid effluvia, and the confined perspiration of bodies labouring in heated rooms, from coarse oil with the general want of cleanliness caused a very powerful nausea to persons entering the buildings.'

It must have come as a great relief to the visitors to inspect the mill of Messrs Jones and Co., at Tyldesley. Here the heat was regulated to 72 degrees and every window could be opened.

> The machinery in this factory and also the steam engine were of highly-polished steel and brass, and the wood principally of mahogany, and the floors and every part of it remarkably clean and neat; no flue was perceptible, the atmosphere was pure, and the workpeople appear to have every comfort and their labour to be only that of attending to the regularity and order of the works.

The mill, which also had a sick club and a Sunday school, was one of the only two listed in the entire collection of reports that aroused any real enthusiasm in the visitors. The other was that of Samuel Horrocks at Bradshaw, near Bolton. The 100 workpeople there had an eleven and a half hour day and their appearance was 'very much healthier' than that of workers in other mills. The mill was 'in excellent condition, very clean and well ventilated.'

The visitors' reports are confirmed and to some extent amplified by an independent publication of 1825 entitled *Sketch of the Hours of Labour, Meal Times, etc., in Manchester*, which also includes the results of a survey made in the previous year of several other manufacturing districts. In Manchester the mills worked on average a fourteen-hour day. Most workers had half an hour for breakfast and some fifty minutes for dinner. There were a few mills that did not stop for breakfast and by no means all the workers had an hour for dinner. The usual starting time was 5.30 or 6 a.m. Finishing time on Saturdays was about 4 p.m. The report, adds, however:

> Although meal times are normally allowed (and the grown-up spinners are released), the children, or piecers, are detained three or four days in each week during these meal times to clean the machinery; consequently they get no exercise or change of air, and what is worse, are driven to the necessity of snatching by mouthfuls their food during the act of cleaning, whilst dust and cotton flue are falling thick around them. This remark applies generally throughout these districts.

The conditions in other areas may be summarised as follows:

Ashton: Fourteen-hour day; half hour for breakfast, one hour for dinner; most mills finished work on Saturdays at 4 p.m., but some went on till 5 and one till 7.

Burnley: Fourteen or fourteen and a half-hour day; no breakfast time; usual Saturday finishing time 6 p.m., but some mills 7 p.m.

Lees, near Oldham: Twelve and a half-hour day; no breakfast time but working hours from 8 a.m. to 8.30 p.m., one hour for dinner; 4 p.m. finishing time on Saturdays.

Oldham: No breakfast time, one hour for dinner. Usual finishing time on Saturdays 3 p.m., some mills 4 p.m.

Colne: Fourteen or fifteen-hour day; no breakfast time; one hour for dinner. 'At Bradley mills, near Colne, Mr William Holt works his mill both day and night and he has done that for ten years past or more.'

11. *Rules of Iron*

In considering the effects of the factory system on the adult workers, it will be worthwhile to look first at the problem of discipline. We have already quoted John Holt's account of the late eighteenth-century mill hands who got drunk on four days out of seven and Richard

Ayton's stories of the well-paid spinners whose lives alternated between periods of toil and bouts of uninterrupted drinking. We have also noted Francis Place's statement of 1819 that the reform movement had gone

Rules from Water-foot Mill, Haslingden, 1851.

RULES
TO BE OBSERVED
By the Hands Employed in
THIS MILL.

RULE 1. All the Overlookers shall be on the premises first and last.

2. Any Person coming too late shall be fined as follows :—for 5 minutes 2d, 10 minutes 4d, and 15 minutes 6d, &c.

3. For any Bobbins found on the floor 1d for each Bobbin.

4. For single Drawing, Slubbing, or Roving 2d for each single end.

5. For Waste on the floor 2d.

6. For any Oil wasted or spilled on the floor 2d each offence, besides paying the value of the Oil.

7. For any broken Bobbins, they shall be paid for according to their value, and if there is any difficulty in ascertaining the guilty party, the same shall be paid for by the whole using such Bobbins.

8. Any person neglecting to Oil at the proper times shall be fined 2d.

9. Any person leaving their Work and found Talking with any of the other workpeople shall be fined 2d for each offence.

10. For every Oath or insolent language 3d, for the first offence, and if repeated they shall be dismissed.

11. The Machinery shall be swept and cleaned down every meal time.

12. All persons in our employ shall serve Four Weeks' Notice before leaving their employ ; but L. WHITAKER & SONS, shall and will turn any person off without notice being given.

13. If two persons are known to be in one Necessary together they shall be fined 3d each ; and if any Man or Boy go into the Women's Necessary he shall be instantly dismissed.

14. Any person wilfully or negligently breaking the Machinery, damaging the Brushes, making too much Waste, &c. they shall pay for the same to its full value.

15. Any person hanging anything on the Gas Pendants will be fined 2d.

16. The Masters would recommend that all their workpeople Wash themselves every morning, but they shall Wash themselves at least twice every week, Monday Morning and Thursday morning ; and any found not washed will be fined 3d for each offence.

17. The Grinders, Drawers, Slubbers and Rovers, shall sweep at least ——— times in the day as follows, in the Morning at 7½, 9½, 11, and 12 ; and in the Afternoon at 1½, 2½, 3½, 4½, and 5½ o'clock—and is——— the Board hung up, when the black side is turned that is the time to sweep, and only quarter of an hour will be allowed for Sweeping. The Spinners shall sweep as follows, in the Morning at 7½, 10, and 12 ; in the Afternoon at 3, and 5½ o'clock. Any neglecting to sweep at the time will be fined 2d for each offence.

18. Any persons found Smoking on the premises will be instantly dismissed.

19. Any person found away from their usual place of work, except for necessary purposes, or Talking with any one out of their own Alley will be fined 2d for each offence.

20. Any person bringing dirty Bobbins will be fined 1d for each Bobbin.

21. Any person wilfully damaging this Notice will be dismissed.

The Overlookers are strictly enjoined to attend to these Rules, and they will be responsible to the Masters for the Workpeople observing them.

WATER-FOOT MILL, NEAR HASLINGDEN,
SEPTEMBER, 1851.

J. READ. PRINTER. AND BOOKBINDER. HASLINGDEN.

a long way towards civilising the untamed men of Lancashire, to whom drunkenness was almost a way of life. When the movement was vigorously suppressed after Peterloo the process was far from complete and large numbers remained firmly addicted to their liquor. Consider that remarkable day in July 1821 when the Coronation of George IV was celebrated in Manchester with a distribution of free food and drink.

Power loom weaving, 1835. The use of cast-iron columns and beams was typical of the improvements in mill design at this time, since they were an element in the prevention of destructive fires— although cast iron could fail, with catastrophic results, and not until the introduction of steel frames later in the century was a fully safe technique available.

Scenes were exhibited [said the *Manchester Guardian*] which even the pencil of Hogarth would fail adequately to portray. At the New Market of Shudehill the meat and loaves were thrown out high from the doors and windows of the warehouses where they had been stored, the populace scrambling for them as they could. It resembled the throwing of goods out of the windows of a warehouse on fire. There was shameful waste and general confusion. At an early hour the stage erected for the applicants to stand on gave way and one person was killed and several were dangerously wounded by the fall. When the liquor was distributing we saw whole pitchers thrown indiscriminately among the crowd, men holding up their hats to receive drink, people fighting and quarrelling for the possession of a jug—the strong taking the liquor from the weak—boys and girls, men and women in a condition of beastly drunkenness staggering before the depository of ale, lying prostrate on the ground under every variety of circumstance and in every degree of exposure, swearing, groaning, vomiting, but calling for more liquor when

they could not stand or even sit to drink it. Every kind of excess, indeed, which the most fertile imagination could conceive or the most graphic pen describe was there witnessed in nauseous and loathsome extravagance. Never did we see, and we hope to God, never again shall see, human nature so degraded. There were two or three lives lost and fourteen persons are in the Infirmary, several of them dangerously injured from the events of the day.

Throughout the manufacturing districts, mill owners were faced with the problem of keeping at regular work men who loved their independence and their ale; and when one remembers that most factory children were employed directly by the spinners—as late as 1833 two thirds of the boys and a third of the girls were under their control—one can readily appreciate the need for severe measures. Unfortunately the measures all too often exceeded the bounds of common humanity; and by an ironic twist of fate, the Lancashire workman's drunkenness, which formerly indicated a carefree independence or an exuberant prosperity, came to indicate his despair and an eagerness to forget his wretched surroundings.

In March 1827, the *Bolton Chronicle* quoted the following extract from a poem written by the clerk to the Haslingden magistrate.

> *The common people are (excepted few)*
> *A filthy, drunken, abject, beastly crew.*
> *So filthy that the very rags they wear*
> *Are less offensive than the stench they bear!*
> *So drunken that all the limits they disown*
> *Save want of cash, long score and landlord's frown!*
> *So abject that they'll beg with whining din*
> *For a few pence to purchase beer and gin.*

After observing that the working classes had few amusements apart from drinking—'If ten or a dozen assemble to enjoy themselves in the open air, they are speedily dispersed by the constable'—the newspaper commented:

Admitting that the poor are thus degraded, what is the reason for it? Because their minds have lost, through a series of oppressions, that independence that formerly was almost the exclusive prerogative of an Englishman; because they are compelled to work more and to endure much greater hardship than negro slaves.

Sets of rules, which controlled life in the mills with a forbidding thoroughness, were drawn up and fines out of all proportion to the seriousness of the offences were exacted, leaving the workpeople considerably the poorer when pay day came round. In his *Political Register*, of 30 August 1823, William Cobbett, quoted the rules of a Tyldesley mill, where a spinner who was five minutes late for work, or who was heard whistling, or who left a window open, or who was found dirty or who was found washing himself was fined a shilling for each offence. Any man who fell sick and was unable to find a substitute had to pay six shillings a day for steam. 'These fines,' said a pamphlet issued by the spinners, 'are as easy to be made as an underling can scratch his pen; and it is entirely at his humour and caprice.' At this mill, which ran for fourteen hours a day, 'the door is locked in working hours, except half an hour at tea time; the workpeople are not allowed to send for water to drink in the hot factory; and even the rain water is locked up by the master's order, otherwise they would be happy to drink even that.'

The rules of Thomas Ainsworth and Sons of Preston, begin by stating that all the workpeople must give a month's notice before leaving, but that 'the masters have full power to discharge any person without previous notice whatsoever.' The following extracts will give some idea of the scope of the 'legislation'.

> Any workman coming into the factory or any other part of these premises drunk shall pay five shillings.
>
> Each person employed in this factory engages not to be a member of, or directly or indirectly a subscriber to, or a supporter of any trade union or other association whatsoever.
>
> Any person taking cotton or waste into the necessaries shall forfeit two shillings and sixpence; and anyone knowing of the same and not giving information thereof shall forfeit five shillings.
>
> Any person smoking tobacco or having a pipe for that purpose in any part of the factory or yard shall forfeit five shillings.
>
> Any spinner whose wheel or wheels are standing either for want of piecers or from any other cause whatsoever during the time the steam engine is going, or not keeping them employed at their usual and proper speed, shall for every hour pay sixpence.
>
> To avoid any misunderstanding or disputes, it is hereby determined that when a breach has been made in any of the rules, and the person committing the same cannot be identified; double the penalty hereby inflicted shall be taken from the people employed in the department where the fault has been committed, whether it may extend only to one room, one overlooker's department or the whole factory.

'The mills of Manchester,' said an anonymous writer in 1843, 'in their extent exceed anything of their kind in the world,' but what impressed him more was the condition of the inmates and the immense influence and authority of the masters. He found that the rules were 'as strict as the articles of war' and that trivial mistakes were frequently punished with dismissal, 'occasioning in many instances the deepest privations and misery.'

James Leach, the Manchester operative, whose *Stubborn Facts from the Factories* was published in the following year, quotes a set of rules under which workers were fined sixpence for talking or whistling or singing. And he adds:

We have repeatedly seen married females in the last stages of pregnancy slaving from morning till night beside the never-tiring

---

Politics and Legislation, 1790–1850

1795	Treasonable Practices Act and Seditious Meetings Act, which limit the rights of individuals to meet and protest.
1799	Combination Act, which gives magistrates the right to ban meetings and political associations of workers.
1801	Suspension of Habeas Corpus Act, which allows detention without trial—the Act is reinstated and then suspended again on several occasions in the next twenty years.
1802	Health and Morals of Apprentices Act, the first factory legislation, forbidding the employment of children under the age of nine as apprentices and imposing a maximum 12-hour day for children.
1811	Framebreaking Act, which imposes the death penalty for machine-wrecking. Unlawful Oaths Act further limits right of association.
1815	Corn Law imposes severe restrictions on the import of grain.
1817	Severely repressive measures against workers' movement and associations; a series of insurrections, marches and major demonstrations in different parts of the country.
Aug. 1819	'Peterloo'. Eleven people killed by yeomanry at St Peter's Fields, Manchester, during radical political meeting.
Dec. 1819	'Six Acts', aimed at preventing illegal military training, forbidding public meetings without licence, curbing freedom of the press, and setting major penalties for 'sedition'.
1823	Transportation Act, slightly reducing the extreme penalties involved in this punishment.
1824	Combination Act modifies the limitations on association.
1825	Cotton Mills Regulation Act imposes a maximum 12-hour day for workers under the age of 16.
1832	Great Reform Act, the first stage of parliamentary reform.
1833	Factory Act, which forbids factory labour for children under 9, and sets a 9-hour day for those under 13.
1837	Chartist movement gathers momentum—major period of activity to 1842.
1842	Mines Act forbids the employment of children under 10 and women below ground.
1844	Factory Act sets a maximum 12-hour day for women and a 6-hour day for children aged between 8 and 13.
1846	Repeal of the Corn Laws.
1847	Ten Hours Act sets a 10-hour working day for women and for children between 13 and 18.
1846	Renewed Chartist activity to 1848.

machines . . . and when they were obliged to sit down to take a moment's ease, were fined sixpence for the offence. In some mills the crime of sitting down is visited with a penalty of one shilling.

'Fines are frequent and heavy, amounting in many cases to several shillings a week,' the factory cripple William Dodd wrote to Lord Ashley from Wigan in 1841, and it is difficult to decide whether by this time the factory rules were being used primarily to enforce discipline or to put extra cash in the masters' pockets. Leach denounced the mill owners as self-elected legislators, who were prompted to draw up their laws solely for 'sordid avarice.' He added:

> The working class will ever look upon this as a brigand system that thus allows employers to assume a power over the law and by a nefarious plotting first create what they are pleased to term offences and then punish them. They are law-makers, judges and jurors.

According to Leach there were masters who deliberately put their mill clocks forward during the night so that they could fine their workpeople. 'On one occasion, we counted ninety-five persons that were thus locked out at half-past five o'clock in the morning . . . These ninety-five were fined three-pence each,'

At the same mill a new cut-looker was asked by the master why he had so little in his 'bate book.'

> The man replied, 'I think there's a great deal. I 'bate the weavers so much that I can't for shame look them in the face when I meet them in the street.' The master answered, 'You be d—d, you are five pounds a week worse to me than the man who had the situation before you, and I'll kick you out of the place.' The man was discharged to make room for another, *who knew his duty better.*

Overlookers as the chief administrators of discipline, were often hated more than the masters. Many used their considerable power to extract extra toil from those in their charge, and incredible though it seems, such men were aided by a number of operatives who were anxious even in those hard times, to do extra work for a little more money. This is one of the themes in a batch of statements taken from Blackburn power-loom weavers in 1847 by Mr Currie, a local surgeon and factory reformer. As one of them observed:

> I always say it's working people as brought the long hours upon themselves. There are people who would go at four o'clock in the morning if the doors were open; all striving to get the most work off. The overlookers are the worst of anybody; whatever one does, they must all do the same, else they must go home. People gone

in at five, never comed out till eight; worked meal times and all to make up: have worked it myself many a time.

Another workman said:

> Poor people have brought factories to what they are: being stingy to get so much work out; and overlookers are a deal of them worse than the masters, because they are paid by the wages of the weaver. The less a weaver gets, the worse it is for the overlooker . . . The hands at so and so's mill tell me they are worse worked now than ever; that the overlookers compel them to produce as much in five days as they did before in six. I don't think masters are to blame for this, only the people themselves . . . I see persons come home who have hardly the power to eat their supper, they are so ill tired. Have seen hundreds taken ill from no other cause than hard work.

12. *Factory Despotism*

After June 1823, workpeople who left their employment without giving notice became liable to three months' imprisonment. The Act was frequently invoked during the next twenty-five years, at first mainly to discipline groups of men who went on a spree, later to punish anyone who dared to disobey his master. 'Fifty years ago,' an Oldham man recalled in 1887, 'it was no uncommon thing if a workman left a mill without proper notice, for him to be deprived of his liberty and treated as a common felon.' *The Manchester Guardian* of 16 April 1825 reported that ten spinners and rovers employed by Stansfield and Rider of Ashton-under-Lyne had been sentenced to two months' hard labour for leaving their work without giving a fortnight's notice which they had engaged to do. At Preston in the previous month a spinner was jailed for three months for a similar offence after his employer had told the magistrates that only a short time before the man and ten others had left their work to go drinking. Another man accused at the same court was said to have bound himself to serve his employers for fifty-one weeks and 'to leave a weekly deposit in their hands by way of security for his good behaviour.' By the 1840s workmen were being engaged on long contracts. At the woollen mills of W. and R. Turner at Helmshore, these often ran to seven years. One unfortunate fulling miller who signed a seven-year contract in 1842, was twice imprisoned for leaving his work, on the first occasion for two months and on the second for three. In 1848 a spinner employed by the same firm was jailed for six months. All were sentenced by their employer who was the local magistrate.

The extremes to which factory despotism were taken may be judged from an article in the *Ashton Chronicle* of 9 December 1848. The author was almost certainly the editor, the Rev J. R. Stephens.

It is notorious that in all the manufacturing towns we ever lived in that the manufacturers constitute for purposes common to their general interest, a united corporate body. The phrase 'black book' or 'blood book' is well understood in the manufacturing districts. The fellow who has dared to speak or act prominently on questions affecting wages or time of working or other points in dispute between men and their masters soon gets what is called the 'bag' or the 'sack'. He is discharged and that discharge is equivalent to a sentence of social extermination. We have known such men in all things besides blameless, tramp scores of miles, and at every mill they call at to ask for work, get but one answer—'No work here for such as you.' Even the children of these men have had to leave their father's house and native town, to seek elsewhere under assumed names the privilege to labour, which they were well aware would be denied them if their parentage were detected. Within the last few days, the threat has been cast at those who have remonstrated against the vexatious arrangements of masters who are violating the Ten Hours Bill: 'If you do not do this and that, you shall neither work here nor anywhere else.' It is impossible for anyone not intimately acquainted with the moral machinery of the factory system to conceive the complete power which the master is thus and in other ways to be detailed, enabled to exercise over his registered workpeople. It is, in fact, almost as difficult for a factory labourer to find a safe harbour elsewhere after receiving a discharge as it is for a foreigner to traverse a hostile country without a passport, or for a branded felon to set up in business when the whole posse comitatus of the detective service is hounding on his track. The interior discipline of a cotton mill is the perfection of social despotism. From the master downwards to the lowest overlooker, there exists throughout an organisation of labour police which nothing can escape. Everything is known and provided for with the most ad-mirable minuteness: and the workman who dares to think and act for himself in any respect contrary to the wish or whim of his employer, must be a rare example of high-mindedness, courage and caution. In one case of persecution, we were the witness to the wholesale eviction of some hundreds of the most industrious and well-conducted of the factory population, who by a secret combi-nation of masters were ruthlessly devoted to starvation because they attended the chapel of a minister whose discourse reproved the sin of covetousness and oppression. These unoffending outcasts wan-dered half England through and were years before they found a home. Beyond the way in which they chose to worship their God, we never heard anything laid to the charge of these persons. They were allowed to be excelled by none either for skill, diligence and fidelity as servants or for their general good conduct as private individuals.

To make the master's hold upon his 'hands' the more secure, recourse is had, in most cases, to the two following expedients:— First, it is the practive whenever possible, to engage whole families, so that each separate member is, as it were, bail-bound for the rest. If one offends, all must quit: father, mother, sister, brother—away they go, at one fell swoop, into the street to seek a living where they can, or—die. Second, the master is an extensive owner of cottages and make the permission to labour in his factory contingent upon the occupation of his houses, for which he charges his own price, always stopping that amount out of the workman's wages. By means of this contrivance the labourer is often forced to leave a better dwelling for a worse and pay from sixpence to a shilling a week more than he paid to his former landlord.

The last sentence brings to mind the reply made by the Lancashire mill master when his workpeople complained that their houses were not fit to live in. 'That's nowt,' said the great man. 'I build factories for you to live in. Houses is nobbut to sleep in.' That attitude, nothing if not direct and robust, was reflected in many areas by the failure of the mill owners to provide housing for their workers. Attitudes varied widely from place to place, from individual to individual. Some owners took a 'responsible' view, and provided accommodation: among numerous other examples, in Over Darwen the mill-owner Eccles Shorrock owned some 12 per cent of the housing stock in the early 1860s, and in Cherry Tree, Blackburn, the Cherry Tree Mill Co. and their successors, the Dugdale family, built considerable numbers of houses for their workers from the 1860s onwards. But elsewhere provision was inadequate or completely lacking, and the resultant shortage, high cost or physical squalor of accommodation was a major and long-standing problem of the workforce.

Though most firms supported the Ten Hours Act, many tried to defeat its intentions either by introducing relays of women and children or by working the men for long periods. A survey made in April 1849 showed that at least 100 Lancashire firms were working more than ten hours a day. There were forty in Oldham alone and another twenty in Ashton-under-Lyne, where there was 'great dissatisfaction' among the operatives. Every Mossley mill was said to be working more than ten hours. During the same month, Henry Knowles and Sons of Burnley, who were running their weaving shed for twelve hours a day, not only ignored a workmen's request for a reduction, but even went so far as to begin recruiting hands to enable the mill to run both day and night. When this failed, they announced that the weavers would have to work fifteen hours a day. Those who refused were dismissed. In August of the same year an example of the spiteful way the relay system was operated came to light when the Colne firm of N. England and Son was fined £1 for overworking a young girl. It was stated that she began work at 6 a.m. but after 15 minutes had to leave the mill until 8.30. She had an hour for dinner beginning at 12.30 and then continued until 7.15 p.m. Thus, while she worked for only ten hours, her working day extending over 13½ hours.

Many Lancashire people were not protected by the Factory Acts, and as late as 1855 a Royal Commission revealed that those in the bleaching, finishing and dyeing trades were toiling under the most disgraceful conditions. The usual working day was 15 or 16 hours and many young children were among those who complained to the Commissioner that excessive work had undermined their health. A boy of 12 who sorted ropes at Blair and Sumner's bleaching works at Bolton said:

I go at 5 o'clock in the morning . . . and go home sometimes at 9, sometimes 10 [at night]. On Friday we work all night sometimes.

Pay day in a cotton mill, by G. P. Jacome Head.

I go on Friday at breakfast time; on Friday night at 6 o'clock I go home to bed for four hours. I feel very tired when I leave on Saturday morning. My feet are often blood raw and they pain me.

Whowell's bleaching works at Tottington ran from 6.30 a.m. to 11 p.m. during the week and then with relays throughout the whole of Friday night and Saturday. Young girls employed to fold cloth often fell asleep at their work and the woman who had to keep them awake confessed, 'My heart is sore for them that I cannot speak to them.'

One learns with surprise that conditions in 1855 were much better than in earlier times. A finisher who worked at Breightmet, near Bolton, and who had been in the trade for 36 years, said that it was once the custom to work throughout the night on Mondays, Wednesdays and Fridays and 'I have scores of times seen both men and children asleep at their work—and dangerous work, too.' Another Bolton witness remembered when the working day for two-thirds of the year was from 14 to 18 hours, and he added, 'I once worked a whole week with only three hours in bed. I slept a little at meal times.'

13. *The Truck System*

Many masters ran shops from which their workers were obliged to buy food and clothing at greatly inflated prices. In remote country districts the provision of houses and shops was occasionally a boon to the workpeople, but usually it was not. David Whitehead of Rossendale records in his autobiography that when he began his first mill at Balladenbrook, a hamlet without a shop, 'the workpeople complained of having so far to go to buy their food. So I began to sell meal and flour and other grocery.' But against this, contrast the following statement by a Rossendale mill worker, Moses Heap:

People were very poor and lived from hand to mouth, day to day . . . They lived under the truck system: the employee had to buy all his necessaries from his master. Thus the master held a whip over his workers' heads in the form of extortionate charges. Even if we only wanted a little meal or treacle, it had to be traded through the employer and one had to be very careful not to overspend one's wages.

Remarkable evidence was given at Manchester in 1827 when a cotton manufacturer appeared in court for paying wages in goods instead of money. One workman, it was stated, had received only two shillings in nine months. The remainder of his earnings 'he was obliged to take from the manufacturer's daughter, who was also the cashier.' Samuel

Orrell's Mill, Stock-port, built in 1834, was an integrated mill with spinning on the upper floors and power loom weaving on the ground floor and in an adjoining shed. Ure, *The Cotton Manufacture of Great Britain* (1836). The engraving is very in-formative in showing the role of road trans-port in the industry, with laden two-horse wagons carrying bales. Note also the separate and orna-mental chimney on the hillside.

Andrew, secretary of the Oldham Master Cotton Spinners and Manu-facturers, in a paper read to the British Association in 1887, showed that the incident was one of many.

It was no uncommon thing in the earlier part of Her Majesty's reign for a shop to be attached to the warehouse or counting house of a cotton mill. Indeed, the shop and the warehouse were often found under one roof. The reckonings and what were humorously called pay days were fortnightly and where a family worked at the mill, they went to the 'tommy' shop, as it was called, for whatever they required; and the value of the articles supplied always stood in the books against the amount of wages earned. I have heard in more than one instance how little money was required to pay the wages. Under the truck system an employer of forty or fifty work-people would pay them all, using one sovereign for everyone's wages. I heard a tale to illustrate this, which I have good reason to believe to be true. On the pay day the workman would go into the counting house, which was in the bottom storey of the building, the shop being over it, to reckon. He would receive the sovereign for his wages and perhaps some change. On leaving the counting house he would go into the shop and tender his sovereign for the demand of his shop score, which said sovereign would be dropped down a tube into the counting house below to pay the next comer, who would repeat the same process. It is said by way of a joke that this sovereign had done duty so often that both head and tail were worn off; but perhaps the funny part was that after the factory master had paid his wages, this sovereign was always left in his pocket.

In 1842, Dr P. M. McDouall of Ramsbottom told the Select Committee on Payment of Wages that in the district between Manchester and Haslingden he knew of only one textile firm, Ashton's of Ramsbottom, who were not involved in the truck system. The difference between Ashton's workers and those at other mills was very great. Under the free system the people were better dressed, had better furnished homes and appeared more independent and comfortable on their scanty means. 'Ashton's mill,' he said, 'is the only mill in the district where there are to be found any of the people owning property. I lived in a house belonging to a working man in the mill, who had saved money out of his wages to build a house; I know five or six similar cases; I know one man worth £200 or £300.' The truck system made people improvident.

> They have no calculation among themselves as to the amount of goods they receive in payment of their wages. They procure whatever they may require without considering the results, consequently a great majority of them are debtors to the masters; besides, when they receive any money they squander it with a reckless spirit like schoolboys . . . There is also a gambling habit introduced in consequence of the truck system, which is injurious to their morals. Whenever they want a little money, 20 persons collect together, principally women; each puts down 1s. and all raffle for the sum by throwing a dice to decide which shall have the 20s. The women leave their houses during the absence of their husbands to attend those meetings. The 20s. are repaid at the rate of 1s. per week. The object is to have the command of a sum of money.

McDouall said that truck shops were usually carried on in the name of the factory manager or book-keeper. One book-keeper at Bury sold both clothes and coal.

> I saw a person a fortnight ago who received 3d. for a week's wages in consequence of the deduction for clothing . . . I have known of

The 'Yellow Factory' or Yard Works, built by John Horrocks in Church Street, Preston, in 1791. The nickname arose from the cream-colour wash with which the factory was painted. This was Preston's first purpose-built mill, and the beginning of the great Horrocks cotton empire (from Hewitson's *History of Preston*).

one case of 1½ d. being paid . . . The men are constantly assailed by the masters to know where they bought their clothing.

The truck system, however, was not operated as blatantly as it had been in 1835, when the cotton trade enjoyed a period of briskness. Then, said McDouall, the masters carried it to such an extent that some of them bundled cheeses into people's houses so that less money would be needed on pay day.

McDouall described how workpeople employed by the Grants of Ramsbottom were given a wage ticket which they had to take to a public house owned by the firm. The landlord changed it for them but only after deducting threepence for each person which they had to take in drink. 'Are they obliged to spend it on beer?' asked a member of the committee. The doctor replied, 'Yes. The little boys in the dye house are paid there. I have seen them come down drunk.' The public house stayed open until midnight or one o'clock on Saturday evening and 'I have known workpeople remain there until they have exhausted their credit and their money.' When another questioner asked what would happen if a man insisted on begin given his threepence instead of drink, McDouall answered, 'There would be a complaint made regarding him, and it would be easy to find fault with his work.'

14. *Tied to the Engine*

Of all the evils of the factory system, the destruction of the dignity of work was the most lasting. Men became subservient not only to hard taskmasters, but also to water-wheels and steam engines; and as Dr James Phillips Kay said of the labouring population of Manchester in 1832:

> They are drudges who watch the movement and assist the operations of a mighty material force which toils with an energy ever unconscious of fatigue. The persevering labour of the operative must ever reflect the mathematical precision and incessant motion and the exhaustless power of the machine.

A Bolton spinner, giving evidence to the Factories Commission in the following year, spoke in much the same vein:

> The occupation is not like that of other labouring men, the spinner or card-room hand cannot get away for a day without great inconvenience; then the occupation is incessant all day long. The man is tied to the engine; he must go along with it and cannot stop; this continuing every day and all a man's life, they get peevish at it and want repose.

'In a cotton factory', from Grindon's *Lancashire: Brief Historical Notes*, 1892. This imaginative re-construction of the early years of the industry shows—if artistic accuracy is assumed—a barefoot child carrying raw cotton, and a very old-fashioned mill, with wooden plank floors and wooden rafters.

The respect which had been accorded to the humblest of workmen in the days before the Industrial Revolution was entirely absent from many factories and in some the dehumanising process seemed almost complete. William Hall said in 1826 of the Preston mill where he had worked as a boy:

> When a piece of board was nailed over the twist pulley so that the workers could put their breakfasts there instead of on the dusty floor, it was considered an indulgence. Previous to that favour they had to stoop and snatch a bite and sup from the floor as they ran half naked and reeking with perspiration from one wheel to another. In this wretched and humiliating manner the piecers are still treated in the numerous factories where no pause of labour is allowed for breakfast time.

Many Lancashire people who found themselves in such hostile and degrading surroundings would have agreed with the Manchester work-man who declared in February 1833, at a meeting to support Sadler's Ten Hours Bill, that an English prison was a palace compared with an English factory.

Dr Andrew Ure said the machines in the Manchester mills were 'without parallel among the works of man,' but as the machines were made even more wonderful they sometimes increased rather than diminished the toil and insecurity of the operatives. Larger mules meant fewer spinners and faster looms demanded extra effort and attention. Thirty-six Manchester thread mills which employed 1,088 spinners in 1829 had only 488 in 1841, though the number of spindles had increased by more than 53,000. In 1847, a Blackburn surgeon said of recent improvements to the power loom, 'The machinery is going too quick for those who had been accustomed to the slow; the shuttle often flies out and sometimes knock their eyes out.'

For women, factory life could be particular debasing. A Bury doctor told a public meeting in 1846 that some mothers who could not afford to stay at home or pay a child minder gave their babies opium or other drugs. Many babies died and—so contemporary observers and moralists believed—those that survived often grew up to be idiots. The *Ashton Chronicle* of 9 December 1848 outlined a number of other evils.

> We were in a house last week, in which a woman told us that after two confinements she had suckled her own child and her daughter's at the same time to let the mother go to the mill to earn her bread. Another of her daughters was in the act of nursing her infant in the hurried moments of the dinner time, and when we asked whether the baby was in good health, she answered that to keep the milk from getting sour whilst locked up in the mill, she had to milk herself many times in the course of the day. We have now before us, as we write, that unhappily most common, but disgraceful utensil called a nipple glass, used by mothers in the factory for the unnatural purpose above mentioned. These glasses when filled with a mother's milk are taken by that mother and emptied down the factory privy.

Two months later, at a time when a number of mill owners were attempting to circumvent the provisions of the Ten Hours Act, the same paper described what work had come to mean for many thousands of Lancashire people:

> Industry is the name given to the practice and habit of our factory neighbourhoods; but it is a strange and most unwarrantable misapplication of a term which originally described an honest and meritorious activity of man's natural faculty for labour. There is no word with which we are acquainted to express the species and amount of toil endured by the millworkers of this locality and concealed from moral observation under that misused designation of industry. Slavery itself does not adequately convey a true idea of what this extraordinary race of people undergo.

The effects of excessive factory work on health and longevity were studied by the Leeds surgeon, C. T. Thackrah, who wrote in 1831:

> I stood in Oxford-row, Manchester, and observed the streams of operatives as they left the mills at twelve o'clock. The children were almost universally small, sickly, bare-footed and ill-clad. Many *appeared* to be no older than seven. The men, generally from 16 to

24 . . . were almost as pallid and thin as the children. The women were most respectable in appearance, but I saw no fresh, or fine-looking individuals among them . . . Here I saw, or thought I saw, a degenerate race—human beings stunted, enfeebled and depraved—man and women that were not to be aged; children that were never to be healthy adults. It was a mournful spectacle.

Perhaps the tragedy of the factory system was best summed up in a few words that were painted on two banners carried in a Manchester and Salford Ten Hours Bill procession in August 1832. The first banner depicted a deformed operative and bore the question 'Am I not a man and a brother?' The second was carried by a group of factory children, one of whom held an overseer's whip and a strap made into thongs. The inscription was 'Behold and Weep'.

15. *The Masters*

What kind of men were the mill masters? In answer, one may begin by quoting William Dodd, the factory cripple, who wrote to Lord Ashley from Wigan in 1841:

> On looking into the origins of the manufacturing firms in this town, I find that the masters have, almost to a man, begun with nothing and risen by little and little till many of them have got to be very wealthy. One man, Mr William Wood, died in the early part of this year, worth £300,000, nearly all of which had been acquired by the factory system . . . As men of figures [the masters] are almost without parallel: they can tell to a nicety how much money will be gained by reducing their hands 6d. per head throughout the factory or to what a fraction of a farthing per pound or per yard upon the goods produced will amount. To their ability in calculating these minute details may be attributed much of their success as accumulators of wealth.

Among the first generation of masters were weavers, who had saved or borrowed enough to go into business; craftsmen who had helped to build the early carding and spinning machines; and yeomen like the first Robert Peel, who invested money made from farming in cotton spinning and calico printing. (Peel's son, the first Sir Robert, when a young man, regularly sold milk in Blackburn before returning to superintend a group a cotton spinners who worked in a barn on his father's farm). But the 'rags to riches' view of the masters, so beloved of the Victorians and so much in keeping with their philosophy of self-help and 'pulling yourself up by your bootstraps', has been challenged in recent years. Study of the textile masters active between 1830 and 1860 has shown that most of these men came from families with a substantial existing wealth, and with landed property, while among the first generation pioneers from the late eighteenth and early nineteenth centuries only 5 per cent were definitely from the 'ranks of shopkeepers, artisans and operatives', with another 20 per cent of untraceable and perhaps humble origins. That still leaves three-quarters of the 'pioneers' with identifiably moneyed origins. This did not affect the image-making, and the powerful image of the self-made industrialist was a potent symbol of the times.

Robert Owen described the early mill owners as 'plodding men of business with little knowledge and limited ideas, except in their own immediate circle or occupation,' and the *Poor Man's Advocate*, looking back half a century observed in 1832: 'The owners of spinning establishments were plain, industrious men, who seemed to belong to this world and who associated with the workmen for the purpose of courting them to work the machines, then rude and small and few in number.'

The plain, industrious factory master was a familiar Lancashire figure throughout the nineteenth century for the cotton trade, despite its vicissitudes, continued to draw men with its irresistible promise of great and quickly-accumulated fortunes. James [later Viscount] Bryce said of East Lancashire in 1868:

> Men almost, sometimes wholly illiterate, have risen to prodigious wealth and indulge in a profuse luxury which strangely contrasts with the primitive simplicity of their own manners. A millionaire has cousins and even brothers among the operatives, and is socially on a level with his own workpeople, to whose class he belonged a year or two before. Of course, it is the ambition of everyone to tread in his steps. The man who has saved a little money, sometimes a pushing mechanic, throws it into machinery, hiring 'space and power' (as they call it) or raising a weaving shop of his own. If the venture succeeds, he extends his operations and makes a fortune; if he fails, he emigrates or goes back to the big mill to earn his weekly wage.

One thinks of James Bullough, who died aged 69 in the year that the above passage was written. Bullough began work as a handloom weaver in his native Westhoughton at the age of seven and lived among looms for the rest of his life. He became a mill manager and after making important improvements to the power-loom, went into business as a manufacturer and machine maker at Accrington. Though he acquired a fortune, Bullough wore clogs to the end of his days.

Another industrious Lancastrian was J. R. Barnes of Farnworth, who in 25 years from 1809 increased his labour force from fifty handloom weavers to more than a thousand workpeople in three large mills. Simeon Dyson, in his *Local Notes and Reminiscences of Farnworth*, said of him:

> I well remember Mr Barnes both before and for years after he had his first power looms, regularly rising at five o'clock in the morning, going into his warehouse in Moses Gate and hand warping until seven o'clock, after which he went to his breakfast; and on market days—Tuesdays, Thursdays and Saturdays—he washed, shaved and dressed and then walked to Manchester and did an ordinary day's work there. He had no fire in the warehouse on the coldest day and his only refreshment consisted of bread and cheese or a twopenny meat pie. After walking home again and after getting his tea, he went into his warehouse again, where he worked until ten o'clock.

The growth of a managerial class enabled men with little or no knowledge of textiles to become masters, a development neatly illustrated by the following mill nick names from Blackburn:

'Th' Lather Box' (started by a barber), 'Th' Butter Tub' (a grocer), 'Th' Stocking Needle' (a hosier), 'Th' Glory Hoyle' (A Methodist), 'Th' Twelve Apostles' (twelve men active in church work), 'Thunder and Leetnin'' (A Primitive Methodist preacher noted for his 'fire and brimstone' sermons) and 'Th' Physic' (financed by a doctor).

Bryce noted that while a manufacturer was making his fortune, he often continued to live simply, indeed roughly, in a three-roomed house, associated on equal terms with his workpeople and sent his children to the National School.

But when his fortune is made, when his income begins to exceed a thousand or two per annum, he suddenly expands from the chrysalis into a butterfly, turns away from the class out of which he has risen and strives to attach himself to that composed of the older manufacturing families, or, if it be possible, even to the landed gentry. The first step is to send his children away from home to boarding school, nominally to get rid of the dialect, but really to get rid of the cousins, to form genteel connections and acquire manners more polished than those at home. The older manufacturing families are themselves not wholly

An unpopular mill master.

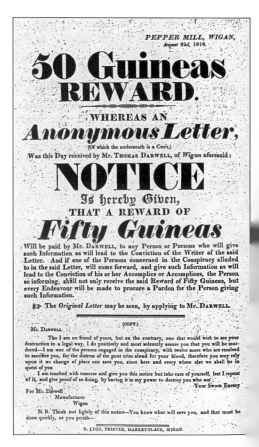

exempted from similar feelings. They have almost an exaggerated horror of the roughness of Lancashire people; they are anxious that their sons should make no acquaintance among their social inferiors.

The gap that separated the successful entrepreneurs from their work-people sometimes widened into an abyss when the pioneers' sons and grandsons took charge of the family firms. Very few took any close interest in their employees' welfare, and as Timothy Grimshaw of Bolton observed in 1838, 'It is laid down as an axiom by too many mill owners that the more ignorant the man, the better the servant.' Several writers in the 1840s commented on the growing division in society. 'There is no town in the world,' the Rev Richard Parkinson wrote of Manchester in 1841, 'where the distance between the rich and the poor is so great, or the barrier between them so difficult to cross.' And he went so far as to declare:

> There is less *personal* connection between a master cotton spinner and his workmen, between a calico printer and his blue-handed boys than there is between the Duke of Wellington and the humblest labourer on his estate or than there was between good old George the Third and the meanest errand lad about his palace.

Cooke Taylor, during his tour of the manufacturing districts of Lancashire in the following year, wrote that England had been divided into nations as distinct as the Normans and Saxons and concluded:

> In our wisdom we have improved on the proverb 'One half of the world does not know how the other half lives,' changing it into, 'One half of the world *does not care* how the other half lives.'

Disraeli, who had visited Lancashire, makes a character in his novel *Sybil*, of 1845, describe the rich and poor as 'two nations, between whom there is no intercourse and no sympathy, who are as ignorant of each other's habits, thoughts and feelings as if they were dwellers in different zones or inhabitants of different planets.'

As early as 1832, the *Poor Man's Advocate* mocked the second generation of mill masters as 'polished dandies' who had been educated at great expense and in 1843 another writer described a cotton lord as 'a man who will not upon any account whatever allow his grandfather to become the subject of discussion: for no consideration on earth will he trace his genealogy further back than his noble self.' Isolated by wealth and power from the class from which they sprang and from the aristocracy by their lack of rank and breeding, the mill owners were often lonely figures in society. And even within their own class there were sharp divisions. When one of the newer Haslingden masters was nominated for the local bench in 1860, he was vigorously and success-fully opposed by his more established neighbours. The wife of one wrote to her daughter, 'I am certain he will not be appointed: it is most ridiculous to put him forward when twelve or fourteen years ago he was a clogger and wore a leather apron.'

Success gave many masters a contempt for those they employed and was seen by the religiously-inclined as a mark of divine approval. 'Glory be to God!' wrote David Whitehead at the end of 1825. 'He has made our business to prosper and kept our hearts right with Him.' Another account of assistance from the Almighty was given at Bury in 1846 during a meeting in support of the Ten Hours' Movement. Henry Rostron, of Radcliffe, a manufacturer who opposed long hours, told the audience that 'one of the great mill owners' had recently informed him that 'The Lord has prospered me,' a claim which prompted the retort: 'I should wish to hear from your operatives how you have prospered them!' Rostron was loudly cheered.

The relentless pursuit of wealth too often became a way of life. 'There are men engaged in the cotton trade who, we verily believe, would squeeze one half of creation out of existence, were it possible, if, by doing so, they could increase their gains,' said the *Poor Man's Advocate* in March 1832 and a Manchester aesthete, deploring 'the want of taste for literature' in the city, wrote in 1835:

The thorough Manchester man sees more beauty in a row of bricks than he would in 'groves and alleys green'; he hears more music in the everlasting motion of the loom than he would in the songs of the lark or the nightingale. For him philosophy has no attraction, poetry, no enchantment, mountains, rocks, fields, streams excite not his delight or admiration; genius shrinks at his approach.

> The only thing he asks or wants to know
> Has but one aim – to learn how markets go.

The *Pictorial Times* in November 1843 was a little more generous, but though it found that many Manchester manufacturers cultivated refined literary tastes and distinguished themselves in politics, science and letters, it concluded:

Generally speaking, your manufacturer is a plodding man of business who is to be found in his counting house at hours when his Liverpool and London rival is snugly reposing in the bosom of his family . . . The complaint against the majority of Manchester men is well founded, that they are incessantly engrossed in business to have little time and inclination for the more elegant pursuits of life.

Not every master grew richer as the years went by. The Lancashire saying 'Clogs to clogs in three generations' sums up the rise and fall of many families, and there were some men who made and lost fortunes in the space of a few years. Thomas Darwell, a Wigan cotton spinner, started a small cotton mill at the beginning of the nineteenth century and by ruthlessly exploiting his workpeople was able to build the large Sovereign Mills. So notorious did these become that some verses satirising conditions there were issued as a broadsheet. The poem begins:

Those Sovran Mills, those Sovran Mills,
If you go there, you'll get no ills:
For daily working fourteen hours
Will only renovate your powers.

The poet was not exaggerating. In February 1828, Darwell and his partner William Wood (the man referred to by Dodd), were reprimanded by the Home Office after the Wigan factory visitors reported that children under sixteen were working from 5 a.m. until 9 p.m. 'Some few,' they added, 'are allowed to go to their home to breakfast and dinner, but by far the greater number are not suffered to go out of the premises between the hours mentioned.'

As Darwell prospered, he went to live first at Ince Hall and then at Standish Hall, which was even grander. He was Mayor of Wigan in 1823 and 1830, but shortly after his second term in office his business failed, his wealth disappeared and he died in poverty in Patrick's Row in a working-class area of the town.

The power of many masters was enormous and often extended far beyond the walls of their mills. East Lancashire can show scores of communities which were dominated by a single family or even a single man. John Graham, the historian of calico printing, wrote in 1846 of John Hargreaves, proprietor of the Broad Oak Works, Accrington, 'He is the owner of all the property in the neighbourhood and reigns like a king.' One could say much the same of William Turner (1793–1852) the largest Lancashire woollen manufacturer of his day, who ruled Helmshore single-handed for nearly thirty years. He was a strict disciplinarian and is reputed to have once used his authority as a magistrate to send a workman to prison for 'spinning thick' and then to have cut the supply of gas to the village Primitive Methodist Church when its members signed a petition for the man's release. On the other hand, Turner built substantial houses for his workpeople, maintained a good school and built the parish church. The district benefited from his close interest in the East Lancashire Railway, turnpike trusts and the improvement of much local farm land. His mills provided regular work for about two thousand people, many of whom had no alternative but to leave the district when the firm ceased production on his death.

16. *Life in the Mines*

I was just under seven when my father took me down the pit; and because we went down ladders, he carried me on his back. There were eleven ladders at 'Tyldesley Fowt' pit and fifteen in that in Wardley Wood.

The Worsley woman who began her working life in such fearsome circumstances was born in 1802 when the Lancashire mines, by later standards, were comparatively small. But as the demand for coal grew rapidly, mines became deeper and more extensive, and earned the reputation of being the most noisome places of toil in the county. That so little has been written about pit life is not surprising, for, as a Government official observed in 1842, 'What passes under ground in dark tunnels in which people work is not known even to the overlooker.'

A notebook compiled in the early years of the century by Thomas Bury, manager of the Duke of Bridgewater's collieries in Worsley, gives a few glimpses of the miner's life. Not only had they to sign 12-month contracts, but they had also to agree to forfeit 2s. 6d. for every day or part of a day they were absent without good cause and 'to suffer such punishment as the law directs and as His Grace's agent may think proper.' Candles were used to test for explosive gases, and Bury, obviously writing from long experience, noted:

> If the flame spurts up and begins to lift, it is an invariable rule that [the gas] is just going to fire. Again, if the flame be broad at the top and bright at the sides, then it is certain you are far enough, for it will fire almost immediately.

Candles, which the miners had to buy themselves, were used for many years after the invention of the safety lamp in 1814. Simeon Dyson in his *Local Notes and Reminiscences of Farnworth*, writes of miners at the Hulton and Grundy Collieries working by candle light in the 1830s, as safety lamps were unknown in the district.

> The colliers' candles were very small (24 to the lb) and very green; this being because of arsenic used in their manufacture, which, it was said, prevented their tendency to gutter or run in the draught caused by the ventilation of the mine . . . The colliers were commonly seen returning from their work in the afternoon with unburnt pieces of green candle stuck in the loop-hole made for the purpose of their working caps. There were also a number of women employed down the pits and people thought nothing of seeing these amazons returning clad only in rough men's trousers and short petticoats,

Women drawing coal in a Lancashire mine in 1842 (British Parliamentary Papers. Children's Employment Commission, Appendix to the first report of the Commission on Mines, Part 2 (1842).

This famous picture, part of the popular image of nineteenth-century industry, was one of a series of engravings which shocked middle-class sensitivities in the mid-1840s.

rough jackets made from a coarse woollen cloth and their legs enclosed in stockings without feet, called 'whirlers'.

Conditions in the Lancashire mines were first brought to public notice by the report, published in 1833, of the Commissioner for Factories, Mr Carleton Tufnell, who declared after visiting the Bridge-water Collieries that 'the hardest labour in the worst room in the worst conducted factory is less hard, less cruel and less demoralising than the labour in the best of coal mines.' A seventeen-year-old miner from Walkden Moor told Tufnell that 'many a time we never see daylight for three or four days together' and a boy from a Worsley pit said he was one of a hundred children and young men who worked in seams three feet thick by the light of candles, which they had to provide themselves. Frequently they went nine hours 'with nothing except a sup of cold water' and at best a bit of bread and cheese; and often they were unable to eat even that because of the dust, dampness and 'badness of the air.' The mine, said the boy, was as hot as an oven and 'sometimes I have seen it so hot as to melt a candle,' but on other occasions we had to work in places where he was unable to keep the dripping water out of his eyes. Beaten by the men they worked for and bruised by low roofs and protruding walls, the mine children 'seldom slept with a whole skin' and few grew up who were not maimed or deformed. Promiscuity was rife underground and many women had children before they were married. Explosions took a regular toll of life, and any miner who survived the numerous hazards of his occupation knew that he would be unfit for work at fifty and that he would almost certainly end his days 'in misery and sorrow.'

The 1842 Report on the Employment of Children, which was quickly followed by Lord Ashley's Act prohibiting the employment underground of women and girls and of boys under ten, gives a much more detailed picture of life in the mines. Most women and children spent their time pushing or drawing tubs from the coal face to the 'pit-eye' or to levels where there were horses or ponies. In narrow or inclined seams, they had to adopt an almost horizontal position and by constantly pressing their heads against the backs of the tubs they occasionally rubbed off so much hair as to become almost bald. At a number of pits, particularly in Clifton, Bolton, Outwood, Lever, Worsley, Blackrod and St Helens, the old method of drawing baskets or wooden sledges ('sleds') was still used.

The drawer is harnessed by means of a chain attached to the 'sled'; the other end of the chain passes between his legs and fastens in front

Boys in a mine, 1842.

to a belt round the waist. When thus harnessed and moving along on his hands and feet, the drawer drags after him the loaded basket; if he is not sufficiently strong he has a helper rather younger than himself, and these latter children are called in Lancashire 'thrutchers'.

A sixteen-year-old girl at Bridgewater Colliery said she drew a 'sled' of coal along a 180-yard passage ten, twelve and occasionally more times a day. Another girl, who was nearly eighteen, said she drew her basket more than eight miles each day, and Betty Harris, aged thirty seven, a drawer in a Bolton mine, gave this account of how she earned seven shillings a week by working from six in a morning until six at night:

> I have a belt round my waist and a chain passing between my legs and I go on my hands and feet. The road is very steep and we have to hold by a rope, and when there is no rope, by anything we can catch hold of. There are six women and about six boys and girls in the pit I work in: it is very hard work for a woman. The pit is very wet where I work and the water comes over our clog tops always, and I have seen it up to my thighs; it rains in at the roof terribly: my clothes are wet through almost all day long. I am very tired when I get home at night; I fall asleep sometimes before I get washed. I am not so strong as I was and cannot stand my work so well as I used to. I have drawn till I have had the skin off me: the belt and chain is worse when we are in the family way. My feller [husband] has beaten me many a time for not being ready. I were not used to it at first and he had little patience. I have known many a man beat his drawer. I have known men take liberty with the drawers, and some of the women have bastards.

Betty Wardle said she had given birth to a child at Outwood Colliery near Little Lever and had brought it to the surface wrapped in her skirt. When asked if she were telling the truth, she replied, 'Aye, that I am. It was the day after I was married—that's what makes me know.'

Mary Glover, aged thirty eight, who worked at Ringleybridge, went into the mine at seven and began work as a drawer:

> I never worked much in the pit when I was in the family way, but since I gave up having children, I have begun again a bit. I go at half-past five in the morning and I come out between 4 and 5 in the afternoon, and sometimes later. I wear a shift and a pair of trousers when at work, and I will always have a good pair of trousers. I have had many a twopence given me by the boatmen on the canal to show my breeches. I never saw a woman work naked, but I have seen men work without breeches in the neighbourhood of Bolton. I remember seeing a man who worked stark naked: we used to throw coals at him.

'A good pair of breeches' was rarely seen, however, and many children were 'in rags and in a disgusting state of dirt.' Cleanliness was hardly considered. Peter Gaskell, a collier who worked near Worsley, was questioned on this subject:

> *How often do the drawers wash their bodies?*—None of the drawers ever wash their bodies: I never wash my body. I let my shirt rub the dirt off—my shirt will show that. I wash my neck and ears and face, of course.
>
> *Do you think it is usual for the young women to do the same as you do?*—I don't think it is usual for the lasses to wash their bodies. My sisters never wash themselves, and seeing is believing. They wash their faces and necks and ears.
>
> *When a collier is in full dress he has white stockings and low shoes, and a very tall neck shirt, very stiffly starched, and ruffles?*—That is very true, Sir, but they never wash their bodies underneath: I know that, and their legs and bodies are as black as your hat.

The youngest children were employed as trappers (air-door minders) and their extremely monotonous job was said by a sub-commissioner to be 'one of the most pitiable in a coal-pit.'

> Their whole time is spent in sitting in the dark for twelve hours, and opening and shutting a door to allow the waggoners to pass. Were it not for the passing and repassing of the waggons, it would be equal to solitaty confinement of the worst order.

Progress in a coal mine was described by a collier at Patricroft:

> It is the custom to consider a man as divided into eight parts. When first a boy begins to work, he is considered to be equal to one eighth part of a man; at ten years he is two-eighths: thirteen three-eighths, fifteen one half, a girl at sixteen one half; a boy at eighteen three-fourths. At this age a boy begins to get coal. Girls and women never get coal and always remain drawers and are considered to be equal to half a man.

Joseph Wild, the Chief Constable of Oldham, listed several fatal accidents which occurred when young boys who had been placed in charge of steam engines failed to stop the winding gear, with the result that miners being hauled from the pit bottom were carried over the beam and thrown down the shaft. Four youths were killed at Chamber Lane Colliery when a boy of nine turned away from the steam engine to look at a mouse. 'The inducement to employ these children,' said the Chief Constable, 'is merely that their services can be obtained for perhaps 5s. or 7s. a week, instead of the 30s. a week which the proprietors would perhaps have to pay a man of full years and discretion.'

Mr Wild also gave an account of the maltreatment of the mine children. Supposed delinquents were always punished 'according to barbarous rules' drawn up by the workers. Generally the victim was beaten on the bare posterior with thin pieces of wood while his head was held fast between another miner's legs.

> However the one punished may cry; they stick to him: and in the last case, where a hungry lad had stole a pit dinner, they mangled his body seriously. In other cases the injured parties could not work at all for some time. In the case mentioned, the offenders were made to placard the town with an apology, to render some compensation in money and promise not to follow any such course in future.

Accidents were so frequent that they aroused no surprise and little sympathy. The Chief Constable said 'a great amount of rude callousness' was shown by the colliers and their families, an uneducated, hard-drinking, hard-gambling set of people, who went to cock-pits, races and fights. When a miner was killed, they would say, 'Oh, I am not a bit surprised: I expected it—I expected it.' And within a day or two, even the wife and children seemed to have forgotten the accident. Mr Wild said, 'People generally feel, "Oh, it's only a collier!" There would be a hundred times more feeling if a policeman were to kill a dog in the street.'

The 1842 Act was often deliberately ignored and as late as 1845 it was estimated that two hundred women were still working in Lancashire pits. At Fletcher's Colliery at Outwood, ladders were placed near the entrance to a shaft to enable women to go down secretly to their work.

In 1846, when a miner was discovered working at the age of seventy five, great and understandable astonishment was displayed by the Lancashire newspapers. The *Manchester Guardian* on 16 May said:

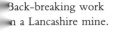
Back-breaking work in a Lancashire mine.

There is now living in the township of Butterworth, near Rochdale, a man named Josh Taylor, aged seventy five years, who, at the age of five began to work in a coal pit. At the age of ten he commenced working as a regular miner and has continued to work in a low mine in the pit up to the present time, a period of seventy years. He can manage to get eight loads of coal at sixpence per load in one day. He never worked in a mine above two feet in height and never worked out of the township.

In the same year, John Rushton, a boy of thirteen, began work at Cinder Field Pit, Walkden. His first job, he wrote in later life, was to push a basket of coal which was hauled by his uncle by means of a belt and chain. Explosive gases were an ever-present threat:

> Our coal-getters worked with candles and on one occasion one of our men observing the flame on his candle, noticed the presence of gas. He immediately cried, 'Candles out! Gas is upon us!' The other men instantly obeyed. With all possible speed we secured our clothing and not waiting to dress, hurried to the shaft in the darkness.

Once a coal-getter's candle did ignite the gas. 'It was a mere flash,

Horse- and man-power combine in moving huge loads of coal underground. This appears to be an underground horse-gin, a winding drum which raised coal from lower levels towards the surface.

but sufficient to cause a shock and a smarting as if he had received a stroke from a birch rod.'

Sometimes the coal-getters would work in the gas-polluted workings until they were almost unconscious, rather than suffer a loss of earnings, and Rushton remembered how his safety lamp grew so hot in such conditions that he dared not touch it.

Most mine owners showed little interest in their workpeople's welfare and as late as 1855 the Government Inspector for the Manchester district found a number of them attempting to enforce rules that few despotic mill owners would have considered. An Act of that year allowed colliery owners to put forward regulations to cover particular local conditions, but among the rules proposed was one requiring all miners 'to attend Divine services at least once on the Lord's Day' and another forbidding the men to begin work on a Monday morning dirty or with an old beard.

A number of employers, however, took a close interest in their workpeople. The Earl of Ellesmere, who inherited the Bridgewater estates in 1837, opened day schools and later evening technical classes, which every boy employed in the mines was obliged to attend. A qualified teacher was appointed to lecture on such subjects as ventilation, machinery and gases that were explosive or injurious to health. After the introduction of the 1842 Act, the Countess opened a domestic science school at Walkden Moor for the women and girls who were displaced. It was the first of its kind in the country.

17. New Towns, New Horrors

'The south-eastern quarter of Lancashire,' said Mr Bryce in his report on the county's schools in 1868, 'is a district to which it would be hard to find anything comparable in England or indeed in Europe.'

Within a circumference of some 90 miles, it contains nine towns with a population exceeding 30,000 and 16 others with a population of more than 6,000 each, towns which have mostly sprung into greatness within the last thirty or forty years and which continue to increase at a rate as rapid as ever. The total population of the district may be roughly estimated at 1,200,000, excluding Manchester and Salford; its area at 500 square miles, giving something like 2,400 persons to the square mile. Even these figures, however, give but a faint idea of its aspect to the traveller. From Burnley to Warrington, from Wigan to Stalybridge, it is one huge congeries of villages, thickening ever and anon into towns, but seldom thinning out into anything that can be called country. Between Bury and Bacup, for instance, or between Rochdale and Ashton-under-Lyne, the line of

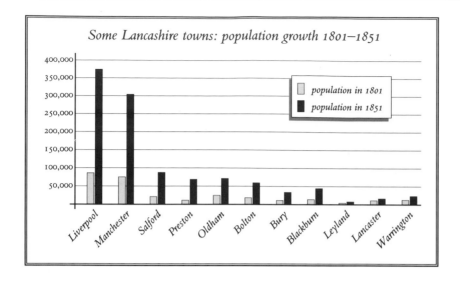

Some Lancashire towns: population growth 1801–1851

population in 1801
population in 1851

Liverpool, Manchester, Salford, Preston, Oldham, Bolton, Bury, Blackburn, Leyland, Lancaster, Warrington

railway is almost everywhere fringed with factories and houses, thickest along the banks of the larger streams, but also climbing the slopes of the great bleak moors that hang over the smoky valleys and only stopping where cultivation itself stops—at the edge of the heathery domain of the grouse.

Towns were built with scant regard for the people who had to live in them. As a Haslingden man observed, there were no buildings or sanitary regulations in the early years of the nineteenth century and anyone with land could build a pigsty or a mansion and face it to any point of the compass no matter how greatly it might offend his neighbours. 'St Helens,' said *Chambers' Edinburgh Journal* in 1846, 'seems to have been built in a hurry, the attention of the inhabitants being so absorbed in advancing manufacturers that they would care little about the kind of house they should provide for themselves.' Three years later, the Rev J.R. Stevens outlined the growth of Ashton-under-Lyne:

Within a narrow ring of what a few years ago was clay bed and moorland, with a stretch of hill and a sweep of lovely dale, now swarm not less than a hundred thousand souls. Suddenly, as if by spell of fairy or fiend, stray hamlet scattered township and straggling parish have run together and have become one vast unbroken wilderness of mills and houses, a teeming town where the ceaseless whirl and rattle, clink and clank of groaning wheel and flying shuttle bespeak the presence of an industry unparalleled in its nature, its intensity and its duration.

Manchester had grown so large by 1840 that a local surgeon remarked that those who lived in the more populous quarters 'could seldom hope

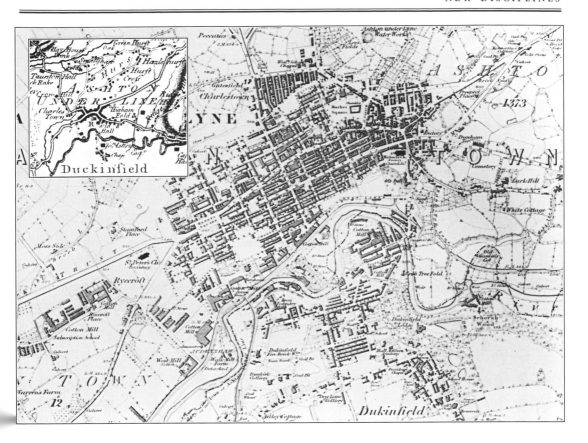

The growth of Ashton-under-Lyne is clearly demonstrated here, in a comparison of Yates' map of 1786 (inset) and the 1st edition Ordnance Survey map of the 1840s. Much of the growth is attributable to the planned new town laid out by the landowner, the Earl of Stamford, from the late eighteenth century. The rigid grid pattern of streets contrasts sharply with the old main road which winds across the town.

to see the green face of nature,' and the economist Nassau W. Senior, after visiting Ancoats, 'Irish Town' and 'Little Ireland' described how small speculators with utter disregard for everything except immediate profit were adding to the Manchester sprawl:

> A carpenter and a bricklayer club together to buy a patch of ground and cover it with what they call houses. In one place we saw a whole street following the course of a ditch in order to have deeper cellars (cellars for people not for lumber) without the expense of excavation. Not a house in this street escaped cholera. And generally speaking, throughout these suburbs the streets are unpaved, with a dunghill or a pond in the middle: the houses built back to back without ventilation or drainage; and whole families occupy each corner of a cellar or a garret.

In 1841, Charles Mott, an assistant Poor Law Commissioner, found Manchester streets being built with neither cellars nor foundations and 'with a rapidity that astonishes persons who are acquainted with their flimsy structure.' The walls were only half a brick [4½ ins.] thick and the whole of the materials were 'slight and unfit for the purpose.'

I have been told of a man who had built a row of these houses;

and visiting them one morning after a storm, found the whole of them levelled with the ground; and in another part of Manchester, a place with houses even of a better order has obtained the appellation of 'Pickpocket Row' from the known insecure nature of the buildings.

Life in the poorer parts of the large towns and cities can scarcely be imagined. As early as 1801, the Manchester Board of Health drew attention to cellar dwellings which were sometimes so dark that patients could not be seen without the light of a candle and which were so badly ventilated that the doctor had difficulty in staying at the bedside long enough to discover the nature of the patient's disease. The report adds:

> The bedclothes frequently consist of the tattered remnants of tar-paulings and cotton bags. Not seldom half a dozen are sick at one time, of whom three or four are panting in the same bed together; or destitute of a bed, some are stretched along chairs; or not being possessed of chairs, are laid upon the ground; or there not be sufficient space for them on the floor, are shoved below looms or cooped up in corners among lumber. Very often the physician repeats his visits only to witness misery he cannot alleviate; and at last to record in the books of the infirmary that the friend of the Wretched—Death—has brought relief.

Dr J. Farriar in the proceedings of the Board of Health in 1805, again referred to Manchester's underground population.

> The number of damp and very ill-ventilated cellars inhabited in many parts of the town is a most extensive and prominent evil . . . They consist of two rooms, the first of which is used as a kitchen, and though frequently noxious by its dampness and closeness, is generally preferable to the back room. The latter has only one small window, which, though on a level with the outer ground, is near the roof of the cellar. It is often covered with boards or paper and in its best state is so much covered with mud as to admit little either of air or light. In this cell, the beds of the whole family, sometimes consisting of seven or eight, are placed. The floor of this room is often unpaved: the beds are fixed on the damp earth. But the floor when paved is always damp. In such places, where a candle is required even at noonday . . . I have seen the sick lying in rags; they can seldom afford straw.

As thousands from all parts of the country and from Ireland flocked to Manchester to meet the insatiable demand for mill workers, the scenes described by Dr Farriar were multiplied enormously. No remedial action was taken, but in 1832, following the arrival of cholera in

In less than a generation, from 1824 to 1848, Preston, like most other industrialising Lancashire towns, grew prodigiously. Comparing Shakeshaft's map (top) with the 1st edition Ordnance Survey map shows the huge expansion of industry and housing south of Church Street, along Marsh Lane and north along North Road. Already in the early years of the century the Lancaster Canal and its associated tramway cut through the west of the town but by 1848 it had been supplemented by a growing railway network.

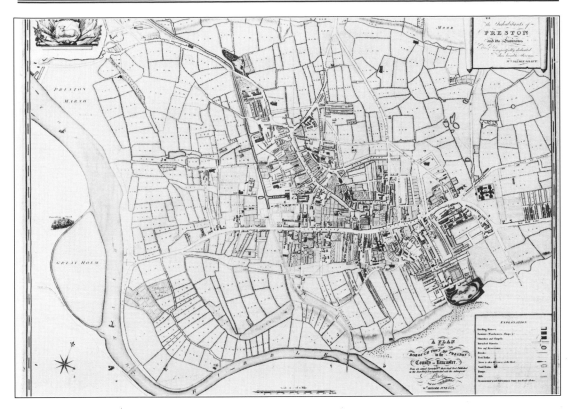

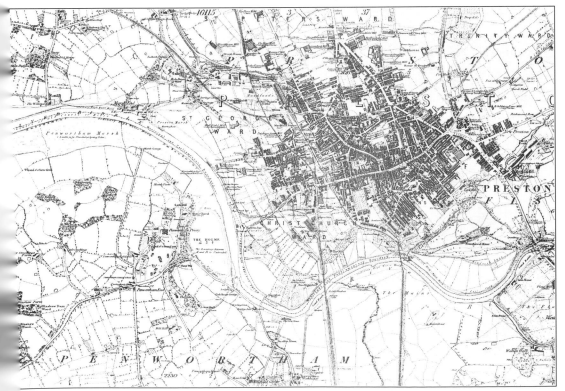

England, boards of health were set up in the main centres of population. That in Manchester was the most active and the investigations of its secretary, Dr James Phillips Kay (later Sir James Kay-Shuttleworth), led to the publication of one of the most important reports of the nineteenth century. As G. M. Young put it, 'There was no reason to suppose that Manchester was any worse than any other towns, and the inevitable conclusion was that an increasing portion of the population of England was living under conditions which were not only a negation of civilised existence, but a menace to civilised society.'

Dr Kay called his report *The Moral and Physical Condition of the Working Classes Employed in the Cotton Manufacture in Manchester*. The following extracts will give some idea of his findings:

> The habitations of the Irish . . . can scarcely be said to be furnished. They contain one or two chairs, a mean table, the most scanty culinary apparatus and one or two beds loathsome with filth. A whole family is often accommodated on a single bed: and sometimes a heap of filthy straw and a cover of old sacking hide them in one undistinguished heap, debased alike by penury, want of economy and dissolute habits . . . One family lived in a damp cellar containing only one room, in whose pestilential atmosphere from twelve to sixteen persons were crowded. To this fertile source of disease were sometimes added the keeping of pigs and other animals in the house with other nuisances of a most revolting character.
>
> A portion of low, swampy ground, liable to be frequently inundated, and to constant exhalation, is included between a high bank over which the Oxford-road passes, and a bend of the River Medlock, where its course is impeded by a weir. This unhealthy spot lies so low that the chimneys of its houses, some of them three storeys high, are little above the level of the road. About two hundred of these habitations are crowded together in an extremely narrow space and are chiefly inhabited by the lowest Irish. Many of these houses have also cellars, whose floor is scarcely elevated above the level of the water flowing in the Medlock. The soughs [drains] are destroyed or out of repair: and these narrow abodes are in consequence always damp, and on the slightest rise of the river, which is a frequent occurrence, are flooded to a depth of several inches. The district has frequently been the haunt of thieves and desperadoes who defied the law, and is always inhabited by a class resembling savages in their appetites and habits. It is surrounded on every side by some of the largest factories of the town, whose chimneys vomit forth dense clouds of smoke which hangs heavily over this insalubrious region.
>
> In Parliament-street there is only one privy for 380 inhabitants, which is placed in a narrow passage, whence its effluvia infest the

adjacent houses . . . In this street also, cess pools with open grids have been made, close to the doors of the houses, in which disgusting refuse accumulates, and whence its noxious effluvia constantly exhale.

The Irk, black with the refuse of dye-works erected on its banks, receives excrementious matter from some sewers in this portion of the town—the drainage from the gas works, and filth of the most pernicious character from bone-works, tanneries, size manufacturers, etc. Immediately beneath Ducie Bridge, in a deep hollow between two high banks, it sweeps round a large cluster of the most wretched and dilapidated buildings of the town. The course of the river is here impeded by a weir, and a large tannery eight storeys high (three of which storeys are filled with skins exposed to the atmosphere, in some stage of the processes to which they are subjected), towers close to this crazy labyrinth of buildings. This group of buildings is called 'Gibraltar', and no site can be more insalubrious than that in which it is built.

One nuisance frequently occurs in these districts of so noxious a character, that it ought, at the earliest period, be suppressed by legal interference. The houses of the poor sometimes surround a common area, into which the doors and windows open at the back of the dwelling. Porkers, who feed the pigs in the town, often contract with the inhabitants to pay some small sum for the rent of their area, which is immediately covered with pig-styes and converted into a dung heap and receptacle of the putrescent garbage which is now heedlessly flung into it from the surrounding dwellings. The offensive odour which sometimes arises from these areas cannot be conceived.

Liverpool, too, had its 'dark, damp, confined and ill-ventilated cellars'—the Manchester Statistical Society counted 7,493 in 1836—and scenes which were almost beyond belief. Dr W. H. Duncan, who found that between 35,000 and 40,000 people were living underground, reported in 1839:

From the absence of drains and sewers, there are few cellars entirely free from damp; many of those in low situations are literally inundated after a fall of rain. To remedy the evil, the inhabitants frequently make little holes or walls at the foot of the cellar stops or in the floor itself; and notwithstanding these contrivances, it has been necessary in some cases to take the door off its hinges and lay it on the floor supported by bricks, in order to protect the inhabitant from the wet. Nor is this the full extent of the evil; the fluid matter of the court privies sometimes oozes through into the adjoining cellars, rendering them uninhabitable by anyone whose olfactories retain the slightest sensibility. In one cellar in Lace-street I was told

LEFT AND OPPOSITE: Manchester cellar dwellings (*Pictorial Times*, 1847). Cellar dwellings were exceptionally insanitary; not only did they have no drainage themselves, but they often received effluent, surface water and floodwaters from other dwellings and from the street. Most were perpetually damp and verminous, and the stench overwhelmed the sensitive noses of outsiders. It was these dwellings which were the first object of attention from the newly appointed medical officers in the 1850s and 1860s.

that the filthy water thus collected measured not less than two feet in depth; and in another cellar, a well, four feet deep, into which this stinking fluid was allowed to drain, was discovered below the bed where a family slept!

It is hardly surprising to find that the average age of the 5,597 working-class people who died in Liverpool in 1840 was only fifteen or that sixty two per cent died before reaching the age of five. The statistics for Manchester were only slightly better, and Edwin Chadwick in his monumental *Report on the Sanitary Condition of the Labouring Population of Great Britain* of 1842 pointed out that for many children mill life there was less damaging than home life.

> However defective the ventilation of many of the factories may yet be, they are all of them drier and more equably warm than the residence of the parent; and we have proof that weakly children have been put into better-managed factories as healthier places for them than their own homes. It is an appalling fact that, of all who are born of the labouring classes in Manchester, more than 57 per cent die before they attain five years of age; that is before they can be engaged in factory labour, or in any other labour whatsoever.

Sanitation and housing in the small industrial towns were little better than those in the cities and in general took longer to remedy. The ever-assiduous Manchester Statistical Society, on investigating living conditions in Bury, found that of 2,755 dwellings examined, only 1,668 could be described as comfortable. Some sixty three families were discovered with five persons sleeping in one bed, and there were some with six. In hilly districts like Rossendale, where 'good' building land was that which could be used for no other purpose, rows of back-to-earth houses were built into the sides of the numerous valleys and cloughs. Bacup, the outstanding example of this kind of town, had a population of between 8,000 and 10,000 in 1849, but in the words of a Government inspector:

> The civil and municipal character are very peculiar . . . it is neither a parish nor a market town. It does not possess any local government whatever, nor has it, with the exception of the Mechanics' Institute any of the institutions and arrangements usually found where large masses of people are congregated together.

The inspector recorded that after visiting some dwellings he had the greatest difficulty in continuing with his duties. Three diseased pigs were living within a yard of a cottage window and in a cellar, which

The back lane be-
tween Paradise Street
(*sic*) and High Street,
Lower Darwen,
photographed in the
1870s. The small slate-
roofed sheds con-
tained ash-pit privies
which were empted
but infrequently. This
picture was used,
with others, by Black-
burn Corporation as
part of its evidence to
Parliament in pro-
moting the 1879
Blackburn
Improvment Act,
which allowed the
authorities to take re-
medial action and
tackle such problems.

was in 'a most filthy state', he was not surprised when the wife told him, 'we have never been well since we came here. We have had low fevers.' The family paid a shilling a week and had to walk 170 yards to a lavatory. A mill owner, in need of a lavatory while in the town, often had the greatest difficulty in finding one fit to use.

I have had to go to half a dozen privies before I could get to one without pollution. I have started at the top of Irwell-street, gone down Back-street and visited all I have come at; some I have found occupied and others as I have already described. I have gone round by the watercourse and given them all a call in the same way and then come out at the top again without any success. I have then proceeded up Union-street and have been compelled to skulk behind a wall.

The lavatories were often facing the streets and were without doors, drains and seats. It was customary 'for two females to go together and for one to stand outside and spread her garments to screen the other.' It was the lodging houses, however, that really appalled the inspector.

Men, women and children and frequently dogs form a promiscuous herd, all sleeping in the same close confined room from where every breath of pure air is excluded; while their unwashed bodies, filthy stinking clothes and frequently evil straw beds produce an atmosphere that is horrible on first entering the room. Most of the lodgers sleep in a state of absolute nudity, and decency with the greater portion of them has long ceased to be thought of.

Preston housing (from the report of Revd Clay). The narrowest of lanes between the rows of back yards has become, in effect, an open sewer. These houses—Elizabeth Street and Ann Street—were part of 'New Preston', a large area of industrial housing which grew from the 1820s on open land east of the old town.

In one lodging house the inspector found four beds occupied by six females and eight males. There were five persons in one of the beds. In another house there were six beds containing four females, nine males and a dog. One room of another lodging house had seven beds used by nine men and seven women.

Bacup's water supply was totally inadequate and the inspector saw some people filling cans with what looked more like liquid manure than water. Other townsfolk walked half a mile to a well. The overcrowded graveyards gave off nasty smells and the Irwell was so full of rubbish that the level often rose and flooded cellars. The dilapidated state of the streets was 'little to be wondered at' because no highway surveyors had been appointed for three years and no highway rate had been collected.

The streams and rivers of East Lancashire, once renowned for their romantic beauty and the excellence of their trout and salmon were choked with the refuse of countless houses, mills, mines, quarries and workshops until the Irwell, into which the accumulated pollution was swept, became the most overworked and most abominable stretch of water in the world. By the early 1860s the river bed in Manchester had risen so high that main sewers and mill goyts were blocked and

Brave souls in mid-nineteenth-century Manchester paddle in the Irwell just below the walls of Chetham's Hospital near the Cathedral. The river, which in the seventeenth century had been noted for its fish, had by this time become an open sewer.

serious flooding occurred after heavy rain. Even at Warrington, eighteen miles from the nearest culpable factory, large banks of cinders were deposited by the Mersey into which the Irwell poured its overburdened waters. 'It is demonstrable,' wrote Thomas Coates in 1862, 'that more than 75,000 tons of cinders are annually cast into the rivers; and the quantity of other solid matter which is so deposited is incalculable.' Coates, who published a short illustrated pamphlet in support of the Mersey, Irwell, &c., Protection Bill of that year, describes some of the methods used to dispose of refuse. Mills adjoining streams usually had an inclined plane down which the ashes from the boilerhouse were shot into the water. Several manufacturers had built tramways to the nearest stream and a mine owner 'sends boat loads of colliery refuse for a considerable distance along the Bolton and Bury Canal to a point where the canal runs close to the Irwell, and there discharges the contents of the boats into the river.' Whole villages, said Coates, contributed to the choking of the streams, and at Bacup, where there was no public tip, a heap of rubbish rose sixteen feet from the bed of the Irwell to the top of a wall adjoining the main street.

'Such is the absence of civil economy in some of our towns,' wrote Edwin Chadwick in 1842, 'that their condition is almost as bad as that of an encamped horde of undisciplined soldiery.' The statement remained true of many parts of Lancashire until well into the second half of the century.

3

New Ideas

1. *The Two Lancashires*

HE working classes are looking for something besides eating, working and dying,' said a note from a group of operatives at Shoe Mill, Accrington, who sent 5s. 6d. to the Lancashire Short-Time Committee in March 1847. Their statement was prompted by an exchange which had occurred earlier in the month during a Commons debate on the Factories Bill. Joseph Brotherton, MP for Salford, had asked: 'Shall it be allowed that to eat, to drink, to work and to die shall be the lot for a large portion of our fellow countrymen?' Sir James Graham, the former Home Secretary, who spoke next, had a ready answer. 'I grieve to say,' he told the House, 'that not in this country only, but throughout the whole of this world of sorrow and care, the lot of eating, drinking, working and dying must ever be the sum of human life among the mass of a large portion of the human family.' Had Sir James been better acquainted with Lancashire, he might have modified his remarks, for the whole county had become a veritable whirlpool of ideas as men from all walks of life struggled to bring order out of the chaos of the new industrial age. From the debate and discussion there had emerged an astonishing number of political, religious, educational and social movements, which, though they represented the widest range of views, were inspired by the same intense and serious determination. The militant Chartist sharpening his pike, the model employer building his school, the co-operator weighing out butter and cheese in his makeshift shop, the nonconformist preacher tramping across the moors to conduct a service in the next valley, the humanitarian (Brotherton was a notable example) championing factory legislation of free libraries—all were united in a desire to change society.

Thousands of people, it is true, were debased by intolerable living and working conditions, but large numbers were influenced by Sunday schools, mechanics' institutions, co-operative societies and the like with the result that there developed within the less prosperous of the 'two nations', the two Lancashires, represented on the one hand by the toper and on the other hand by the enlightened working man. The excesses of the first group blinded many observers to the achievements and even the existence of the second and the determined pursuit of knowledge, culture and a better life was only occasionally acknowledged. To appreciate the triumph of these men and those who devoted their time to helping them one has merely to consider their unpropitious surroundings. Joseph Livesey, the temperance pioneer, spent his childhood at the hand-loom in a damp cellar, but, as he records in his autobiography:

> This cellar was my college, the breast beam my desk, and I was my own tutor. Many a day and night I laboured to understand Lindley Murray [an English Grammar] and at last by indomitable perseverence, what appeared as a hopeless task was accomplished without aid from any human being. Anxious for information and having no companions from whom I could learn anything, I longed for books, but had not the means with which to procure them. There were no public libraries and books of all kinds were expensive; and if I could succeed in borrowing one I would devour it like a hungry man would his first meal.
>
> I seldom got a meal without a book open before me at the same time, and I managed to do what I have never seen any other weaver attempt—to read and weave at the same time. For hours together I have done this and without making bad work. For hours I have read by the glare of a few embers left in the fire grate with my head close to the bars.

The life of James Sharples (1825–92), the boilermaker-artist, is another example of intellect and industry battling against almost insuperable odds. At the age of ten, Sharples, who was one of thirteen children, started work in a Bury foundry and regularly spent fourteen hours a day heating and carrying rivets for the workmen. By studying early in the morning and late at night and by attending Bury Mechanics' Institute, he developed a talent for drawing which he discovered when he sketched designs on the workshop floor. At eighteen, he began his most famous painting, *The Forge*, a detailed interior of an engineering shop which took three years to complete. Sharples received great help from his brother James who sometimes got up as early as three o'clock to pose for him and who also undertook some of his work at the foundry to allow him to devote more time to the picture. But even more remarkable than the painting of *The Forge* was the engraving of it. In 1848, Sharples bought a steel plate twenty one inches by eighteen, but being unaware of the acid process, spent the spare time of ten years cutting the design with needles.

The Forge, by James Sharples (on loan to Blackburn Museum and Art Gallery from Miss Marion Sharples, reproduced by kind permission of Blackburn Museum and Art Gallery).

A fine painting of early industry—here is shown a transition phase between the individual craftsmen and the large industrial enterprise, an important stage in the development of most industries in the late eighteenth and early nineteenth centuries.

A correspondent of *The Working Man* in 1866 told a similar story.

Many years ago I was a lad working in a dye-house in a Lancashire village. At that time, much work and little leisure was the rule; and those of us who had any desire to educate ourselves found considerably more difficulty than do the lads of today. We very frequently had to labour week after week at an average rate of sixteen hours a day, and not seldom spent the whole night at work. Looking back at that time, it seems to me strange indeed that the desire to know and understand was not utterly destroyed by the irksomeness of our physical life . . . Even in the dye-house we found occasional half hours when we might steal away with our Walkingame [a popular book on arithmetic] or Lindley Murray, or hide ourselves in the murk and steam between the 'becks' at which we laboured, and there enjoy such books as we could then obtain. Some of us could repeat long passages from the versified romances of Walter Scott; others were deep in Burns and Byron; others again discussed questions of theology and politics; others were well read in biography—knew all about Franklin and his kite, about Newton and his dog Diamond, and could repeat long lists of names of men, who from positions as lowly as our own, had risen to honour and renown. Some of us, even in those early days, wrote rhymes for ourselves. We had no pens, pencils or paper, and so took small, pinky, soap-encrusted boards from the becks and scribbled upon them with wooden skewers.

Physical discomfort was only one of many obstacles confronting these men. We have described Manchester's inglorious coronation festivities of 1821: ten years later drunkenness remained one of the city's favourite pastimes. On New Year's Day 1831, Livesey found the dram shops 'in full operation' and saw 162 persons, two thirds of them women and young girls, enter one shop in half an hour. In May of the same year he observed in his magazine *The Moral Reformer:*

> Drunkenness is so prevalent that I doubt whether it would be possible to travel half a dozen miles in any public road in Lancashire without seeing some indication of it.

Livesey found Bolton even more obnoxious than Manchester. 'Boys will drink like men, and children often come to sup with their mothers,' he wrote, adding that women went to public houses as a matter of course and 'in open day may be seen sitting with long pipes in their mouths and their glasses before them.' After visiting Bolton on Easter Day, he told his readers:

Joseph Livesey, born at Walton-le-Dale, near Preston, was a man of many talents—cheese factor, newspaper editor, local politician, writer and—for which he is best known to posterity—temperance reformer and advocate of many social and moral causes.

> From the surrounding country there was an influx of many thousands of young persons. Rude, uneducated and exceedingly vulgar in their habits, some of these fellows when they get into liquor are almost like mad bulls. They come purposely for a spree and when they return to work, if they cannot boast of a good fuddle and recount a number of lawless exploits, they would consider they had fallen short of acting their part. The streets were crowded early in the afternoon and numbers were staggering and vociferating under the influence of drink. But in the evening the scene was still more affecting. So many drunken men were prowling along the streets that it was scarcely possible to move without being entangled with them.

Of Bolton on Easter Monday 1832, Livesey wrote: 'I witnessed such scenes of drunkenness and brutality, particularly in the country people, as I believe could be found in no other place.'

Twenty years later, the Sunday school teachers of Burnley and Habergham Eaves, in a memorial to the local magistrates, spoke of being 'painfully impressed with the low standard of morals among a large portion of the population.' A thousand drunken people could be seen in the town on a Saturday night and on Sundays 'large numbers in a state of disgraceful intoxication may be seen wending their way, to the annoyance of the virtuous and sober, with tottering steps from one scene of dissipation to another.' Prostitutes openly exhibited themselves and 'the spread of the vagabond practices of pigeon flying and dog racing' had created the greatest concern. Gambling had gripped the young, who seemed to the memorialists to be hastening along a road 'which must inevitably terminate in the destruction of their temporal prospects and happiness and in blasting their hopes for eternity.'

If drinking was the working man's favourite recreation, fighting was his favourite 'sport'. The *Bolton Chronicle* of 5 November 1836 reported:

> On Monday last a fight for £1 a side took place at Heywood between William Hutchinson, alias 'Old Irons', a collier, and John Standering, a moulder. The men fought what is called Lancashire fashion, i.e. kicking and throttling. The young man Hutchinson was kicked in the most brutal manner. Messrs. Taylor and Leach, surgeons, have attended him, but have no hopes of his recovery. Standering has left the country.

In May 1838, the paper described a 'purring' match near Bury at which, for £25 a side, two men 'nearly in a state of nudity, kicked each other with shoes heavily toed with iron and studded with jagged nails so as to tear skin and flesh away at every kick.' The report added that 'fair' kicking was that confined to the shins and knees.

Similar news items appeared regularly and the following, published in the *Manchester Courier* in November 1848, indicated that fighting had lost none of its popularity ten years later. The paragraph is headed 'Lancashire cannibal'.

> Early on Saturday morning a police office of the C division observed a man, having the appearance of an excavator, busily engaged searching a field off Store Street for something which he appeared to have lost. The officer went up to and questioned the man, who at first seemed remarkably taciturn and indisposed to answer questions, but at last he gathered that the fellow he was addressing had that morning been engaged in an up and down fight, Lancashire fashion, and that he was looking for one of his ears—*which his antagonist had bitten off!* Commiserating with the poor wretch, the police officer assisted him to look for his ear, which after a while he found, when the officer strongly advised him to appear at the Borough Court next morning to apply for a warrant against the brute who had so maimed him. 'Noa, noa,' rejoined the fellow, cooly depositing his stray ear in his waistcoat pocket, 'aw'st do nowt

at soart; it was a fair gradely stand-up battle, un aw want nother law nor warrant.'

Superstition had a considerable hold on the country people and according to a report in the *Liverpool Mail* in March 1846, five persons in the neighbourhood of Smallbridge, near Rochdale, earned a living by 'fortune telling, relating the planets and looking through glasses.' Many persons in the vicinity were said to believe in witchcraft and to wear charms on their clothing to prevent injury by evil spirits. The enlightened citizens of Liverpool were doubtless amused to read about their benighted neighbours, but the credulity of many of their own townspeople was exposed only a few days later. Towards the end of the month notices appeared in Liverpool announcing that 'Don Edward Heuson, the Modern Daedalus, recently arrived from New York,' would ascend from Clayton Square by means of 'a winged machine' and fly to St Patrick's Chapel, calling on his way at the Town Hall and the Customs House. Huge crowds thronged the square at the appointed time, but the 'Modern Daedalus' did not appear. It was 1 April.

Dr Kay, in a letter to the 1833 Select Committee on Public Walks, said the labouring classes of Manchester were 'ignorant of all amusements, excepting that very small portion which frequents the theatre.' And he added:

> The few hours which intervene between labour and sleep are generally spent either in the tavern or in making necessary family arrangements. On Sunday the entire working population sinks into a state of abject sloth or listless apathy or even into more degrading conditions of reckless sensuality.

Joseph Fletcher, secretary of the 1840 Handloom Weavers' Commission, wrote in almost identical terms and regretted that the Manchester operatives, instead of 'walking abroad with their wives and children' on Sundays were 'too numerously at home in their dirt.' The need for public walks and places of recreation was reiterated in the following year by Charles Mott, an assistant Poor Law Commissioner, who said it was not to be wondered at that thousands flew to beer shops and dancing houses on Saturday nights. Edwin Chadwick quoted Mott's account in his own great report of 1842, but he followed it with the revealing story of how Manchester celebrated the wedding of Queen Victoria on 10 February 1840.

The Old Cock Pit, Preston, from Hewitson's *History of Preston*. Cock-fighting was a sport of gentlemen: the Preston pit regularly saw local gentry and nobility, including Lord Derby, entertained by the spectacle of their own birds fighting, and special cockfights between the 'mains' of the leaders of society were a prominent attraction at eighteenth-century Preston Guilds.

Drunkards in the reading room of a public house (photograph courtesy the Harris Museum, Preston). Reading of newspapers seems to be only a minor occupation: drinking and haranguing the assembled multitude were seemingly more popular.

Extensive arrangements were made for holding a Chartist meeting, and for getting up what was called a demonstration of the working classes, which greatly alarmed the municipal magistrates. Sir Charles Snow the Chief Commissioner of Police, induced the Mayor to get the Botanical Gardens, the Zoological Gardens and Museum and other institutions thrown open to the working classes at the hour they were urgently invited to attend the Chartist meeting. The Mayor undertook to be personally answerable for any damage that occurred from throwing open the gardens and institutions to the classes that had never before entered them. The effect was that not more than 200 or 300 people attended the political meeting, which entirely failed, and scarcely 5s. worth of damage was done in the gardens or in the public institutions by the workpeople who were highly pleased. A further effect produced was, that the charges before the police of drunkenness and riot were on that day less than the average of cases on ordinary days.

Here was a side of working-class character that most commentators never discovered. Nor did they realise what important changes were taking place in the towns they were so quick to condemn. Once men and women had learned to read, to write and to reason—and in this the Sunday schools did an enormous good—the quest for enlightenment was often zealously pursued. A Haslingden schoolmaster, who complained in 1816 of 'the great need for a library to beget something of literary, scientific and general inquiry among the inhabitants,' noted in his diary only eight years later: 'There never was such a rage for periodical publications as there is at present,' and in 1830 he recorded:

The periodical literature of Great Britain is at the present day completely astonishing. Every art, science, branch and department; every denomination, political and religious, has its organ or publication. Knowledge of all sorts is an overflowing stream, which adapts itself to all palates and conditions of men. Most individuals are now enabled to read, many to understand and many to reason. A new era seems to have arisen among men, and a new order of things is adapting and preparing itself for the new opening state of the human mind. These things will ultimately lead to a new order of establishments and institutions, both of a political and theological nature.

An indication of the enthusiasm for reading among working people can be found in the following passage written in 1839 at Preston by A. B. Granville during his tour of the Northern spas.

A licensed hawker having advertised the importation and intended sale of three thousand volumes of cheap books had been so successful in his operation, which was carried on in the open market place, that he felt it necessary to apologise to 'the reading public' because his large stock had been exhausted a day sooner than he had anticipated. He promised, at the same time, to return soon with a still more splendid supply for their accommodation.

Even in the public houses, which so many writers denounced but few visited, the quality of the conversation was remarkably enhanced. A Bolton witness told the Factories Commission in 1833:

Twenty seven years ago you might sit in a public house and wait till the crowd had gone and you would not have heard one word about political matters; if a person had introduced a subject of that kind he would have been considered a Jacobin; but now . . . you cannot sit ten minutes in any public house in this town or in any other I am acquainted with without hearing men discussing politics and other measures of government, and often as rationally as if they were legislators, though probably they could not write five sentences.

Another Bolton man, Timothy Grimshaw, writing in 1838 at the age of 61, described the tremendous improvement which he had seen in the manners and customs of local people.

There was a time when the great bulk of the Boltonians were very little removed from barbarians—being almost without education and seldom travelling beyond the precincts of the wild moors by which they were circumscribed. It was by no means unusual for the shopkeepers in Deansgate and Churchgate to close up their doors and windows in consequence of some set fight and that, perhaps, on market day. The fights were of the most brutal kind: kicking one another, up or down, from one end of the street to another. While the vulgar were thus amusing themselves, another and *higher* grade were enjoying a more elevated and *intellectual* pastime understood by the term *trotting*, which was nothing more or less than imposing upon or ridiculing any stranger who might have the ill luck to fall into their company . . . Thanks to the Sunday schools, or rather conductors of them, all these vulgarities have vanished away. Strangers pass along our streets unmolested, enter our inns and are received with civility, ask for information and assistance and are answered by the voice of hospitality. Even that most frightful and obnoxious creature, an *Irishman*, is now perfectly free from the jibes and jeers of the trotters and from the still more rude insults and purrs of the unwashed . . . Deane, Tonge and Halshaw moors are now crossed by the traveller without fear of being slutched or stoned by the wild natives.

The change that came over many working men was described by a reactionary Stockport manufacturer at a meeting held appropriately on All Fool's Day 1839.

The lower orders were not now what they used to be. The labouring poor used to be submissive and respectful to their employers and superiors. They spent their summer evenings at cock fights, bull baits and other athletic sports and during their long winter nights sat around the blazing faggot telling hobgoblin stories and in playing at blind man's buff and other innocent amusements. Now they spent their evenings both summer and winter, at Radical meetings, mechanics' institutions, lyceums and public house bars where they learned every species of insubordination. He knew for a fact that some of these fellows had become so dangerously cunning that they had not been a month in any mill before they knew the amount of the master's profits as well as he did himself, and depend upon it, as soon as those profits became high, their hands would turn out for higher wages; aye, and would obtain their demands, too. Why, they must either raise the wages of their workpeople or else they must incur the expenses of fetching a great number of families from Ireland or Buckinghamshire, and by the time they had made good hands of these people they would be as saucy as the rest.

Change, however, was not confined to working men. There were 'two Lancashires' at all levels of society and the model employer as well as the factory despot was a significant, if less familiar, figure of the age. The middle classes gave strong support to the churches, backed the mechanics' institutions from their inception in the mid-1820s and grew increasingly enthusiastic about most of the reform movements that held the stage in the 1840s and beyond. Few 'Ten Hour' meetings took place without speeches from at least one manufacturer, clergyman and doctor; and it was men such as these who led the agitation for free libraries, public parks and improved sanitation.

2. The Churches

The religious groups which sprang up in such great numbers during the nineteenth century influenced Lancashire people more than any other movement. Besides inspiring or enforcing a disciplined way of life, they provided education and social centres for the masses, and gave people who were denied a say in local and national affairs a sense of responsibility that came from helping to run an organisation of their own. They also narrowed the gap between the employing and working classes, which the factory system made so dangerously wide.

'People were religious in those days,' the Accrington industrial chemist, John Emmanuel Lightfoot (1802–1893), once remarked near the end of his life, recalling that as a young man he used regularly to

---

Attendance at worship, 1851

The 1851 Census of Religious Worship gives useful, although not always totally reliable, statistics for attendance at churches in each of the main denominations. In Lancashire the percentage of the population which attended worship ranged from 62% in the Clitheroe area to 26% in Oldham. Below are some figures for the relative strength of each denomination, as measured by Poor Law Union area:

	Church of England	Roman Catholic	Other Protestant
Clitheroe	26%	10%	20%
Garstang	27%	14%	7%
Warrington	25%	7%	11%
Lancaster	25%	4%	5%
Liverpool	11%	12%	5%
Chorlton	12%	2%	10%
Oldham	9%	1%	12%
Haslingden	19%	1%	37%

(adapted from C. Phillips and J. Smith, *Lancashire and Cheshire from* A.D. *1540* (1994), p. 220.)

Cannon Street Baptist Church, Accrington, from A. H. Stockwell's *Baptist Churches in Lancashire* (n.d.)

Early nonconformist denominations usually built modest and plain places of worship, often converting existing buildings, but by the nineteenth century a creeping tendency to worldliness, and a desire to advertise their wares more prominently, encouraged many to adopt more elaborate architectural styles. In this case the church is scarcely distinguishable from contemporary Anglican designs.

School attendance in Lancashire, 1843 *(figures relate to 'manufacturing districts')*		
	Sunday Schools	*Day Schools*
No.	768	2,195
Schools	218,412	121,455
Average no. at each school	284	55

(adapted from C. Phillips and J. Smith (1994), p. 207, table 3.23)

attend six or eight services every Sunday at the Wesleyan Methodist chapel of which he was a member. There was a prayer meeting at 7 a.m., Sunday School at 9 a.m., morning service, afternoon school, love feast and evening service, before and after which there were usually additional prayer meetings to make the day complete. Strict codes of conduct governed the lives of the church members. The Primitive Methodists of Haslingden decided in 1832 that

> If any [Sunday school] teacher be found guilty of Sabbath-breaking, frequenting public houses, card tables, dancing rooms, cricket playing or gaming of any kind, or any other practice contrary to the Word of God, they shall be admonished for their conduct. If they reform, well: if not, they shall be expelled from the society.

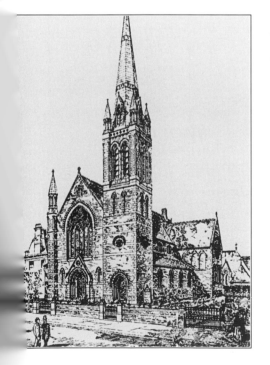

During the week the teachers were to take particular notice of the conduct of their scholars, and any swearing, quarrelling and calling ill names was to be reported to the Sunday school superintendent so that a reprimand could be given. Cricket, dancing and card games were widely denounced and in 1858 the United Free Methodists of Clitheroe added draughts and dominoes to the list of 'foolish and degrading pastimes which darken the mind and lead the heart away from God.' The scholars who attended the Baptist Church in Accrington were expected to stand 'with almost military precision' from the opening of the Sunday school until its close. The classes were arranged in semicircles with the girls and boys toeing wires stretched along the ground. A number of large cards inscribed 'Dunce', 'Careless', 'Swearer' and so on were held in readiness by the teachers and hung around the necks of any young offenders who had then to

149

the 'stall of repentance' in front of the super-intendent's desk.

The early records of the Nonconformist churches contain numerous criticisms of members who failed to attain the required high standards. A woman was excluded from Goodshaw Baptist Church, Rossendale, in 1841 'for dancing in a jerryshop at a wedding and refusing to acknow-ledge herself in error,' and preachers were just as likely to be censured. Any arriving late at the Helmshore Primitive Methodist Chapel at this time could expect to be fined at least threepence.

The growth of the churches can be seen from the statistics compiled by Edward Baines, Jnr., in 1843 and published as *The Social, Educational and Religious State of the Manufacturing Districts*. He found that in Lancashire there was church and chapel room for 42¾ per cent of the population, compared with 30 per cent in London, and that there was one Sunday scholar for every 5⅔ in-habitants, as against one in twenty in London.

Chorlton Road Con-gregational Church, Manchester, by H. E. Todmarsh in his *Man-chester Old and New*, volume 3.

The population of the county had increased by 148 per cent since 1801, but church and chapel room had increased by 241⅔ per cent. Turning to the Haslingden district for a more detailed picture of this development, we find in 1825 the despondent minister and deacons of the Pleasant Street Baptist Church referring to the inadequate means of moral and religious instruction in the town and declaring that many of the inhabitants 'have for a long time been immersed in ignorance and accustomed to habits of indecency and vice.' By 1857, however, it was estimated that 2,790 Haslingden people, almost one in every three, attended Sunday schools, 'a greater number in proportion to the population than any place in Lancashire.' In 1866, when the proportion was nearer a half than a third, Mr James Stott said when he laid the foundation stone on the new Wesleyan Chapel at Helmshore:

> I can remember when the chief sport of the people in winter was running down hares by tracking their footprints in the snow. That was more especially the pastime on the Sabbath day; and on the days after this followed feastings of hare, mutton and beer. In such a condition were the people of the neighbourhood that they were called 'Musbury Turks'. But since the erection of our chapel, the chapel of our Primitive Methodist friends and the [parish] church close by, a great change has been wrought in the condition of the inhabitants. The young people have been gathered together in

Sabbath schools and have exerted an influence for good on their parents.

In the following year Sir James Kay-Shuttleworth summed up the contribution of the Sunday schools to education. He wrote to the scholars of the Bamford church where he had once been a superintendent:

> Long before even enlightened statesmen and leaders of public opinion cared for the education of the people, the congregations had begun to work in the Sunday schools. When the Government first attempted to organise national education, it not only found its machinery ready to hand, but also found that the churches and congregations contained within themselves the zeal and purpose as to public education.

The instruction offered by the Sunday schools, though extremely limited, was of inestimable value and was the key used by many people to unlock the doors to richer storehouses of knowledge. The Haslingden Primitive Methodist school welcomed children of all denominations, 'provided they be free from offensive and contagious distempers' and set out to teach them 'to read tolerably well, to write legibly and to understand the addition, subtraction and multiplication of money.'

The churches were equally important in the emotional lives of the people, particularly during the wretched times that made up so much of the first half of the nineteenth century. It gave to many who saw no prospect of improving their lot on earth the hope of a reward in heaven and in the words of V. S. Pritchett:

> The hot exotic scenery of Palestine with its kings, champions, prophets and savage wars, its tales of destitution and treasure, rags and precious stones, of glittering possessions and peculiar animals, provided a complete allegorical world in which the poor of a cold, damp, unjust society could feel truculent and imagine themselves rich. How satisfying to the imagination, as well as to the sense of social justice, to be able to tell the oppressive squire or ironmaster that he was a camel trying to get through the eye of a needle.

Church services were frequently touched with drama. 'Oh Lord! punce [kick] into me wi' thi clog irons,' a penitent Helmshore man cried out on one occasion. On another a Haslingden minister roused his congregations by shouting, 'Fire! Fire! Fire!' and on being asked where, retorted, 'In Hell for sleepy sinners!' Stephen Clarke, in his *Clitheroe in the Railway Days*, describes how the volleys of 'Amens', 'Glories' and 'Hallelujahs' which punctuated Methodist services in the town could be heard several streets away and how the excited hearers thumped the pews and forms so heavily during powerful sermons that they sometimes caused considerable damage. A similar enthusiasm by the Methodists of Pilling prompted the local squire to remark:

> In the tavern there is no loud shouting or singing on Sunday evenings, but in the preaching-house the noise is so great until late at night that the neighbours cannot go to sleep.

These outbursts did not last, however, for the restraining hand of the employing classes soon held in check the excesses of all but the most wayward sects. Many churches were built and largely maintained by landowning or manufacturing families who made regular attendance on the Sabbath a condition of employment: and where membership was not insisted on, it was certainly an essential for any workman seeing advancement. Almost every church in Haslingden had a close link with a textile mill at some time during the second half of the nineteenth century and a similar pattern could doubtless be found throughout the whole of East Lancashire. Leonard Horner, who visited the Grant brothers of Ramsbottom in 1837, observed: 'They have built at their sole expense a large and beautiful church with a tower and bells, and strange to say, it is a Presbyterian church, and they have a full congregations.' Some masters saw churchgoing as a wonderful aid to discipline and wholeheartedly endorsed that part of the catechism which enjoined the poor man 'to order myself lowly and reverently to all my betters and to do my duty in that state of life into which it shall please God to call me.' Countless sermons were preached on the virtues of hard work and thrift; and many a master who nodded in approval regarded his success in business as a sign of divine reward. Yet those who believed they were so favoured were often passionately concerned to improve society. David Whitehead, of Rawtenstall, was a fervent Methodist who, by building a church, a school and good houses, by starting a savings bank and by encouraging temperance, did much to transform the 'wild men' of the Rossendale Valley into responsible citizens.

Church membership, whether voluntary or enforced, gave to large numbers an austere respectability that was in sharp contrast to the easy-going vulgarity of the previous generation. It also gave a sense of companionship and opportunities for self expression; and though it often produced an outlook so narrow and uncharitable as to create considerable hostility among the rival sects, its tremendous civilising force cannot be overestimated.

3. *The Chartists*

The steady growth of the churches was very different from the fluc-
tuating fortunes of the Chartists, the working-class reformers whose
programme was set out in the famous Six Points—universal suffrage,
vote by ballot, equal electoral districts, abolition of the property
qualifications for MPs, payment of MPs and annual parliaments. The
movement was strongest when times were bad, but even at its height
it was divided into physical and moral force factions and never seriously
threatened the country with the revolution which some of its leaders
hoped to promote. The Chartist 'Hymn', *Sons of Poverty Assemble*, was
certainly stirring:

> *Rouse them from their silken slumbers*
> *Trouble them amidst their pride:*
> *Swell your ranks, augment your numbers,*
> *Spread the Charter far and wide:*
> *Truth is with us,*
> *God himself is on our side.*

Most of the movement's supporters, however, would have been content
with a good house, a well-paid job and sufficient to eat and wear; and
when, in Gibbon's words, prosperity relaxed the nerves of discipline,
many lost their enthusiasm for the cause and others turned to activities
which offered more immediate if more mundane rewards than the
overthrow of government.

The Lancashire Chartists came into prominence in 1838 and 1839
when they organised huge torchlight meetings on the hills—one at
Kersal Moor in September 1838 drew a crowd of 50,000—and when
the more militant members obeyed the call to arms that was made so
passionately by a number of their leaders. In March 1839, the *Bolton
Free Press* reported an 'extensive speculation in the pike trade' with
common halberds fetching 9d. to 1s. 3d. and those with 'a sharp-edged
hook for cutting horses' girths' as much as 2s. 9d. However, in August
when Parliament rejected a petition for the Six Points, the 'Sacred
Month' of strikes, which was supposed to have followed, failed entirely.
Many Chartist leaders were arrested and others fled. A package containing eighteen pikes and a number of musket balls was found under
the floor of the Mechanics' Hall of Science in Bury during a search
by the authorities and elsewhere a great weapons many were buried
and forgotten until they were dug as curious relics longs after Chartism
had become a memory. On 21 September, the *Bolton Free Press* announced that the cause of physical chartism was almost extinct and that
'a great many deadly weapons' had been sold as old iron.

The distress at the start of the new decade revived the ailing movement and many Chartists were among the rioters who roamed the
manufacturing districts in August 1842, stopping mills and mines by
drawing the plugs from the boilers of the steam engines. Cooke Taylor
wrote of the Lancashire people's 'heroic endurance of unmerited su-
fferings' at this time, and among the rioters there was an almost total
absence of that blind fury with which the loom breakers of 1826 went
about their business. The only clash which resulted in loss of life was
at Preston where five men died from wounds received when soldiers
fired on a mob after being attacked with stones. The 'Plug Plot', which
was, in fact, a spontaneous outburst of discontent, failed as the 'Sacred
Month' had failed and showed that the Chartist leaders, who were
unable to control the situation, were not the men to lead the working
classes to instant emancipation. Many Lancashire Chartists turned to
the Ten Hours, the trade union and the co-operative movements and
some joined the factory masters and merchants, whose Anti-Corn Law
League seemed likely to remove at least one of the major grievances
of the age. By 1846, the once fanatical Chartists of Mossley had become
advocates of free trade and Corn Law repeal. 'The assembly room at
Brookbottom,' said the *Manchester Guardian* of 9 May, 'is now closed
and the boards where the orators held forth and made known the
principles of the *Northern Star* are converted into a resting place
for swine.'

It would be easy to conclude that the Chartists were rash or im-
practical men who attempted to achieve what in the mid-nineteenth
century was an unattainable ideal. But to say that would be to do them
an injustice. In the decade after 1838 Chartism focused attention on
the problems of a disjointed society; and it was determination and not
defeatism that led a great many of its supporters to concentrate their
efforts on single issues rather than on pursuing the panacea of universal
suffrage. Most of the working-class movements that developed in the
1840s, '50s and '60s, in particular Co-operation and the miners' trade
union, owed much to men who later had the satisfaction of witnessing
the widespread acceptance of the programme for which they had fought.

4. *The Co-operators*

The Co-operative movement, the most successful of all nineteenth-
century working-class achievements, sprang from the idealism and sound
sense of the Rochdale Pioneers, whose methods quickly spread throughout the country and abroad. Several societies had been started before
the Pioneers opened their first shop in 1844, but credit trading destroyed

most of them in times of distress. The Rochdale Friendly Co-operative Society, formed by a group of Owenite weavers in 1830, crashed after a few years, but it helped to prepare the ground in which the Pioneers sowed their seeds. Several of these early co-operators together with a number of Chartists, were among the twenty eight men who opened the famous store at No. 31 Toad Lane on the evening of 21 December. The historian of the movement, George Jacob Holyoake, has described the momentous occasion:

> It had got wind among the tradesmen of the town that their competitors were in the field, and many a curious eye was that day turned up Toad Lane looking for the appearance of the enemy; but like other enemies of some historic renown, they were rather shy of appearing. A few co-operators had clandestinely assembled to witness their own *denouement*: and there they stood, in that dismal cellar room of the warehouse like the conspirators under Guy Fawkes in the Parliamentary cellars, debating on whom to devolve the temerity of taking down the shutters and displaying their humble preparations. One did not like to do it, and another did not like to be seen in the shop when it was open: however, having gone so far, there was no choice but to go farther, and at length one bold fellow, reckless of the consequences, rushed at the shutters and in a few minutes Toad Lane was in a titter.

The entire stock consisted of 28lb of butter, 56lb of sugar, 6cwt of flour, a sack of oatmeal and some tallow candles, all of which had been bought for £6 11s. 11d. The beginnings were humble, but the principles on which the business was based, in particular that of distributing dividends to registered members, ensured success. For three months the store opened on Saturday and Monday evenings, after which it was found necessary to extend the opening to every night except Tuesday. The society was by now prosperous enough to declare a dividend of 3d. in the pound and to pay the two shopmen at the rate of 3d. an hour. The first year's trading produced a profit of £21 and membership almost trebled. The titterings in Toad Lane were heard no more and Rochdale listened respectfully when the Pioneers had anything to say. There was an assured and satisfying ring to their announcements. 'The objects of this society are the moral and intellectual advance of its members. It provides them with groceries, butcher's meat, drapery goods, clothes and clogs.' For innumerable families, co-operation on these terms became a way of life.

Not least among the advantages of the movement was the guarantee of pure food. In the 1840s beer, bread, tea, coffee and many other items were adulterated with additives and colouring matters, most of them dangerous and some acutely poisonous. Holyoake told a meeting of working-class people in Rochdale shortly before the formation of the Pioneers' Society:

> Anybody can see that the little money you get is half wasted because you cannot spend it to advantage. The worst food comes to the poor which their poverty makes them buy and their necessity makes them eat. Their stomachs are the waste baskets of the State. It is their lot to swallow the adulteration of the market.

Pure rather than cheap food was the Pioneers' aim, but adulteration was so widely accepted that when they set up their own corn mill, they had some difficulty in selling the flour, because it was darker than the treated kind to which people were accustomed. As late as 1856, the Third Report of the Select Committee on Adulteration of Food noted that some co-operative societies had so much trouble in selling uncoloured tea that at least one had engaged a lecturer to tell customers what the genuine article looked like. A Liverpool firm, however, had no hesitation in deceiving the public when, in 1851, it took out a patent for a machine which compressed chicory into the shape of coffee beans.

News of the Pioneers' success soon inspired others. The Bacup Chartists, whose meeting place was an attic, became enthusiastic co-operators in 1847 and for several months took turns to walk to Rochdale or Todmorden to buy goods. After a year they were able to take over the whole building and to buy a horse and cart. Thomas Newbigging, the Rossendale historian, said of their early endeavours:

> They had a good deal to learn and made mistakes in buying. One of the mistakes, I remember, was the purchase of a small cargo of Dutch or American cheeses. These, when they came to hand, proved to be so hard that a knife blade stood no chance with them. They were more like grindlestones (as one of them expressed it) than

LEFT TO RIGHT:
'The Pioneer Store in its original state', 1844, from J. Holyoake, *History of the Rochdale Pioneers* (1893); Central Stores, Toad Lane, 1863 (ibid); The Co-operative store in Camden Street, Liverpool, the first registered office of the C.W.S. (from W. Henry Brown (ed.), *Story of the Liverpool Cooperative Society Limited*.

cheeses. What was to be done? It would never to do throw them away—that was out of the question. So Adam o' Bobs, who was equal to the emergency, brought his handsaw one night and divided them out into a number of saleable pieces. When cut, they had the appearance of brown ivory, and they were nearly as hard. There must have been some aching teeth and jaws before those same cheese were finally polished off.

The Haslingden Co-operative Society was also started by a group of Chartists. After collecting £10 they sent one of their number to Blackburn to buy stock, which was sold from a house at the bottom of Pleasant Street. Above the door they put up a signboard embellished with four stars to mark their 'indebtedness to the *Northern Star* for the light they had obtained on social and economic questions.'

A correspondent of *The Working Man* discussing in 1866 the beginnings of co-operation in Rossendale, recalled that:

In some places the men were so susceptible to the ridicule which might be thrown upon their amateur shopkeeping that they drew lots to decide who should open the shutters on the first night.

On the opening day of a store near Haslingden:

The poor fellows were busy arranging things so as to display their goods to the best advantage. I suppose treacle was there, as it was elsewhere in Lancashire, an article of large consumption amongst children; but as the co-operators had not the orthodox can from which shopkeepers pour that thick fluid, it was placed in a large mug. One of the men passing this mug with the half-cheese which was the whole dairy produce they proposed exhibiting, was so clumsy as to let it go souse into the treacle. The consternation was great, but the fault was mended.

The early minute books of the Haslingden Society, besides recording rapid expansion, make it plain that for large numbers of people co-operation was a matter of passionate and absorbing interest. So concerned in the day-to-day running of the business were the members that they frequently dismissed their officers at packed and stormy meetings and on one occasion set up a committee to superintend the committee of management.

These were the days [says the society's historian, Sir Rhodes Boyson] when committee members were fined 1s. 10d. for telling tales outside the committee room, when members were appointed to stand outside the committee room to make sure they were no key-hole listeners, and when members signed complaints and placed them in a box outside this room.

By the middle of the century, the Co-operative Movement was firmly entrenched—there were 130 societies and more than 15,000 members in 1851—and the formation at Manchester in 1863 of the North of England Co-operative Wholesale Society—a federation of local consumers' societies—inaugurated an era of even greater influence and importance.

Some indication of the achievements of the first co-operators will be seen from Holyoake's account of the Pioneers' Society in 1857.

The industrial districts of England have not such another sight to show as the Rochdale Co-operative store on Saturday night.

At seven o'clock there are five persons serving busily at the counter, others are weighing up goods ready for delivery. A boy is drawing treacle. There are two sides of counters in the grocer's shop, twelve yards long. Members' wives, children of members, as many as the shop will hold, are being served; others are waiting at the door . . . On the opposite side of the lane, three members are serving in the drapery department, and nine or ten customers, mostly females, are selecting articles. In the large shop on the same side of the street, three men are chopping and serving meat in the butcher's department, with from twelve to fifteen customers waiting. Two other officers are weighing flour, potatoes, preparing butter etc., for other groups of claimants. In other premises adjoining, shoemakers, cloggers and tailors are at work or attending customers in their respective departments. The clerk is in his office attending to members' individual accounts or the general business of the society.

The news room over the grocery has twenty or more men and youths perusing the newspapers and periodicals. Adjoining, the watch club, which has fifty-eight members, is collecting its weekly payments and drawing lots as to which shall have the repeaters which the night's subscriptions will pay for. The library is open, and the librarian has his hands full in exchanging, renewing and delivering books to about fifty members, among whom are sons, wives and daughters of members. The premises are closed at ten o'clock, when there has been received during the day for goods £420, and the librarian has lent out two hundred books.

Buyer and seller meet as friends: there is no overreaching on one side and no suspicion on the other; and Toad Lane on Saturday night, while as gay as the Lowther Arcade in London, is ten times more moral. These crowds of humble working men, who never knew before when they put good food in their mouths, whose every dinner was adulterated, whose shoes let in the water a month too soon, whose waistcoats shone with devil's dust and whose wives wore calico that would not wash, now buy like millionaires, and, as far as purchasers of food goes, live like lords. They are weaving their own stuffs, making their own shoes, sewing their own garments and grinding their own corn. They buy the purest sugar and the best tea, and grind their own coffee. They slaughter their own cattle, and the finest beasts of the land waddle down the streets of Rochdale for the consumption of flannel weavers and cobblers . . .

The teetotallers of Rochdale acknowledge that the store has made more sober men since it commenced than all their efforts have been able to make in the same time. Husbands who never knew what it was to be out of debt, and poor wives who, during forty years, never had sixpence uncondemned in their pockets, go every week into their own market with coins jingling in their pockets; and in that market there is no distrust and no deception; there is no adulteration and no second prices. The whole atmosphere is honest. Those who serve neither hurry, finesse nor flatter. They have no interest in chicanery. They have but one duty to perform—that of giving fair measure, full weight and a pure article.

5. *Humble Scholars*

When Leonard Horner, the factory inspector, visited Rochdale in 1836, he 'was very much amused' on looking over a list of factory children to find one called Xantippe.

> I thought [wrote Horner] that that name had been dropped since the wife of Socrates made it so famous. I learned that she was the daughter of a weaver who is passionately fond of ancient history, and they shewed me another list, the names of two others of his daughters, Diaphantes and Pandora; but think what a word was added to each, a word which the poor weaver could neither change nor modify; Barraclough—Pandora Barraclough!

The Rochdale weaver was one of many Lancashire working men, who, by tremendous self-sacrifice, pursued knowledge of all kinds and often became skilled scientists and scholars. Their story is remarkable and inspiring, but it is also tinged with sadness, for few of these men were able to use their talents as they would have wished and most were obliged to spend the greater part of their lives at menial and laborious employment. Professor Sedgwick, the geologist, paid them a sincere tribute when he addressed a meeting of the British Association in Manchester in 1842. During his walks through the city, he said, he had met operatives whose brows were smeared with dirt and whose hands were black with soot, but whose intellects gave proof of high character. 'I conferred with men,' he added, 'who in many ways were my superiors.' Two years later in his *Walks in South Lancashire*, Samuel Bamford wrote:

> The working class of South Lancashire are the greatest readers; can shew the greatest number of writers; the greatest number of sensible and considerate public speakers. They can show a greater number of botanists; a greater number of horticulturalists; a greater number who are acquainted with the abstruse sciences; a greater number of poets and a greater number of musicians, whether choral or instrumental. From the loom they will bring out anything that has ever been worked in Europe, in mechanics they are nowhere surpassed and in mining rank with the best. They probably turn out a greater amount of work than any equal number of people under the sun.

The novelist, Mrs Gaskell, referred to some of the scientific artisans in *Mary Barton*, published in 1848:

> There is a class of men in Manchester, unknown even to many of the inhabitants, and whose existence will probably be doubted by many, who yet may claim kindred with all the noble names that science recognises. I said 'in Manchester,' but they are scattered all over the manufacturing districts of Lancashire. In the neighbourhood of Oldham there are weavers, common hand-loom weavers, who throw the shuttle with unceasing sound, though Newton's *Principia* lie open on the loom, to be snatched at in work hours, but revelled over in meal times or at night. Mathematical problems are received with interest and studied with absorbing attention by many a broad-spoken, common-looking factory hand. It is perhaps less astonishing that the more popularly interesting branches of natural history have their warm and devoted followers among this class. There are botanists among them, equally familiar with either the Linnæan or the Natural system, who know the name and habitat of every plant within a day's walk from their dwellings; who steal the holiday of a day or two when any particular plant should be in flower, and tying up their simple food in their pocket handkerchiefs, set off with single purpose to fetch home the humble-looking weed. There are entomologists who may be seen with a rude-looking net, ready to catch any winged insect, or a kind of dredge with which they rake the green and slimy pools; practical, shrewd, hard-working men, who pore over every new specimen with real scientific delight.

One of the outstanding mathematicians was John Butterworth (Jack o' Bens), who lived at Haggate, near Oldham, where he was born in 1774. He became a jenny spinner at the age of six and was almost twenty before he was able to read and write well. For most of his adult life he was a fustian weaver and never earned more than 15s. a week.

By the 1840s weaving brought him only 8s. a week and to earn a few extra coppers he ran a school in 'a small, narrow room, two yards in width.' Yet as a geometrician Butterworth was said to be 'scarcely excelled by any other man in the kingdom,' and was a contributor to all the leading mathematical journals of his day. It is worth noting that during the early nineteenth century candidates for a mathematics degree at Cambridge were not expected to progress much beyond the extraction of cube roots and the solution of what to men of Butterworth's calibre were exceedingly simple problems.

The Lancashire botanists were active well before the turn of the century. Artisans' societies were flourishing in Oldham and Eccles by the late 1770s and others were formed in Manchester, Ashton and Middleton shortly afterwards. The Oldham members met for nine months in the year and paid 2d. a month for books and 4d. for liquor. The entrance fee to the Eccles Society's Sunday afternoon meetings was 3d., and, although all of it went on drink the gatherings were held 'with the decorum of a religious service.' By 1795, the Oldham Society had 20 books and 1,500 specimens and the agriculturist John Hall found that members had been as far afield as Liverpool, Lancaster, Chester, Nottingham and Hull and that 'one had undertaken a voyage as far as the Western Parts of America to botanise under the patronage of John Lee Philips of Manchester.'

The late eighteenth-century enthusiasm for botany coincided with the prosperity that followed the great textile inventions: in the difficult years that followed, when it might have been expected to disappear, it increased considerably and became the delight and consolation of innumerable working men. The *Preston Chronicle* of 16 July 1825, reported that several hundred botanists from Lancashire and Yorkshire had met at Newchurch-in-Rossendale on the previous Sunday and had exhibited 'a rich store of rare and beautiful plants.' To attend the meeting, many of them would have had to walk great distances, but it is certain that few would have thought much of it. The stamina of the botanists was astonishing. James Crowther, of Manchester, after a day's work would often walk fifteen or twenty miles to collect a plant he had been told about. He usually managed to reach his destination before dawn and return to the city in time for work. Crowther's story was told in December 1843, when a society was formed in Manchester 'for the relief and encouragement of scientific men in humble life.' He was born in a Manchester cellar in 1768, the son of a labourer, but received some schooling before being set to work as a drawboy at petticoat weaving. Crowther became a leading figure in the Manchester Society of Botanists, a group of working men who met once a week in the spring and summer to discuss their findings. He made many nightly excursions, but notwithstanding all his precautions, he was often pursued and had many narrow escapes from being captured. He often contrived to elude his pursuers by his extraordinary swiftness in running. Many were the chases he had, but the most severe was with Mr. Hopwood's keepers in Hopwood Park. They once pursued him three or four miles across the country without stopping and he considered it nearly a miracle that he escaped them.

Another prominent Manchester botanist was Richard Buxton, who, when over sixty, regularly walked more than thirty miles a day looking for specimens. Like most of his colleagues he was extremely poor and eked out his income from shoemaking by selling Sunday newspapers. In 1849 Buxton published a book on the plant life of the district within sixteen miles of Manchester. 'Fields and woods,' he wrote, 'although the rich man's heritage, may still be the poor man's flower garden.'

John Horsfield, of Besses o' th' Barn, learned the classical names of the plant classes from lists pinned on the post of his hand loom, and Edward Hobson, of Manchester, became an acknowledged authority on natural history despite a lifelong battle against poverty. When he died in 1830, aged 48, his friends placed a memorial tablet in St George's Church, Hulme. Its inscription sums up not only Hobson's achievements, but also those of a whole group of remarkable men.

> Though of humble parentage and scanty education . . . and amidst privations and difficulties, he, by assiduity and zeal rendered himself a most skilful naturalist, as his scientific works and ample collections lastingly testify. Entomology, botany and mineralogy were his favourite pursuits. Many celebrated men in their writings and privately in their correspondence with him have acknowledged his great attainments.

6. The Quest for Knowledge

During the 'Plug' riots of 1842 when the mills of Lancashire were halted by bands of starving workpeople, a group of young men from the Royton Temperance Society met together to decide how best they could improve their education. They hired a room for 1s. 2d. per week and began what proved to be one of the most successful of all Lancashire working-class ventures, the Royton Temperance Seminary.

> The members were all lads, some one or two of the dozen being, perhaps, twenty-two or twenty-three years old. Their subscription was, of course, small. In a very short time they doubled their numbers, and when the mills were opened again, they determined

to continue the little educational work they had commenced. They framed rules, the first of which was that all members should be pledged teetotallers; and the second that all members should be prohibited from gambling. With these stringent rules they prospered and had considerable influence for good upon those by whom they were surrounded.

The young men soon built their own premises where they were able to use a good library, study maps and globes and even play an organ. Several members formed a fife and drum band and others gave secular and religious instruction to several hundred children in a room at a nearby mill.

The story of the Seminary was given in *The Working Man* in 1866 by a correspondent who recorded the progress of its founders. One was a clergyman, three were schoolmasters, five were master cotton spinners, two were managing mills in Russia and most of the rest had obtained respectable positions as foremen, etc.

Every Lancashire town and most villages had societies which catered for the educational pursuits of working people. Many, like the Royton Temperance Seminary, were supported entirely by the members' subscriptions, but others, particularly the mechanics' institutes, received substantial backing from the employing classes. John Higson has described the societies that flourished, if only fleetingly, in the village of Droylsden. A Young Man's Mutual Improvement Society was founded in 1839 and was followed two years later by the Chemical Society, which met in a cellar beneath a shop. ('In this humble laboratory the members studied the rudiments of chemistry and manufactured blacking and furniture paste which were sold to defray expenses.') In 1842 came the Fairfield and Droylsden Naturalists' Society out of which grew the Droylsden Mechanics' Institute. The Droylsden Temperance Society was active in the late 1840s and went so far as to run a night school in a cottage, where spelling, reading and writing were taught free.

Rochdale in the 1840s had the Equitable Pioneers, the Literary and Philosophical Society, the Debating and Conversation Society, the Independent Odd Fellows' Society, the Botanical Society, the Church Institute and the People's Institute. A reporter of the *Rochdale Pilot* who visited the last named of these bodies in 1849 noted:

Two hundred assemble nightly for instruction. All the people sit in one large room at tables without distinction as to progress or ability. A boy perplexed by simple addition is elbowing a youth deep in the mysteries of cubes and squares, while with an utter disregard of order, the voice of the teacher is heard above the hum of the arithmeticians loudly putting questions to all in grammar.

Though classes of this kind were usually overwhelmed by their own confusion, others were extremely successful. Outside the churches, some of the earliest endeavours in adult education took place in the mechanics' institutes, the first of which were opened at a time when the idea of educating the masses was by no means widely held. Not everyone agreed with Lord Brougham, who promoted the movement, that knowledge was the 'forerunner of liberality and enlightened toleration,' but as the years went by his statement was seen to be correct and support by the upper and middle classes was increasingly given.

The formation of the Lancashire institutes—the first was at Manchester in 1824—disclosed a tremendous thirst for knowledge among working people. It is, of course, possible to exaggerate the impact of this movement. That many working people wanted to learn is undoubtedly the case, but the institutes and societies could only cater for better-paid and already semi-literate members of the working class. The movement towards self-help education was of major importance, but to a minority of the working class, and not until the 1870s, and more-or-less universal elementary education, were all sections of society touched by the fingers of literacy and learning. The Preston Institution for the Diffusion of Knowledge, distant ancestor of the town's university of the 1990s, attracted only a small membership in relation to the size of the local population after it was founded in 1849. A serious lack of elementary education prevented many would-be students from taking some of the courses that were provided. It was often found necessary

Burnley Mechanics' Institute (Burnley Library Local Studies Collection). This building, which still survives as a major element in the cultural life of East Lancashire, was one of the finest of all such institutes. Its proud and prominent place in the town centre highlights the key role in the community which its founders expected it to play.

to give a grounding in the three Rs before starting the scientific instruction for which the pioneers of the movement were so enthusiastic. Dr W. H. Pilkington, one of four Haslingden professional men who began evening classes in 1838, remembered:

> Some of the young men who entered as students could only read and write imperfectly while others could not read or write at all. We could not commence our classes until after eight o'clock for the working people in those days were employed from half past five in the morning until eight in the evening so that little time was left for instruction.

The institutes met with varying success, but throughout the nineteenth century, and in particular during the bleak years before the passing of the Ten Hours Bill, they were among the few beacons in the dark and often frightening world. Some, like that at Burnley, were begun entirely by workmen, others, like those at Manchester and Liverpool, by some of the cities' chief citizens. The founders of the Burnley Institute were 'a few poor men,' who started a library in 1834 helped only by 'a few tradesmen of slightly better position.' An ironmonger was the secretary and a pawnbroker their 'friend and adviser.' For several years they met in an old house at a street corner where 'reading begat arguments, and debates took place.' Classes in reading, writing and speaking attracted new members, and from these humble beginnings the institute developed into the town's most influential body with members in all ranks of society. In the words of an annual report, 'It grew until it became famed throughout the country as a training

The Oldham Lyceum, from Butterworth's *Historical Sketches of Oldham* (1856).

ground for men of high talent and the hope and inspiration of many a working lad.'

A similar tribute was paid to the Oldham Lyceum by the local historian Benjamin Grime. In his *Memory Sketches* of 1888, he wrote that in the 1840s and 1850s the Lyceum 'began to inspire young men with a relish for something beyond the mere elementary knowledge of reading and writing' and was 'the first to promote among the working classes of this district a longing for mental culture, and for acquiring the graces and adornments of social life.' Grime was one of the earliest members of the Lyceum, and from laying out books and slates for the teachers, he became a teacher himself and was often engaged by groups of students for private tuition. For many years, a class of adults—married men with families—met at the home of one of the members from six to eight every Sunday morning to study grammar under Grime's direction. His fee was 1s. 6d.

The first public lecture sponsored by the Manchester Mechanic's Institute proved dramatically that thousands of working men were eager for knowledge. The Rev Andrew Wilson was engaged to speak on 'Mechanical Philosophy' and to mark the occasion free tickets were issued.

The Warrington Perambulating Library in 1851 (*Illustrated London News*). Access to literature, whether high- or low-brow, ephemeral or of permanent value, was a main aim of educationalists, social reformers and individuals with ambition to 'better themselves'.

> Long before the appointed time every avenue to the Theatre was completely blocked up, and when the doors were opened, a tremendous rush took place, and in a very few minutes the building was crowded to excess.

Some 1,400 were present and as many were unable to gain admittance. The lecture had to be repeated at a later date.

Besides organising lectures, the Manchester Insitute ran numerous classes—there were seven hundred students by the late 1840s—established a library and sponsored exhibitions, social events and concerts. The exhibitions were staged to pay off the institute's debts and in the days before public museums and art galleries they proved enormously popular. The first, from December 1837 until February 1838, attracted 50,000 visitors, and the last, from December 1844 until March 1845, more than 100,000. People from all classes went to see the exhibits, which ranged from stuffed birds and machinery to paintings by Leonardo da Vinci, Titian, Rembrandt and Van Dyck. There were demonstrations of glass blowing, pictures from the magic lantern and, among other wonders, Austin's Happy Family, a collection of two hundred animals and birds which lived peacefully together in one big cage. The displays gave unbounded delight and if the special newspaper, the *Exhibition Gazette*, is to be believed, at least two pickpockets were so fascinated by what they saw that they completely forgot to ply their trade.

One of the very first students of the institute was the Rev Johnathan Bayley, the Swedenborgian minister, who began classes in 1824 while still a boy of fourteen. Twelve years later, when he took charge of the church in Accrington, he started a mutual improvement society, which set such a high standard and gave such a range of instruction that it resembled 'a little college' more than a night school. Writing, arithmetic, grammar, geography, elocution, Latin and chemistry classes were all available and the enthusiasm that was aroused led in 1851 to the foundation of the town's Mechanics' Institution.

The war against ignorance took many forms, one of the most effective of which was the Warrington 'perambulating library.' In the summer of 1858, the directors of the Mechanics' Institute, who were anxious to increase borrowing from the library, determined to buy a one-horse van, fill it with books and send it once a week 'to every door in Warrington and the vicinity.' The proposal aroused great enthusiasm and it was decided to hold a flower show and a bazaar to raise money for what was almost certainly the first mobile library. By October the *Warrington Guardian* was able to report:

> Not only have many of our wealthy townsmen given their pounds, but women—some of them poor widows—have given their mites. Two hundred working men's wives and daughters, at their homes, have stitched, darned or knitted articles for the Bazaar.

The sale of some 2,000 of these articles, including toys and clothes, raised £250.

On Monday, 15 November, the 'perambulating library' began to tour the streets of Warrington and was frequently seen 'some miles beyond the municipal boundary.' Its success was immediate and the number of books issued from the institute rose from 3,000 a year to 12,000.

Education in Lancashire was helped enormously by the success of the public library movement, in which Joseph Brotherton was the leading figure. Salford and Warrington were the first towns in the country to open public libraries and others soon followed. The Manchester Free Library, formerly the Chartist Hall of Science, was opened on 6 September 1852, a day long remembered by hundreds of working men. A reporter of the *Manchester Examiner*, who went along during the first week, found a policeman on duty to keep back the borrowers crowding round the issues desk. All the tables were occupied in the evenings and 'We saw young men who were perhaps tired enough with the day's toil, standing patiently to read and forgetting their fatigue until closing time [9 p.m.] was announced.' Among the books over which 'many thoughtful heads were bent' were works of philosophy, mechanics, history and astronomy, an official report on a coal pit accident and Shakespeare's plays. Before the end of the week the patrons were asking for the opening hours to be extended. 'The success of the library,' said the *Manchester Guardian* after its first year, 'surpasses the most sanguine expectations of the promoters.' There were 4,857 readers.

Perhaps one may sum up the achievements of the workingmen's quest for enlightenment by quoting from an essay written by the Rev T. G. Lee of Salford in 1850:

> The intelligent and industrious operatives constitute by far the most important class in the community . . . Diligent study has thrown open their understanding and the tide of intellect has begun powerfully to set in.

7. *The Teetotallers*

While Bacchanalians madly sing
   And magnify impiety
We'll load the passing zephyr's wing
   With praises of sobriety.

The boys and girls who sang those lines at the Great Juvenile Gathering in the Bolton Temperance Hall on 4 February 1851, were members of the first great propaganda movement of modern times—a movement which had been started in Lancashire almost twenty years earlier to combat the devastating effects of prodigious drunkenness. The problem, as we have seen, was immense, but the astonishing progress of the teetotallers, particularly during the years 1832–37, is without parallel in the annals of secular asceticism and was one of the most remarkable achievements of the nineteenth century. The dedication of the pioneers was extraordinary and the temperance societies they founded in almost every town and village produced one of the greatest civilising forces of the age.

As early as 1809, the Rev W. Cowherd, of Salford, and a small band of followers—the 'Cowherdites'—had renounced intoxicating drink and in the same town ten years later Joseph Brotherton had issued a pamphlet urging total abstinence, but the movement did not come into being until 1832 when Joseph Livesey, the Preston cheese merchant, philanthropist and social reformer, drew up the first teetotal pledge. A number of 'moderation' societies had met with only slight success, and

The demon drink as seen by *The Struggle* in 1842.

Livesey, who had launched his *Moral Reformer* in 1831, saw that a more resolute spirit was needed. In the July issue he wrote:

> So shocked have I been with the effects of intemperance, and so convinced of the evil tendency of *moderate* drinking, that since the commencement of 1831 I have never tasted ale, wine or ardent spirits.

Throughout the first half of 1832, there were heated discussions in Preston about the wisdom of advocating total abstinence. Livesey and a few others decided it was the only course possible, and on 23 August he and a friend, John King signed a pledge to that effect in Livesey's shop. A week later after a public meeting, at which the question was again debated, Livesey, King and five others pledged themselves 'to abstain from all liquors of an intoxicating quality, whether Ale, Porter, Wine or Ardent Spirits, except as Medicines.' The 'Seven Men of Preston' were soon joined by others, among them Richard ('Dicky') Turner, a reformed drunkard who was to give the new movement its name. This occurred at a Preston temperance meeting in September 1833 when Dicky, in the course of a passionate speech, declared that nothing but the teetotal would do. The word caught the imagination of the audience who cheered loudly, and Livesey cried out, 'That shall be the name, Dicky,' Though an unlettered man, Turner was never at a loss for a word, and as Livesey later recalled, 'if a suitable one was not at his tongue end he coined a new one.'

Though the teetotal movement made rapid progress during 1833, it faced much opposition. One 15 June, the *Preston Pilot* reported:

> The temperance fanatics collected another mob on Sunday last, and the Sabbath was again desecrated by their insane proceedings. Indeed, the only way we can account for the intemperate conduct of these people is by supposing they are always drunk.

The paper went on to describe how the 'anti-hypocriticals' of the town assembled in considerable force and after a battle of words with the teetotallers, 'advanced pot in hand and pipe in mouth and forced their way into the enemy's quarters.'

Despite setbacks of this kind, Preston had two thousand teetotallers before the end of the year. 'We felt,' said Livesey, 'that we were really engaged in a "Temperance *reformation*". We gave heart and soul to it. We seemed as if we would turn the World upside down.' And Joseph Dearden, writing of this year in his *Dawn and Spread of Teetotalism*, said:

> Some rough work had to be done: the 'fallow ground' had to be ploughed; and men were forthcoming for the fight—men who regardless of all opposition, never faltered, never waited, but were ever ready 'in season and out of season.' The leaders of the movement were soon supported by a little army of advocates in the persons of reformed drunkards, whose experiences, as related by them, had great influence upon the masses. As early as this date there could be numbered 20 speakers engaged, not only in Preston, but extending their labours to all the surrounding villages. Every village within nine miles of Preston had been visited.

'Preston,' says Livesey in his autobiography, 'was soon regarded as the Jerusalem of teetotalism from which the word went forth in every direction,' and he describes how he and six companions with a horse and cart, 9,500 tracts and a white flag bearing a temperance motto, set out in July 1833 to convert the manufacturing districts. Livesey had by now perfected his 'Malt Liquor Lecture', the first scientific attack on strong drink, and he was to give it over and over again with telling effect to audiences that were astonished to learn that beer was not replete with nourishment. During a week's tour, the missionaries visited Blackburn, Haslingden, Bury, Heywood, Rochdale, Oldham, Ashton, Stockport, Manchester and Bolton, as well as numerous villages. Nowhere did they fail to attract an enthusiastic audience.

> At Rochdale we drove through the main street with our flag flying. The bellman was not at home, so we left his fee and took the bell and rang it ourselves. A large congregation was collected; several powerful addresses were delivered, and although sneered at by a lawyer and openly opposed by a liquor merchant, it was evident that many people were deeply affected. It is not too much to say that the success of co-operation in Rochdale owes something of its vitality to the results of this meeting.

When the party reached Stockport at three o'clock one afternoon, they found themselves without a meeting place and it was not until half past six that they secured the Primitive Methodist chapel.

> Up to that time no notice had been given of any meeting. What was to be done? 'Have you a drum?' said I. 'And a man that can beat it?' 'Yes.' Both were immediately procured; I ordered the cart out, and off we started. We drove rapidly through the streets,

Preston Temperance missionaries in Blackburn, 1833 (photograph courtesy of the Harris Library, Preston). Proclaiming the message from wagons and street corners, and waving the banners to carry the word—the methods of the temperance reformers were identical to those of more obviously religious evangelical groups.

stopping at every crossing. One beat the drum, another called out the meeting and the rest of us showered out the tracts. The result was an excitement of a kind I never saw before or since.

The triumphant tour ended at Bolton where 'the effect of the addresses by our reformed drunkards was shown by the tears that were shed and by every other demonstration of feeling.' The Bolton Temperance Society advocated abstinence from spirits only, but as a result of the visit, a new society, which offered a teetotal as well as a moderation pledge, was formed in the following week.

Teetotalism, with its missionaries, hymns, sermons and confessions, spread like a new religion until the whole country within a short time knew of its doctrine. Tea parties, organised ostensibly to promote a better understanding between the classes, were used to spread the cause; and for those beyond the influence of such gentle methods, impassioned pleas, such as that signed by thirty reformed working men of Preston in December 1833, were directed in the form of posters at all 'tipplers, drunkards and backsliders.' On 1 January 1834, Livesey launched the *Preston Temperance Advocate*, the first teetotal newspaper. Its pages relate the triumphant progress of the movement and the disappearance of the moderation societies. By the end of the year more than 28,000 Lancashire people had signed the pledge.

The first out-and-out teetotal society was formed, not at Preston

A Temperance procession passing the Town Hall in Preston (photograph courtesy of the Harris Library, Preston). The temperance reformers also fully appreciated the powerful message which could be conveyed by an organised public event: processions, showmanship and cheap but cheerful carnivals could attract the crowds and impress the image very effectively.

where the members had a choice of pledge until 1835, but in the village of Miles Platting, near Manchester. There Dr R.B. Grinrod began cottage meetings in July 1834 and attracted such enthusiastic support that he was soon obliged to lecture to audiences of up to 3,000 in the open air. (A Preston youth's total abstinence society had been formed three months earlier, but its members needed only sign the pledge for a year at a time). An active teetotal society was formed in Warrington in October 1834 and followed the example of the Preston pioneers in sending out missionaries to the towns and villages in the neighbourhood. Manchester was much enlived in June 1835 by a week's temperance festival, which included lectures, tea parties and a huge procession with a cart displayed the 'fruits of teetotalism'—a sack of flour, a ham weighing 65lb, a cheese of 85lb and a loaf of 60lb. During the same year at one of Dr Grinrod's lectures a Manchester carpenter John Cassell—founder of the great publishing house—was inspired with the new ideal and became a voluntary temperance missionary, going from village to village in many part of the country and collecting his audiences by shaking a watchman's rattle. Marriage enabled him to begin a printing business which he used to further the temperance cause, first by issuing tracts and later by publishing journals like *The Working Man's Friend*. It was also during 1835 that the Preston teetotallers engaged the Blackburn theatre for six successive nights. The meetings were crowded, and the result, said the *Temperance Advocate*, was that '350 persons, including a considerable number of the most degraded characters in the town have signed the pledge.' A year later when a national temperance conference was held in Preston, more than ten thousand people took part in a procession, after which four meetings were held simultaneously.

The teetotallers used all methods to further their aims. There were temperance halls, temperance seminaries, temperance lectures, temperance processions, temperance bands, temperance songs and temperance poems. In darkened halls throughout the country the magic lantern chilled temperance audiences with such cautionary tales as Cruickshank's 'The Bottle!' a series of illustrations depicting fifteen years in the life of a drunkard. From scenes of courtship, marriage and the happy home, the story proceeded, with occasional pauses for temperance hymns, via the public house and the pawnshop to murder and the madhouse. Youth groups formed an important section of the movement from the outset and were instructed with stern Victorian thoroughness. 'Children with dirty faces will be liable to expulsion,' was a familiar injunction on the concert programmes of the Bolton Society, and one that was well heeded judging by the large numbers who regularly sang of Bacchanalians and 'the draught from the crystal spring.' Songs were a much-used means of propaganda:

I'm very fond of a social glass,
   But it must be filled with water;
Water pure doth brighter shine
   Than brandy, rum or sparkling wine.

Broken-hearted drunkards and noble teetotal gentlemen figured prominently in the songs; and total abstinence was even equated with sex appeal. In *The Water Nymph*, a maiden sings of a suitor:

Though he comes till he's tired and woos on his knee,
   If he will not drink water, he shall not have me.
Should he not come again, I'll not sit and cry;
   There'll be men who drink water for all by and by.

There were few towns which did not hear Livesey's Malt Liquor Lecture, which always ended with the ceremonial burning of the spirit distilled from a quart of beer. When this was done at Burnley, a man cried out, 'I've drunk as much of that as would have lit all the lamps in Manchester.'

We have noted the splendid success of the Royton Temperance Seminary: somewhat less ambitious were the teetotallers of Droylsden, whose educational endeavours were limited to evening classes, but they had a strong missionary spirit and in 1849 persuaded 267 villagers to sign the pledge. 'In the following year,' wrote the local historian John Higson,

> tracts on total abstinence were circulated in the village at the rate of four hundred per week and a first-rate procession was got up on the Monday of the Wakes Week. The members wore white rosettes and the juveniles were distinguished by a strip of blue. A red herring borne on a pole was inscribed 'A drunkard's bullock' and an empty barrel was labelled 'To Let'. A wooden-legged personator of an inebriate riding on an ass was abused in Fairfield by a real tippler, who was as 'drunk as a Lord' and evidently averse to shams.

The temperance cause was actively supported by the nonconformist churches and by a number of evangelical bodies, among which was the Hallelujah Band, a group of working-class enthusiasts who were prominent in Haslingden during the 1860s. Hymns sung to the popular tunes of the day and graphic confessions by reformed jailbirds and drunkards ensured packed meetings at the Town Hall. Major David Halstead has described a memorable occasion on which a local 'character' known as Blue Tail volunteered some account of his reformation.

He began by drawing attention to the blessings and comforts of a home from which drink was absent; how since he reformed he had been able to live in comfort, save money and furnish a house; how he spent his nights at the fireside with his wife instead of in the tap room as formerly; how at that moment a big fat pig belonging to him was hanging in the shop of 'Dick Butcher' decked out with blue ribbons and bearing the label 'Hallelujah pig'; how this would be cut up and sold during the approaching week, and he hoped everybody present would buy a bit. Hearty applause encouraged him to begin to describe his life prior to joining the Hallelujah Band. But here our hero overdid it, for he out-Heroded Herod. He described the many scenes in such vivid detail as to shock everybody. He finished by telling how 'last Belle Vue Monday' he chalked up thirty two pints at Owd Ned Barnes's all of which he 'supped hissel' as he never thrat (treated) nobody because nobody thrat him; then how he returned home at midnight, 'dragged t' wife eawt o' bed bi' t' yers ov her yed, torn'd her eawt o' th' heause i' her shift, un' locked do'r on her'—and this was recounted with many horrible details. Women screamed, men rose in anger; epithets most uncomplimentary were hurled at the speaker; threats to murder him, calls to hang him, appeals from the audience to throw him from the platform—'Send him to Botany Bay!' 'Fotch th' police!' Pandemonium reigned for some time and if some of the women could have reached poor old Blue Tail, he would have been torn to pieces. Only with the appearance of the big burly figure of Police Sergeant Shaw did the disturbance subside.

Had the teetotallers been able to offer a satisfactory substitute for alcohol, they would doubtless have made even greater progress than they did; but not every thirsty workman found water a sufficiently powerful counter-attraction to beer, nor did every workman prefer to temperance hall to the public house. Livesey, who had once believed that strong drink would be driven out of the country for ever, had to admit in old age that the problem remained enormous. The over-whelming triumphs of the pioneers were never repeated, and though the movement remained strong, it met resolute opposition. When a man was accused of assaulting a woman during a temperance meeting at Whitworth in 1852, his solicitor told the magistrates that the reformers went round with a band of music and at each beerhouse 'set up a shout which was calculated to irritate those who were not disposed to be teetotallers.' Four years later, William Gregson, a Blackburn tem-perance advocate, visited Crawshawbooth and began to lecture from a lorry near the Black Dog Inn. The village publicans retaliated by loading a barrel of beer on to a lorry of their own and drawing it alongside that of their opponent. 'Pint pots were handed round to all present and one was given to the speaker,' the Rossendale diarist Moses Heap recorded. Gregson threw away the contents, but kept the pot. 'When the drink began to operate, then commenced a lively time with singing, shouting and fighting.' During 1855 Henry Lees and Brothers, of Victoria Mills, Ashton, found the effects of drunkenness so serious that they began to pay their sober operatives on Fridays and the tipplers on Saturdays. This, said the *Ashton Reporter*, was 'in order to extinguish the appearance of lassitude frequently exhibited by some of the worshippers at Bacchus' Shrine' on the morning after pay night. At the first meeting of the Trades Union Congress, which was held in Manchester in 1868, the delegate of the Glass Bottle Makers' Society said to applause that night drinking affected working men injuriously 'a great deal more than their physical toil during the day.'

The universal menace of drunkenness was overcome only after the civilising forces of Victorian England had been at work for many years. To the teetotallers must go the credit for a large share of the success; but it is ironic to reflect that it was the widespread adoption of the much criticised habit of moderate drinking rather than of total abstinence that had a decisive impact on one of the most virulent social evils of the nineteenth century.

8. *Model Mills*

The dismal picture we have painted of the factory masters is relieved by the shining endeavours of a small band of men, who, by taking a close interest in their workpeople's comfort, education and welfare, created some of the happiest and most intellectually stimulating communities of nineteenth-century Britain. A tradition of benevolence grew up during the years of the hand-loom weavers' prosperity, and despite the fierce competition that later bedevilled the cotton trade, it was never wholly extinguished. Many of the earlier manufacturers were remembered with affection. 'The weaver was as happy and independent as a prince. He loved his employer and his employer loved him, their interests were mutual,' an Eccles man recalled in 1852, and John Higson in his *Historical and Descriptive Notices of Droylsden*, of 1859, said that in the halcyon days before 1812

> Masters competed, not which should get his work done at the lowest rate, but which should give the highest remuneration for labour. A strife arose in this respect between Mr. John Orrell, of Ashton, who afterwards erected the extensive cotton mill at Openshaw, and Mr. Lewis, of Ryecroft, each trying to exceed the other in high wages. Eventually the contest was gained by Mr. Orrell, when his weavers subscribed and presented him with a silver cup to commemorate the event.

We should remember that benevolent paternalism and benevolent despotism were on either side of a fine dividing line, and that deference, obedience and subservience were the expected returns from a workforce treated in this way, but this should not reduce the achievement of these 'model employers', or detract from the success and virtue of their efforts. We should, perhaps, compare them with their contemporaries, and not with our own views on the ideal relationship between employer and employee.

Faced with the worsening conditions, many men of this stamp withdrew from business, leaving, as the 1823–24 factory visitors' reports show, only a handful of masters who did anything to improve their workpeople's lot. It would be wrong to say that all the rest were unconcerned. Even in the late eighteenth century the Peels provided schools for the children employed at their calico printing works, and in May 1825 several Manchester mill owners petitioned Parliament to regulate the hours of work. They were, they said, deeply interested in the health and welfare of the factory operatives and believed that none should have to work more than eleven and a half hours on weekdays or more than eight and a half hours on Saturdays. They would cheerfully adopt this arrangement provided there was a fair prospect of its becoming general, 'but if others did not act upon the same principles, the petitioners would not be able to compete and would be compelled in self defence to revert to the former system.' Parliament ignored the masters' plea and ahead of the factory reformers there lay a bitter struggle that was to last for more than twenty years.

The model mills of the kind pioneered by Robert Owen at New Lanark were hardly to be met with in Lancashire at this time. That of Jones and Co, of Tyldesley, was a rare example. Besides running a clean and well-ventilated mill, the firm treated their employees as human beings and not mere machine-minders. 'If any of the workpeople falls sick, which seldom happens, they are maintained,' the factory visitors reported. 'Messrs Jones have established a sick club in their factory and each person subscribing 1d. a week receives 4s. a week.' The firm opened a Sunday school for their workpeople and any others who cared to attend. Time off was allowed for the local wakes and was made up at the rate of half an hour a day.

The following decade saw an increase in the number of well-run mills; and in January 1837, Leonard Horner, the Factories Inspector, said he could draw up a long list 'where order, cleanliness and attention on the part of the master to the comfort and welfare of his workpeople are conspicuous.'

I have often wished [he went on] that those who so thoughtlessly believe and give currency to tales of the miseries of the factory workers, and of the cruelty and hard-heartedness of their masters, would go to some of the mills to which I could send them, and judge for themselves. They would then see how greatly they have erred in their general condemnation of what they term the factory system, and how much virtue, intelligence, comfort and happiness are to be found among the workers in a well-regulated mill.

The Round Mills (often called the Four Factories) on the outskirts of Bolton, were doubtless of the kind to which Horner refers. A correspondent of the *Bolton Weekly Journal*, who worked there as a boy in the 1820s and '30s, described his experiences in a series of articles published during December 1879. Though the hours were very long and 'punctuality was insisted on with great strictness,' the mills 'were acknowledged to be the best-conducted in the town and neighbourhood' and were free from the worst abuses of factory life. The workpeople were able to look out over a beautiful green land-scape, and 'occasionally we had a sight of the huntsmen following the hare . . . Of course, the spinning would be neglected so long as they remained in sight; indeed, the rules and regulations of the mills were not stringently enforced.' Some of the spinners took guns to the mill and kept a watch for flocks of birds. 'The temptation to these jolly sportsmen could not be resisted. If they could get out no other way, they would top the back gate and were in the fields in a few minutes.'

> The mill yard [the account goes on] was like a large orchard, containing square plots of grass, and apple and pear trees, which in autumn caused many a young lad's mouth to water. The fruit was pretty well watched; nevertheless, the temptation was often too great to be resisted, and many a boy got into trouble, especially led therein by a large jargonnel pear tree that almost wholly covered the gable end of No. 4 Mill. There was a plot reserved for flowers and noted for the quantity and quality of the tulips cultivated there. I think there were also some plum trees against the mill walls. I suppose this outside view did something towards cultivating a taste for fruit and flowers among the workers inside the mills, especially the spinners and piecers. Great emulation existed among the spinners as to whom should have the earliest and largest cucumbers, pots containing the early seed being placed over the steam pipes that heated the rooms with the object of forcing growth. The spinners would look with eager curiosity almost every day for any appearance above the soil; and there was great rejoicing when a young sprout appeared above the surface. No gas being used in the mills, the piecers grew balsams, the rivalry among them being equally as great as to who should have the finest bloom as it was among their masters, the spinners, to have the earliest cucumbers.

The village of Hooley Bridge, near Bury, which grew up around a large cotton mill built in 1826 by Joseph Fenton of Bamford Hall, was an early example of enlightened paternalism. Fenton ran a school, encouraged his workpeople to cultivate gardens and prohibited beer-houses and spirit sellers. The mill closed in 1862. 'The workpeople,' wrote Henry Pitman, editor of *The Co-operator*, in 1869, 'were noted for as the best housed, best fed, clothed and educated in Lancashire.'

During the 1830s the firm of H. and E. Ashworth of Turton and Egerton provided their workpeople with substantial cottages at reasonable rents and arranged periodic inspections to ensure a high standard of hygiene. From 1825 the firm also ran day, evening and Sunday schools and by 1833, Henry Ashworth was able to tell the Factory Commissioners that of the 532 employees, all but seven newcomers could read and 247 could also write. Children were encouraged to broaden their minds and 'when a boy has nothing to do he can walk into the school and read a newspaper or any history, as we keep a library of books for their use.' A washroom with soap, towels and combs was provided. In 1837, Henry's partner Edmund said that many of 'the lower orders' in Lancashire were so ignorant that they did not realise the disadvantages under which they laboured, but the brothers found what few of their colleagues were willing to believe—that people who were educated, comfortably housed and treated with respect made by far the best workers. This was a policy adopted by Hindes and Derham, the large worsted spinners of Dolphinholme, near Lancaster. Leonard Horner wrote in 1838:

The mill is surrounded by the cottages of the workpeople, and they

Low Moor Mill, Clitheroe (photo-graph courtesy of Clitheroe Library Local Studies Collection). The mill, owned by the Garnett family, was noted for its commendable attitude to the employees. The neat and elegant architecture suggests that it was a 'model' in other ways as well.

form quite a community of themselves. There is a most delicate cleanliness observed in the mill and all about it, and the whole group of houses are fresh whitewashed outside nearly every year, and contrast well with the bright green of the trees. The moral conditions of the people is a great object of attention with the proprietors; they pay eighty pounds a year to a clergyman, have built a chapel and schoolhouse and maintain a schoolmaster. From all I hear, it is a most virtuous and happy little colony, one of the instances where a well-managed factory, under the guidance of enlightened and benevolent proprietors, is a blessing to the country. It would be impossible to collect a set of more healthy, tidy, orderly people, than those I saw working in the mill.

Other model employers active at this time were Jacob Bright of Rochdale, the Whitehead Brothers of Rawtenstall and James Thomson of the Primrose Calico Printing Works, Clitheroe, who offered apprenticeships only to those boys who could read and write at fourteen. The result was wholly beneficial. 'Primrose became a seat of learning,' an old resident of Clitheroe recalled in 1898 and Thomson's success in creating a prosperous industrial community 'attracted many artisans who had seen the world and who brought with them well-stored minds.'

The occasional treats and entertainments which for many years were sufficiently remarkable to be reported at length in the Press, were another indication of friendly relations between mill masters and their workpeople. The Grants of Ramsbottom, the Cheeryble brothers of Dickens's *Nicholas Nickleby*, despite their failure to stamp out the truck system, were paternalistic and often generous employers. To mark the coronation of George IV in 1821, their employees marched to Bury headed by two Highland pipers (the Grants were Scotsmen) and on returning were treated to 'a feast of two fat oxen, ten sheep and a waggon load of porter and beer brewed from fourteen loads of malt.' Another 'splendid entertainment' was given in 1839:

The company numbering eight hundred [said the *Bolton Chronicle* of 5 October] assembled in a commodious room elegantly fitted up for the occasion and a sumptuous repast of good old English cheer, roast beef, etc., was provided. After dinner they were regaled with a plentiful supply of ale and porter. An excellent band being in attendance, each joined in a merry dance from the child of six to the matron of four score. At about seven o'clock, John Grant Esq., made his appearance in the room and was enthusiastically cheered: when the cheering had subsided which lasted several minutes, he ascended the orchestra and after acknowledging the hearty welcome he had received, addressed them in warm and friendly terms. Several excellent glees and songs were sung during the evening and the utmost hilarity prevailed. At eleven, the party highly gratified broke up with three times three cheers for the health and prosperity of their worthy entertainers and employers.

The annual treat given by J.R. Barnes and Son of Farnworth was always noteworthy. In January 1845, the 700 workpeople dined to the strains of 'Mr. Fisher's celebrated Cornopean Band' and a set of glee singers. After the meal

A splendid magic lantern with a great variety of astronomical, microscopical, scenic and humorous slides was lent by Mr. Thomas Barnes who gave a short and interesting description of each.

'An electrifying machine' and a demonstration of laughing gas 'completed the philosophical entertainments' after which dancing, singing and recitations added to the enjoyment, prompting the *Bolton Free Press* to remark: 'What a pity it is that there are not more such meetings betwixt employers and employed.' This thought was obviously in the mind of the workman who acted as chairman at the following year's festivities.

He called the attention of other masters in the area (of whom there were several then present) to the pleasing sight of nearly one thousand happy smiling faces, all beaming with social life and harmony, which were thus called forth into lively exercise by the kindness and liberality of one individual.

The sending up of a balloon and a display of fireworks were extra attractions on this occasion.

The gulf between 'the two nations' was agreeably bridged at Low Moor, near Clitheroe, in April 1849, when Jeremiah Garnett, senior partner in the firm of Horsfall and Garnett, celebrated a half century in the cotton trade with a lavish entertainment for his workpeople and friends. Just twenty years earlier, during a period of unrest, he had been busy supervising the construction of a moat to defend the mill: now with equal thoroughness, he prepared for what proved to be a memorable and delightful day. The arrangements occupied more than a month and included the elaborate decoration of two large spinning rooms. Pink and white glazed calico covered the walls, which were festooned with evergreens and flowers. Fluted pillars and 'several valuable paintings in oil' helped to complete the transformation. The festivities began with a dinner for which 'an ox was expressly fed and slaughtered' and in addition there were many extra joints of beef, hams, veal and mutton pies . . . a plum pudding weighing 20lb and 50 weighing 14lb, 'all of the richest and most savoury make.' During the meal at which about 500 were present, a brass band played 'popular and appropriate airs,' and after a tea on much the same scale, about 1,000 people were guests at 'a grand ball.' The two rooms were brilliantly lit with gas and 'relays of sandwiches, punch, lemonade, orange, cakes and wine were plentifully supplied.' 'Factory operatives, gentlemen and ladies,' said the *Preston Chronicle*, 'mixed together in the merry reel, which was kept up with great spirit till daybreak.' And the *Preston Guardian* observed 'We wish that those persons who draw their notions of factory people from fashionable novels had been there to witness the scene: we think they would have left the place with very different impressions from those with which they entered it.'

The 1840s also saw the first mill outings by rail and the introduction of several more lasting benefits. In August 1841, two Blackburn manufacturers, W. H. Hornby and W. Kenworthy, gave their workpeople a playground, which was named the Brookhouse Gymnasium. The half-acre field, said the *Blackburn Standard*, 'is laid out for a variety of interesting games calculated to invigorate the youthful frame, such as quoiting, football, tennis ball, skittles, etc.' and of the workpeople who attended the opening, the paper remarked: 'The glow of health which their countenances presented afforded the conclusive answer to the calumnies and misrepresentations of those self-styled philanthropists who pass such sweeping and indiscriminate condemnation upon the whole body of mill owners.'

The Doubling Room at Dean Mill, Barrowbridge, Bolton, visited by Prince Albert in 1851. Barrowbridge was a well-known 'model' community, with workers' housing, a village institute, organised classes for adults, a school and other facilities.

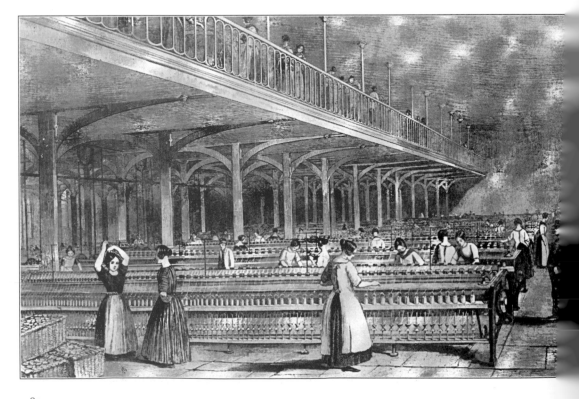

Baths for men, women and children were opened at the mill of P. Catterall and Co, of Preston in May 1844 (the *Preston Guardian* took the then unusual step of publishing a diagram) and in December, Gardner and Bazely marked the opening of their bath-house at Dean Mills, Barrowbridge near Bolton, with a performance of Handel's *Messiah*.

The same year was made even more memorable when Robert Gardner of Preston and Robert Knowles and Sons, of Bolton introduced an eleven-hour day at their cotton mills. With nine hours on Saturdays, the working week was cut from 69 to 64 hours and there was no loss of wages. At a tea party given by Gardner's workpeople to celebrate the first anniversary of the new system, it was stated that output had increased, wages were higher and less time was lost through sickness than when they worked twelve hours a day. Of the six hundred operatives, the number attending night school has risen from twenty seven to ninety six and the young women 'were becoming better acquainted with domestic matters.' Mr Gardner in a letter to the meeting said that he would begin a ten and a half hour day during the winter. In April 1846, the second anniversary of shorter working, a bath-house was opened at the mill. It had a warm bath, a vapour bath and a shower bath 'all fitted up in comfortable style' with towels 'and every other requisite' provided.

The more settled economic climate of the mid-1840s, to which Peel's financial reforms made a considerable contribution, helped to improve relations between masters and men—the Cotton Spinners' Union referred in 1843 to a 'new spirit of cordiality'—and the fact that the once hostile parties were coming to understand each other's problems was made clear at a tea party given in August 1845 by the operative spinners of Bolton for a number of their employers. This commemorated 'the great and important fact' that the masters 'with the utmost cheerfulness and goodwill' had twice advanced wages without the need for strikes. More than 900 people attended the party in the Temperance Hall which was decorated with banners including 'Prosperity to the Cotton Manufacturers—Comfort and Happiness to the Operatives' and 'May nothing separate the interests of the Employers and the Employed.'

The Bolton district was celebrated for a number of model employers who set up well-run village communities. Those of the Ashworths were first to attract attention, but Barrowbridge and Eagley later achieved equal if not greater renown. Barrowbridge was remembered for much more than its bath-house oratorio. In 1851 it was visited by Prince Albert and described by the *Illustrated London News* as 'a well-organised community never equalled in the Utopias of philosophy.' Workpeople who arrived early were able to relax in a well-lit and well-heated room which was supplied with all the latest newspapers and periodicals. After the morning's work, a steam kitchen, where five hundred dinners could be kept hot, and a dining-room well furnished with tables and benches, were available to all. In the evenings the villagers used the room for meetings and the mill's brass band rehearsed there. A co-operative store, started in 1837, and equipped with a blast-oven that baked 150 loaves a day, was run by a workpeople's committee. The firm supported a large school, above which was a lecture room with accommodation for between 2,000 and 3,000 people. Lecturers who provided 'entertainment of amusing or innocent character' were welcomed and no charge was made for gas used in scientific demonstrations. 'With such encourage-ment,' said the *Illustrated London News*, 'a succession of instructive displays are afforded the workpeople.' Some three hundred employees lived in stone cottages built by the mill owners, a large cottage with a plot of ground being let for 2s. 6d. or 3s. 6d. a week. The Prince Consort was much impressed as he toured the village and the mill, where, in the words of the *Bolton Chronicle*, 'the band discoursed sweet music as he went into the doubling room.'

Also on the outskirts of Bolton was the village of Eagley, where Chadwick Brothers, sewing thread and smallwear manufacturers, created a 'Utopia' to rival Barrowbridge. *Bradshaw's Handbook to the Manufac-turing Districts* said in 1854:

> The superior management of these mills is at once apparent in the extreme order and cleanliness which everywhere prevails and a large expenditure is undertaken by the proprietors for promoting the moral and intellectual improvement of the workpeople.

The firm ran 'an excellent school' and the 'otherwise useless land on the reservoir banks, many acres in extent, has been planted and tastefully laid out in walks interspersed with seats and arbours for the recreation of the persons employed in the establishment.' The mill had a library of 15,000 volumes and a reading room which took the local and London daily papers and 'many of the best periodicals.' The account goes on:

> A very small monthly charge is made for admission: and it is pleasing to find that the benefits of the institution are appreciated by neigh-bouring workpeople, numbers of whom are subscribers. It is worth remarking that the best Historical and Biographical works and Voy-ages and Travels are more sought after than the works of a lighter description . . . Music is regularly taught at the evening school and a very good brass band is in operation. Many of the workpeople who have gardens show much taste and skill in the culture of flowers and vegetables. Dining rooms and hot, cold and shower baths are provided without charge.

9. *The Free Traders*

The better feeling that developed between a number of mill masters and their workpeople during and after the 1840s owed something to the Anti-Corn Law League and the burgeoning of Free Trade Liberalism which the movement greatly accelerated. The doctrine of *laissez-faire* was tempered with the humanitarianism of the philanthropists so that goodwill and higher profits, once so remote in the eyes of all but a few Lancashire manufacturers, came to be increasingly allied in the philosophy of their successors.

On 24 September 1838, as Lancashire Chartism reached its zenith at the monster meeting on Kersal Moor, seven men met a few miles away to begin a repeal movement, the success of which was in striking contrast to the decline of its boisterous but less well organised rival. The founding of the Manchester Anti-Corn Law Association set in motion a sequence of events which led, not only to the triumph of industrial over agricultural interests and the adoption of free trade as the official government policy, but also to the widespread belief, held with religious intensity by many, that free trade was the cure for all social ills and the only sure way to international peace.

The Manchester School was how Disraeli described the men who

Reform movement in the early 1840s. A cover picture from Joseph Livesey's *The Struggle*.

kept up the onslaught against protection, for it was from the heart of that city that the National Anti-Corn Law League, which superseded the Manchester Association in March 1839, directed its offensive. The founders of the League—'representatives from all the great sections of our manufacturing and commercial population'—maintained that the Corn Law, besides causing needless distress by keeping food prices high, was depressing home manufacturers and overseas trade. It was argued that foreigners, unable to dispose of their grain surpluses at reasonable prices, could buy few of the British goods they wished for, and that only total repeal would solve these menacing problems.

The movement began with two great advantages: its leaders, in particular Richard Cobden and John Bright, were brilliant and dedicated men, and secondly its members were rich enough to sustain a long and costly campaign. By its direct and powerful methods, the League became the first great political pressure group and its success demonstrated to a far from passive people the effectiveness of peaceful persuasion. Branches were established throughout the country and paid lecturers toured both the industrial and agricultural districts. An official newspaper, the fortnightly *Anti-Bread Tax Circular* was launched in April 1839 and later became a weekly, *The League*. (In December 1841, the indefatigable Joseph Livesey, at his own expense, started in Preston a small illustrated weekly paper, *The Struggle*, which sold for a halfpenny. Its racy style and its crude, but pointed, woodcuts proved extremely popular and earned a circulation of 15,000, which was only a little behind that of *The League*.) By 1843, some nine million tracts weighing more than one hundred tons had been issued from Manchester. Among them was a 108-page booklet which was sent to every voter, full advantage having been taken of the cheaper postal rates introduced in 1840. The booklet's message was forthright and clear:

> You are an elector. To you is entrusted the privilege of choosing the law-makers. It is a trust for the good of others; and upon the right or wrong exercise of this trust depends the happiness or misery of millions of your fellow creatures. At the next Parliamentary election, you will be entitled to choose between a bread taxer (*one who witholds corn from the people*) and a candidate who will untax the poor man's loaf. The choice involves an awful responsibility. Think solemnly and carefully, before you decide. Examine the evidence which is now put in your hands. Ignorance cannot be pleaded after knowledge has been freely given to you. Remember that you will decide for plenty or for scarcity, for comfort or misery, for health or disease, for life or death for many thousands of immortal beings. Remember, above all, that your decision will be recorded on high, and that you will be called on to account for your vote at that dread tribunal when all mankind will be judged—not by their

professions, not by their prayers, but when the blessed will be told, 'I was hungered and ye gave me meat.'

The moral earnestness of the publications was supported by Anti-Corn Law bazaars—one at Manchester in 1842 raised £10,000 in eleven days—anti-Corn Law songs, anti-Corn Law poetry and anti-Corn Law dances. But more important still was the large-scale purchase of land to provide freeholds—and hence the vote—for League supporters. The anti-Corn Law MPs formed a small but dynamic party in Parliament and to increase their numbers, subscribers to a £500,000 fund were recruited, but after the first call of ten per cent, Peel was converted to free trade, and with the Irish potato famine forcing his hand, the Repeal Bill passed on 26 July 1846.

The seven years of agitation gave the country not only free trade, but also a new ideology which inspired most of the best achievements of Victorian Liberalism. Looking back in 1868, Joseph Livesey wrote:

Comparing the last twenty with the previous thirty years, I don't hesitate to say that free trade has saved this country from revolution, and has been the forerunner of that contentment, tranquility and progress which have marked this latter period.

4

New Pleasures

1. *Brighter Times*

LANCASHIRE people who survived the painful changes of the early nineteenth century found that life in an industrial society—a society enriched by scientific discoveries and stimulated by an array of civilising forces—had many new pleasures as well as many new problems.

From that memorable day in 1805 when William Murdoch lit a Salford cotton mill with gas, Lancashire became a brighter place to live in. The benefits of a better lighting were incalculable and it is doubtful whether any other single invention brought more cheerfulness to Victorian England than the gas lamp. There was an early, but short-lived outcry in Manchester about the 'profane way of dissipating God's darkness,' but the general response was one of delight and astonishment. The Manchester Police Commissioners began to manufacture gas in 1807 and installed their first burner above the police office, an event recalled some fifty years later by the chairman of the city's Gas Committee at a meeting of the British Association.

> I well remember the sensation which this lamp produced, and the crowds that night after night gathered in front to gaze at it, manifesting by their eager and intense curiosity a vague sort of impression that an element of nature was being developed that would be useful to mankind.

People went miles to see the lights come on in a big mill, and when the new wonder reached Haslingden, one man was so overwhelmed that he declared that 'daylight was a fool to gas.' There was great excitement in Liverpool in January 1816 when two large gas lamps with three burners each were exhibited in front of the Town Hall. 'The light is so brilliant,' said the *Liverpool Mercury*, 'that a person may with ease discover the hour by his watch at a distance of twenty or thirty yards.' In less-populated areas candles and oil lamps continued

Dear JONES !—At Pendleton last night,
A saw the famed ELECTRIC LIGHT:
And as I know you rather doubt it,
I write to tell you all about it !
Five hundred thousand—more or less—
Of eyes, as near as I can guess,
At nine P.M.—few minutes past—
Were towards "HIS WORSHIP's" mansion cast !
BUILE HILL is where "HIS WORSHIP" lives.

And admirable dinners gives ;
POTTER his name whose cellars flow
With generous wine, as hundreds know :
He's very popular, and rumour
Speaks of his excellent good humour,
His hospitality, good sense,
All exercised without pretence.
I should have told you he's the MAYOR
OF MANCHESTER, and fills "the chair,"
Conscious of dignity and station,
On every public great occasion.
I only wish, as I'm a sinner,
He'd ased me, Wednesday night, to dinner.
Well, never mind ! if he had known
That I, JOHN SMITH, was in the town,
I should have been outside his garret,

Full of "HIS WORSHIP's" matchless claret !
I'd rather far his wine been sipping,
Than standing where I did all dripping,
For the thick rain in torrents flow'd,
Damping the ardour of the crowd ;
Yet still I felt each pelting shower
Whetted one's appetite the more,
Until the light burst forth in glory,
Out of "HIS WORSHIP's" upper storey—
POTTER, Esquire, and friends, the whiles,
Were all of them "upon the tiles,"—
This is a fact, as JOHN SMITH knows,
I saw "HIS WORSHIP" scratch his nose !
You know, friend Jones, my word is law,
I'll tell you, therefore, what I saw :—
The flowers beneath began to blow,
The sheep to bleat, the cows to low,
And the male poultry to crow,—
They quite mistook the light as warning
Of the approach of early morning :
I saw, although my eyes are weak;
Into the middle of next week :
Could read, and be it ne'er forgotten,
Next Tuesday's prices, "stocks," and "cotton,"
If it had been a better-sort-night.

I could have seen into a fortnight.

The clock struck ten ! Oh ! What wondrous change !
The "LIGHT" then took a wider range,
Three miles away, as true as life,
Some one was seen to kiss his wife !
In a small window with a curtain,
There's no mistake, the distance certain,
I saw her blush, then hide a minute,
Not that there's anything wrong in it,
Still it's not nice e'en by one's mother,
To be caught kissing one another !
It's such a startling invention,
That just one other fact I'll mention :
The weathercock on BOWDON steeple
Was seen to wink by several people !
STAITE's "lightning" struck the bird with wonder,
Ten thousand voices pealed the "thunder,"
And JONES, unless I'm much mistaken,
Folks' incredulity was shaken,—
That light's "A FACT" and STAITE will "do it,"
Let clever people look unto it.
Of my impressions you've the pith,

YOURS, VERY FAITHFULLY,
    JOHN SMITH.

Manchester, August 8th, 1850.

The electric light in Manchester. A poem of 1850.

to be used for a number of years and many people, like the Rossendale diarist Moses Heap, must have reflected how 'dreadfully long' the nights of winter seemed to be. In thousands of cellars and lofts hand-loom weavers toiled through the long hours of darkness by the faint light of candles which were usually suspended in sockets of hooked wire from strings stretched along the tops of the looms. Mill conditions were little better. Of his early days in the spinning room a correspondent of the *Bolton Weekly Journal* said in 1879: 'The candles were fixed in very primitive candlesticks that were inserted in the wooden rollerbeam. Two were thought sufficient for each short mule.' A reflector was considered 'a great invention.' When Accrington was first lit with gas in December, 1840, it is easy to understand why, in the words of the *Bolton Free Press*, 'the inhabitants are quite delighted with the change.' Occasionally there was opposition, on financial grounds, to the introduction of gas lighting. The ratepayers of Chowbent (Atherton) voted against it in 1837 and again in 1844 when, 'for two or three weeks the township was much excited upon the subject.' After a poll had been demanded, there was 'an active canvass' by both the advocates of darkness—farmers and the 'lowest description of the working classes'—and the advocates of light, whose ranks were swelled by the clergy, gentry, tradesmen and 'the more intelligent operatives.' On voting day, said the *Bolton Free Press*,

> The whole of the time during which the poll was open was occupied in mustering the forces: sick and lame were all brought up. Two aged persons were wheeled to the voting place in wheelbarrows. Vehicles of a higher character were also employed. Falsehoods of the grossest character were, we understand, uttered by the non-lighting party.

'The opponents of enlightenment' won by 109 votes to 95, but some 251 non-ratepayers also insisted on going to the poll, and as the *Free Press* pointed out, had these votes been legal, the lighting party would have had a majority of 64.

During the late 1840s when gas lamps were a familiar sight throughout Lancashire, reports were received of a rival form of lighting—electricity. William Edwards Staite at that time seemed destined for greater fame than William Murdoch, but his carbon arc lamps powered by galvanised batteries proved far too expensive to be a commercial proposition. Staite took out a series of patents in 1846–47–48 for lamps to illuminate 'public and private buildings, streets, squares and other public places' and he gave demonstrations which astonished all who saw them. On the wet and gloomy evening of 7 August 1850, Staite shone his lamp from the roof of Buile Hill, Pendleton, the home of John Potter, then Mayor of Manchester. Despite the heavy rain, the experiment was highly successful and the *Manchester Guardian* declared that the rays of light 'were seen to have an intensity and brilliancy far surpassing any other artificial light hitherto known.' As soon as the beam shone forth there arose from various points on the roads and in the fields around Buile Hill great cheering and clapping of hands from thousands of spectators who had assembled notwithstanding the heavy rain, to witness the exhibition. Chaseley, the residence of Robert Gardner, Esq., which is some 600 or 700 yards north of Buile Hill, was brought up out of the murky gloom into a distinctness as vivid as if under a brilliant moonlight. The groups of persons in front of the house were distinctly visible to the observers on the roof of Buile Hill, and even ladies could be discerned at the windows. The light was next turned upon various green fields and lawns, all of which were seen to be crowded with persons of both sexes; and the effect of so many upturned faces, all instantaneously brought out of darkness into a dazzling and conspicuous pre-eminence by the light was exceedingly striking. Everywhere plaudits followed the reception of the 'new light,' and the scenes which were revealed to the observers on the roof were like some extraordinary living phantasmagoria; houses, groves and lawns, with numerous gazers,

The first public square outside London to be lit by gas. Preston's market square was illuminated by a gas light at the top of its Obelisk, initially supplied—leakily—by pipes constructed from army surplus gun barrels.

emerging out of darkness, and suddenly disappearing, as the reflector cast the rays of light in a new direction. Several houses at Seedley were quite lit up by the light for a few seconds; and a part of the old Eccles road was seen to be crowded with spectators who cheered loudly as they found themselves lighted up by this artificial sun.

Observers on hills, church towers and other high buildings for miles around took part in the experiment. The scientist John Joule, watching from his home in Moss Side, Manchester, three miles from Buile Hill, found the light 'most brilliant and beautiful' and he said would have been able to read the small print of the *Guardian* if the beam had remained stationary. At the Botanical Gardens, Old Trafford (two miles from Buile Hill), one observer was able to tell the time by his watch, and Professor Calvert read the words 'Latest Intelligence' in his copy of the *Guardian* before the beam swung away. The number of *Guardian* readers waiting with their copies in the pouring rain seems to have been considerable, but the *Manchester Examiner and Times* also had its supporters. After recording Professor Calvert's achievement, it added:

> Further beyond the Botanic Gardens the landlord of the Punch Bowl, near Stretford, was able to read *the smallest print* of the *Examiner*, but this may perhaps be attributed to the greater degree of luminosity which we claim for our articles.

Staite also demonstrated his lamp in the Free Trade Hall, where 'several ladies were observed to smile and shade their faces as the light was turned upon them, as if afraid that their beauty and loveliness would be too prominently brought forward.' In the following year Staite lit Lime Street railway station, Liverpool, in the presence of the directors, but though his 'small electrical machine illuminated the entire station sufficiently for the transaction of ordinary business,' it was not adopted by the North Western Railway Company. The inventor was again in Liverpool during May 1852, and for several evenings his lamp drew large crowds to Prince's Pier. Again no orders followed and electric light was hardly heard of in Lancashire for another sixteen years when it was used to inaugurate floodlit football. A match between Blackburn Rovers and Accrington at Alexandra Meadows in November 1878 attracted nearly a third of the population, for, besides the 6,000 who paid to go into the ground, another 20,000 had a free view from Corporation Park. The light was supplied by two of Gramme's arc-lamps powered by a portable engine.

The lighting was 'a brilliant success,' said the *Blackburn Times*, which added in a passage unique in the annals of football reporting:

> On the players making their appearance on the ground from their respective tents, attired in picturesque costume, the scene was charming and fairylike. For a short time they amused themselves by playing leap-frog and racing. The leather, which was painted white in order to be better seen by the players, was kicked off about a quarter-to-eight o'clock. Although the faces of the players could not be distinguished at any distance, the ball could be seen very well and the players had no difficulty in following it. The Blackburn team succeeded in scoring three goals to none.

2. *Intrepid Aeronauts*

The establishment of gas works had an unexpected side effect. Coal gas, which is lighter than air, proved a boon to balloonists who used it to make ascents from most of the larger Lancashire towns from the 1820s onwards. Any account of ballooning in Lancashire must begin, however, with James Sadler (1753–1828), who went up from Manchester on 12 May 1785, only eight months after the Italian Vincenzo Lunardi had become the first man to ascend from English soil. After exhibiting his balloon in the Exchange, Sadler took it for inflation to the garden of a private house in Long Millgate. Tickets cost 10s. 6d. and 5s. The balloon was slowly filled with hydrogen—made by the action of sulphuric acid on iron filings—and at 1.20 p.m. in the words of the *Manchester Mercury*:

> Sadler ascended in a slow and majestic manner amidst a vast concourse of spectators, who saluted him with a grateful cheer for the pleasure he afforded in so magnificent a sight . . . All hearts and all tongues

seemed to be in unison in praise of his behaviour and of the object before them.

Sadler was in the air for about forty minutes before landing on a sand bed between Blacow Bridge and Radcliffe. He returned to the city in the evening 'amid the plaudits of a crowded multitude.'

Two months later, on 20 July 1785, Lunardi, then secretary to the Neapolitan Ambassador in London, ascended from the North Fort at Liverpool. 'A prodigious concourse' waited in heavy rain during the morning and had almost given up hope of seeing the aeronaut when the weather improved. A changeable wind continued to blow, however, but Lunardi was determined to go ahead with his plans and announced that he would go up at five o'clock. The inflation was exceedingly slow and the tough Liverpool crowd grew hostile when the time passed without any sign of the balloon. Well aware of the danger of delaying much longer, Lunardi ordered a gun to be fired as the signal that the balloon was sufficiently inflated. Unfortunately it was not, even when he threw out two boxes of ballast, his pistols, his speaking trumpet and finally his cork jacket. It was six o'clock before the balloon was ready. The gun was fired again and the crowd who had waited so long and whose patience was almost exhausted at last saw Lunardi rise into the air.

> For a moment [said the *Liverpool General Advertiser*] an awful silence took place, but this immediately gave way to loud and retierated bursts of applause. Again all was still and he saluted the spectators gracefully, waving his hat.

There was a moment of suspense as the balloon swung away towards the Irish Sea, but the wind shifted, and Lunardi came down in a field of wheat at Simonswood, twelve miles from Liverpool, after a flight lasting an hour and twenty minutes. To keep himself airborne he had thrown out his hat, coat and waistcoat, and he suffered considerably from exposure.

In May of the following year Sadler returned to Manchester, and from the same garden made a flight to Pontefract. The wind was much stronger than on his previous ascent, and though he landed safely he was unable to hold his balloon which took off again and eventually fell into the North Sea. Sadler made a third flight from Manchester in June 1812. For three hours thousands waited at Shudehill, until, to quote the *Manchester Mercury*:

> A burst of loud and reiterated shouts announced the interesting and momentous crisis—the ascent of the majestic traverser of the upper regions with the intrepid and venerable aeronaut, unaccompanied, firmly standing up with his hat in his hand, waving it and moving most respectfully to the congregated multitude.

Having risen above the rooftops, Sadler 'exercised two flags with much activity' and was then whisked towards the Pennines by a strong breeze. Shortly afterwards a man driving a horse and cart along a moorland road was alarmed to see Sadler's balloon bearing down on him. He fled in terror as the balloon struck his vehicle. The grappling iron took hold, but then broke loose and the balloon went bouncing over the hills into Yorkshire, finally coming to rest near Sheffield. The 50-mile journey lasted 48 minutes.

Sadler was not alone in discovering that it was easier to go up in a balloon than to come down in one. A Mr Livingstone 'rose majestically' during the Preston Guild celebrations of September 1822, but once the 'cheering shouts of ten thousand voices' had died away he was faced with the problem of descending in a high wind on Billington Moor, near Whalley. 'The ballon,' said the *Preston Chronicle*, 'was dragged over two or three fields and its grappling iron tore up everything that impeded its way.' Three farm labourers managed to wrap the grappling iron round a tree, only to see the tree ripped from the ground. 'After several dreadful rebounds,' the account adds, 'Mr Livingstone was thrown out of the car at the height of 18 feet and fell upon his side, which, we are sorry to say, is much bruised.' The balloon was found at Methorpe, six miles from Selby.

A red letter day at the Vauxhall Gardens, Manchester.

Mr Livingstone does not appear to have resumed his aeronautical career and it was Sadler's son, Windham William Sadler (1796–1824) who next took to the air in Lancashire. Sadler—he was named after the politician William Windham, who accompanied his father on his first ascent in 1785—made several flights in the county. From 1817 until 1822 he was engineer to the Liverpool Gas Company after which he opened a 'warm vapour and medicated bath establishment' in the city.

When Sadler took off from the Cloth Hall, Salford, in April 1824, 'crowds of country people came into the town. Every eminence was thronged with spectators, factories and the tops of houses being similarly occupied.' The balloon reached Knutsford. In the following month, as Sadler descended near Bacup after a flight made to mark the opening of the Rochdale gas works,

the inhabitants of that populous neighbourhood to whom the sight was perfectly novel, crowded around in such large numbers and with such intense curiosity that some trifling damage was done to the balloon.

On 27 May, Sadler and Lt R.H. Peel of the Third Dragoon Guards, 'evincing the utmost calmness on the perilous occasion' stepped into the basket of the balloon—42ft high and 36ft in diameter—in the Liverpool Cattle Market. It was a splendid moment.

> The balloon now appeared in its full magnitude, in alternate stripes of crimson and yellow, and as the sun shone upon it, rendering it semi-transparent, it undulated to and fro as if impatient to bound into the realms of ether . . . Two ladies came forward and presented flags to the aeronauts. Every bosom now throbbed with intense expectation, and in a few minutes the word 'let go' was given and the balloon—with its pendant voyagers, soared majestically from the earth, the sunbeams gleaming on it as on a burnished globe. It is impossible to conceive an ascent more sublime and gratifying than this. The giant bulk of the balloon formed a striking contrast to the diminutive size of the car and the intrepid voyagers, who, suspended beneath the gorgeous orb, sailed calmly and noiselessly through the fields of air. There is an indescribable emotion which arises from the contemplation of so extraordinary a spectacle of human ingenuity and daring.

The balloon landed near Chester after being in the air for 91 minutes.

On 27 September 1824, after a flight from Bolton, Sadler who was accompanied by his manservant, prepared to land at Fox Hill Bank, near Church. The grappling iron was fixed to a tree, but the rope broke and the balloon shot forward, 'sometimes dragging the car on the ground and sometimes dashing it against trees, houses and whatever happened to be in its course.' When the balloon struck and demolished a cottage chimney, Sadler was thrown to the ground and received injuries from which he died the following day. Sadler's servant was flung out at Whalley and broke an arm. The balloon fell into the sea off the Yorkshire coast.

The next balloonist to visit Lancashire was George Green who, only a year after Sadler's fatal accident, made two ascents from Preston and one from Blackburn. Two of the flights were made at very high speeds: 28 miles from Preston to Wigglesworth, near Settle at 79mph, and 65 miles from Blackburn to Braithwell in Yorkshire at 70mph. This was the first balloon ascent from Blackburn and crowds of people flocked to the town to see it. The *Blackburn Mail* of 26 October 1825 said of the inflation:

> About 12 o'clock the magnificent machine began to show its form, and during the remainder of the period occupied in filling it, being

acted upon by the wind, it rolled furiously about, threatening to overwhelm those who approached too near it, and anon violently agitating the ropes which were attached to various parts of the network with which it was encompassed, and indeed for a short period before the filling was complete, it was with difficulty restrained from mounting the airy regions. At length . . . the intrepid aeronaut, with his companion, Mr C. Radcliffe of this town, stepped into the car and the magnificent object being released from its restraints, mounted upwards, bounding off before the gale with the utmost velocity.

The rapidity of the balloon's departure alarmed many spectators and fears for the two men's safety grew when no news of their descent was received before the end of the day. Their return next morning was marked by the ringing of church bells.

Green made two flights from Blackburn in 1828, the first notable for the fact that he successfully dropped a fowl by parachute and the second for the fact that it was his 50th ascent—the 'Grand Jubilee Ascent', as he called it. Green's balloon with the basket attached stood 60 feet high and had crimson and gold stripes. It was also 'painted with a variety of allegorical subjects, principally from heathen mythology.'

On one side [said the *Blackburn Mail* of 9 April] were Flora, Agriculture and Plenty with a representation of Cybele drawn by a car of lions. In the centre of the other side was Juno with a figure of Aeolus at one end, having the winds chained in his cave and apparently watching the progress of a balloon, seen in the distance, with great anxiety.

'The number of visitors to the town was excessive,' said the report, 'and every window that commanded a view . . . was literally crowded to suffocation.' The balloon was blown towards Preston, where, said the *Preston Chronicle*, 'it afforded a high treat for crowds of people who hastened to the south side of the town to witness the majestic spectacle.' Green landed at Longton after travelling 14 miles.

During a flight from Bury to Edenfield in the following June, Green safely dropped three kittens by parachute. In the same month, as he was descending near the Leeds and Liverpool Canal on the outskirts of Blackburn after an ascent at Preston,

a boy caught hold of the grappling iron for the purpose of fixing it in the ground, and not getting disengaged from it, he, when Mr Green thought proper to rise again, was carried into the air, and having the presence of mind to retain his hold of the rope, was safely transported with the balloon across the canal without sustaining any other injury than a few slight scars on the face.

There was a similar incident at Salford on 16 October 1837, when Charles Green (1785–1870), brother of George and the most celebrated of the nineteenth-century aeronauts, ascended in the *Great Nassau Balloon*, which had caused a sensation in November of the previous year by carrying Green and two companions 480 miles in 18 hours from London to Weilburg, in the Duchy of Nassau, Germany. As Green began his 252nd ascent, a workman who attended the balloon, was seen hanging on to one of the ropes. The spectators watched in silence as the balloon rose above the city, but the workman, who was an old sailor, began to climb up the rope and to a tremendous outburst of cheering reached the basket when the balloon was about 250 feet from the ground.

In 1837, Lancashire also had a visit from the balloonist Mrs Graham, who made two ascents from the Liverpool Zoological Gardens while her husband stood by in a steamer in case the wind carried her out to sea. Both flights were uneventful.

On at least one occasion the spectators of a balloon ascent found themselves in danger. On 13 August 1849, Green took off from Preston in the 60ft high *Rainbow* balloon. It was the first ascent in the town for 21 years and vast numbers went to watch. 'Every available standing or clinging place from the lamp post to the church steeple had its respective occupiers,' said the *Preston Guardian*. There was also a number of 'venturesome gentlemen,' who had perched themselves near the cupola of the Corn Exchange. To everyone's alarm, the balloon struck the weather vane on the building and received an 18-inch tear as it almost wrenched off the letter 'S'. The car of the balloon swung violently and the gentlemen 'were in no small peril of having their craniums damaged.' Green brought down the balloon safely and before the end of the month made another flight to Accrington, where such a large crowd collected that he had great difficulty in leaving the town.

3. *Off to the Sea*

The rapid growth in Lancashire of a vast industrial society stimulated an insatiable demand for holidays by the sea. On foot, in carts and carriages, and then by packed excursion trains came an ever-swelling torrent of pleasure-seekers until large stretches of the county's once-deserted coast were as crowded as the new towns from which they drew so much of their support. As early as 1788, when Blackpool was 'a few houses ranged in a line with the sea,' Catherine Hutton, daughter of the resort's first historian, found there not only the Lancashire gentry and the opulent merchants of Liverpool, but also 'a species called

Boltoners'—rich, rough, but honest cotton spinners and manufacturers who were greatly enjoying the first fruits of the new era. It was the craze for sea-bathing that began the trek to Blackpool, Southport, Lytham and Morecambe Bay. The resorts had little else to offer, though by 1795, Blackpool, ever a pacesetter in matters of entertainment, boasted a news-room and circulating library, a company of comedians, a new chariot for the ladies and the Rev Mr Elstone 'who delivers most excellent admonitions.' In 1813, the traveller Richard Ayton found Blackpool 'the favourite bathing place of the county' and in his *Voyage Round Great Britain* wrote:

> Among the company are crowds of poor people from the manu-
> facturing towns, who have a high opinion of the efficacy of bathing,
> maintaining that in the months of August and September there is
> physic in the sea—physic of a most comprehensive description,
> combining all the virtues of all the drugs in the doctor's shop, and
> of course a cure for all varieties of disease. It is not, they imagine,
> any peculiar condition of their own systems, in the months I have
> mentioned, that gives the sea its effects upon them; but they conceive
> that during this period it is actually converted into a great dose, by
> the admixture of some ingredients which do not belong to its
> composition at other seasons. Their meaning is perfectly literal,
> when they say that there is physic in the sea, and they submit
> altogether to a very rough probation in order to receive the full
> benefit of it. Most of them come hither in carts, but some will
> walk in a single day from Manchester, distant more than forty miles;
> a tolerable kind of trial by way of beginning, for they rest here
> only three or four days, and in each of these undergo a course of
> seasoning quite as severe as that of the first. The earliest act of the
> morning is a draught of salt water, a quart, and sometimes two,
> which is followed, under the notion of fortifying the stomach by
> an equal quantity of gin and beer. This mixture swallowed, a man
> is properly prepared for the bath, in which he continues to paddle,
> either in or out of his clothes, for the remainder of the day. They
> always select a spring-tide for the time of their visit, when the water
> has most strength they say; and three or four days of it are supposed
> quite enough to prove the utmost effects of the physic, and they
> are generally sufficient to empty their pockets. They bring their tea
> and sugar with them, and pay nine-pence a day each for their
> lodging.
>   Their accommodations at night must not be forgotten in the
> account of their toils and difficulties. A single house here, and not
> a large one, frequently receives a hundred and twenty people to
> sleep in a night: five or six beds are crammed into each room, and
> five or six people into each bed; but, with every art of packing

and pinioning, they cannot all be stowed at one time: those, therefore, who have the places first are roused, when they have slept through half the night, to make way for another load—and thus every one gets his night's rest. A small cottage was shewn me, in which I should not have supposed there was more than comfortable room for the family inhabiting it; but which nevertheless, I was told, sometimes mustered fifty sleepers per night. Such a dose of three days when considered in all its component parts, would scarcely, it might be imagined, be beneficial to anyone; but the people must derive some good from it, or they would not take it with so much resolution and regularity. An occasional riot, that does absolute violence to every part of the body, and turns the whole order of it topsy-turvy, may be of some service to persons leading sedentary lives; and certainly no more effectual plan of general disturbance can be conceived than the annual course of walking, drinking, dipping and lodging, submitted to by these patient manufacturers.

The appearance of the beach here at high water is very remarkable; and, as I cast my eye along it, and saw it, for the length of nearly a mile, darkened with thick clusters of people, full of motion, and continually splashing in and out of the water, it brought to my mind the host of Puffins at Priestholme, as the only scene of life, and bustle, and noise, that could equal it. I could not help admiring the honest confidence with which both sexes, among the lower orders, bathed together, as if really, during this act of immersion,

Blackpool's rise to fame began in the 1750s, when it started to attract middle-class visitors for healthy seaside holidays. Although its image as a 'select' resort was a long time a'dying, by the 1820s it was more notable for the large number of working-class holidaymakers who came despite the still difficult access.

there was a temporary suspension of every feeling of dignity and decorum, which, for the most part, makes breeches and petticoats absolutely necessary. I observed here, and it was a novelty to me, that the ladies who used bathing-machines yielded themselves up to the care of men-guides, whose strength, I was informed, was often found requisite to resist the boisterousness of the sea on this beach. On such a consideration no one could object to their interference; and they are, moreover, steady, discreet men, who, from long familiarity with their employment, are considered as fairly naturalised among the ladies, and are looked upon as nothing more than old women.

On looking at the crowd without doors, one might be puzzled to conceive how they could possibly be lodged within, unless he were acquainted with that admirable economy of space that is practised in the disposal of poorer people. There are four or five boarding-houses for the politer part of the company, and even in these a system of packing is adopted, that is quite as much as can be patiently borne by one accustomed to anything more private than five in a bed. I dined at one of them, in company with nearly a hundred persons who must certainly have slept in families. People

Plan of the intended town of Morecambe from the Board of Health Report for Poulton, Bare and Torrisholme, 1851. Attempts to design a planned town, based on the apparent success of the new town of Fleetwood, were largely ineffective. The town grew in a haphazard and confused fashion, and there has been a problem in defining Morecambe's real role ever since.

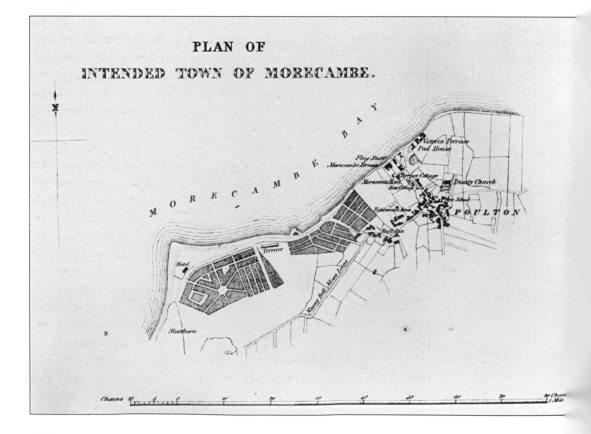

live here, in every respect, on very familiar terms. They meet regularly five times every day, in full concert, to eat together; and a general sense of friendliness and fellowship springs from this community of wholesome indulgences, that renders them little fastidious about the division of their room at nights.

When Ayton reached Poulton-le-Sands, now part of Morecambe, he found it almost as overflowing as Blackpool and learned at first hand how the problem of accommodating large numbers in small spaces was tackled.

I applied for a bed at the first public-house that I came to, but was peremptorily informed that I could neither have one, nor a part of one, there being already a company of sixty people in the house to be accommodated for the night. I had no reason to disbelieve this account, for the noise from within would have done no discredit to six hundred mouths. Unfortunately for me, this was the first day of a spring tide, and the crowd collected in the village were the manufacturers [hand workers] from the inland towns, come for the benefit of the physic in the sea. There was another public-house in the place, where I learned that I might have a bed: a piece of news which gave me quite as much surprise as satisfaction, for there were already men enough in and about the house to people the whole village. Six cart-loads had arrived in the course of the day; and the carts were now lying on their shafts before the house, in humble imitation of the coaches and chaises, and gigs, which we see stopping the way before more splendid establishments of this description. In the style and arrangement within doors, there was a general resemblance to the modes of genteeler boarding-houses, with some variations that were not a little entertaining to me. On entering the parlour of the visitors, which was the kitchen of the family, I found a long table laid out for a public supper, around which there was already collected a considerable party of men, each taking his preparatory pint and pipe. With the fumes of tobacco there mingled the fragrance of a large pan of beef-steaks and onions, and another of eggs and bacon, which were to compose the repast of the invalids. The rooms above the stairs were alive with company, but, on a summons to supper, all flocked together, forming a party of about forty people. There was a large proportion of women among them, many of whom were so gaily attired, that I thought they looked quite out of place in such an atmosphere, though, to tell the truth, they did not seem to be at all discontented with their circumstances. One or two indeed appeared disposed to spoil the common conviviality of the meeting, by some affected airs of delicacy and fastidiousness; but they met with no success, and were speedily

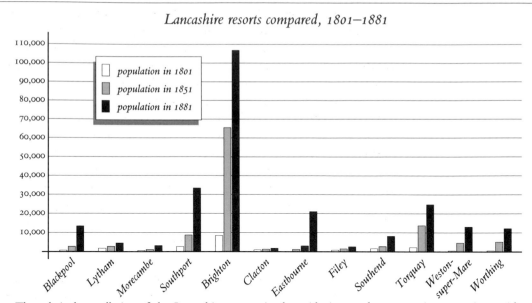

Lancashire resorts compared, 1801–1881

□ population in 1801
▨ population in 1851
■ population in 1881

Blackpool · Lytham · Morecambe · Southport · Brighton · Clacton · Eastbourne · Filey · Southend · Torquay · Weston-super-Mare · Worthing

The relatively small size of the Lancashire resorts in the mid-nineteenth century, in comparison with those of the south coast, is clear, as is the pre-eminence of Southport within Lancashire itself. But the growth rate of Blackpool was far greater than that of neighbouring resorts, and its meteoric rise in the second half of the century is clearly foreshadowed (adapted from statistics in J. K. Walton, *The English Seaside Resort; a social history 1750–1914* (1983), tables 1, 2, 3 and 5).

daunted by the honest and heedless vulgarity of the majority.

During supper no one had evidently any thought but of his plate; but when all that was dressed was eaten, and the pipes were filled, and the ale had made a circuit or two round the table, there burst forth a general uproar of talk and laughter, which became still more animated as the ale continued its revolutions; till a huge fellow, fierce and foaming, rose up, and after thumping the table with a quart pot, till no other sound was to be heard in the room, demanded a song. A song was sung, and again every tongue broke loose; till the gentlemen with the quart pot again interfered, and silenced all clamour but his own. And still the ale performed its rounds, till order was entirely confounded, and all was talking and singing, and laughing, and all together. The entertainment was novel, to me at least; and upon the whole, I was really inclined to think it more amusing than the ponderous decorum of higher company in higher places, with the formal dullness, or tiresome officiousness, of Mr President and Mr Vice.

The amusements of the evening terminated with a dance; but, at the time this was called for, the ale had been at least one round too much; and though every man in the company could rise from his chair, yet no one had any control over his motions, or could stand still, or move as he wished himself, or as others directed. The ladies were merely a little louder and merrier than usual, and were still able to jump about with spirit and precision, had they not been incessantly thrown into confusion by the blunders of their lawless partners, who, in spite of every effort employed to reclaim them, and keep them to the figure, threatened, at every step, to plunge headlong into the fire, or out of the window. There was no music, save the general roar of the room, and some irregular scraping of feet and clattering of quart pots, and a drowsy, crapulous muttering, meant for a tune, from some sick and sleepy guests, who still kept their chairs at the table. Time and exercise might eventually have given more sobriety and regularity to the dance: but, unfortunately, there was still more ale in the cellar, and the general complaint was still of being thirsty. This incorrigible symptom leaving me nothing to hope, I did not wait to witness the final demise of the company, but retired to my bed.

And now my tribulations began. The landlady, a neat, tidy-looking woman, whom I should not have suspected of such atrocities, conducted me up stairs, and opening a door, held her candle immediately under my nose, to guide me safely through several narrow passages, with room only for the legs sideways, made by four beds, which formed a blockade before the one intended for myself. Four people, she informed me in cold blood, were to sleep in each of the four beds, but I was to have only a single partner; and there, sure enough, before my eyes, soundly sleeping, and loudly snoring, lay my destined comrade, who had retired from the riot below, an early victim of ale and tobacco. My conductress, mistaking my silence for contentment, had nearly escaped from the room before I could find voice to arrest her steps, and unburthen my heart. My remonstrances, it may be imagined, did not want emphasis; but she listened to them without any kind of emotion; thought that my scruples were quite unconscionable; observed that we were all Christians, and flesh and blood alike; and finally forced me to compliance, as she supposed, by declaring, that if I did not sleep in the bed that was prepared for me, there was no other for me in the house. There is indeed (she said) a chaff bed in a hole at the top of the house: but I should scarcely think of offering that to a gentleman. Now this was a straw held out to a drowning man, and I eagerly seized hold of it. The chamber, I found was very literally described; but I had to rejoice that it would not hold more than one, and crept into my bed with the further satisfaction of knowing that I was removed, as far as possible, from the noise and smoke below.

On coming out of my hole at seven o'clock in the morning, matters appeared to be in much the same state as I had left them on the preceding night, the company having again betaken themselves to pipes and ale, with appetites sharpened by bathing, and copious draughts of salt-water. They were very lively under their trials, and seemed to be beginning the day with a kind of ease and contentment in their looks and manners, as if there was not the least doubt among them that they were going on pleasantly and prosperously. For my own part, I was almost exhausted, merely as a spectator of their revels, and made my escape from them into the open air with singular satisfaction.

Though the distress that followed the Napoleonic Wars and the harsh restrictions of factory life prevented the mass of Lancashire people from travelling to the coast, there was no decline in the popularity of the resorts. Visits by members of the growing middle classes ensured their progress; and for Blackpool and Lytham there was the additional patronage, if only on Sunday outings, of the working population of nearby Preston.

Southport, said by one writer in 1806 to have been 'scarcely hitherto known,' soon took its place among the leading bathing places, particularly after 1821, when Scarisbrick became accessible by canal from Manchester. In that year, according to the *Liverpool Kaleidoscope*, 'haylofts were let off at a shilling a head as sleeping rooms, without any bedclothes except horsecloths or straw.' The Manchester writer J.S. Gregson, in a poem published in the same periodical three years later, described how 'the busy burghers' of the city delighted in taking their families on the packet boat to 'that far-famed desert strand.' After travelling all day they reached Scarisbrick.

Lord Street, Southport, from Bland's *Annals of Southport* (1887). The quality of planning and design in Southport—including and laying out of the famous Lord Street—were primarily the result of strict controls exercised by the town's two landowning families, the Bolds and the Heskeths. This ensured that, even though it grew to be a very large town, Southport retained its 'quality' air.

> Where, like to claiming customs on the coast,
> The hulk is boarded by a clamorous host
> Of boys and jarvies, lords of caravans,
> Carts, coaches, jaunting cars, and shandy-dans,
> Like hookers-in soliciting pell mell
> To drive to Barlow's or to Clare's hotel.

The attractions of Lytham, unrecorded or perhaps unnoticed by Ayton in 1813, were chronicled in the same year by Captain William Latham.

> One circumstance must above all others render Lytham dear to those who have a strict regard to morality—vice has not erected her standard here. The numerous tribes of gamblers, unhappy profligators and fashionable swindlers find rapine and employment elsewhere. Innocent recreational delights, riding, walking, sailing and other modes of pastime banish cares from the mind, while the salubrity of the air expels disease from the body. Much diversion is found upon the two most excellent bowling greens on which part of the company are frequently seen, enjoying themselves with a revolving bowl.

It was about this time that Jonathan Peel of Accrington, calico printer and son of the first Robert Peel, began to spend his winters at Lytham. Perhaps it was the strict regard for morality that attracted him, for he was deeply religious and devoted much of his time to studying the

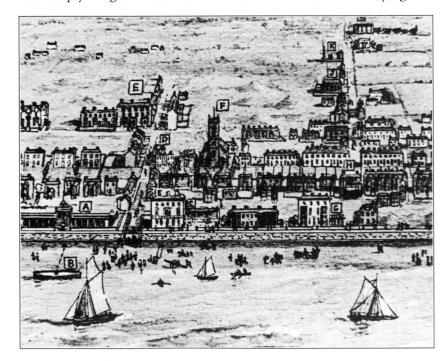

A detail of a *Bird's Eye View* of Southport, 1849, with yachts, bathing machines, and Lord Street running parallel to the beach.

Bible. His granddaughter, Catherine Jacson, wrote in her *Formby Reminiscences*:

> Each weekday he took his regular walk on the green beach . . . and each Sunday one of the two bathing machines the place was endowed with carried him and one or two elderly friends to the small white-washed church in the fields.

The Lytham she knew in the late 1820s consisted of 'a few houses down to the beach and some fishing cottages behind with one wide street across.' As in Blackpool considerable profits were made by the owners of these simple dwellings. The *Preston Chronicle* of 14 August 1824 said of Lytham and Blackpool:

> We may venture to say that these two watering places never witnessed such crowds of visitors of various classes as have this week continued to flock to them in search of health, pleasure and relaxation. Cottages calculated to lodge with comfort not more than half a dozen persons each, have been for many nights the receptacles for 20 or 30 inmates. Some idea of the vast influx of company may be formed from the fact that no less than 100 carts containing an average of eight persons each passed through Clifton turnpike on Saturday last.

By 1828 the trek to Lytham, particularly on the August 'Bathing Sunday', had become a stampede:

> The village was much thronged by visitors on Sunday last [said the *Preston Chronicle* of 30 August]. Almost every vehicle in Preston was in requisition to convey the company, and we were sorry to observe that the poor animals doomed to drag some of them, were under guidance of merciless brutes; in fact, it was actually difficult for the sober pedestrian to keep from under the wheels of some of the carriages, or for those who wished to travel at a moderate rate from being upset. One horse was so much overdriven that it expired soon after its arrival, while another received a severe injury from being driven over the battlement of a bridge.

Astonishing numbers continued to find accommodation in the cottages along the coast and something of a record must have been set at Blackpool in 1827 when crowds from East Lancashire slept in shifts, sixteen to a bed. People who had known the resorts in less turbulent days grew apprehensive at the disturbing trends that were appearing. The mixed bathing at Southport alarmed 'a scholar and gentleman,' who wrote in the *Liverpool Kaleidoscope* in 1823:

> At the height of the tide every machine is in motion, carrying indiscriminately, occupants of either sex, at no unsociable distance from each other, not even with screens which are common at all

continental bathing-places, but left to the uninterrupted gaze of the passing crowd.

Gregson, however, who had an appreciative eye for the 'lovely damsels' on the shore, said of their bathing:

Heedless of being seen by vulgar men
They dash and splash and splash and dash again
And though these feats the grinning beaux discern
They scorn to show a symptom of concern.

Lytham from the beach, from *Six Views of Blackpool and Lytham*, n.d.

Lytham was developed as a small resort after 1795, initially without much overview by its landowners, the Clifton family. From 1830, however, strict covenants and control over building ensured that a select and genteel community was created.

The girls may not have been concerned, but the authorities were and in 1824 or 1825 introduced regulations to govern the bathing. The sexes were segregated and a vacant space of one hundred yards was marked out by posts between the two bathing areas. Boat owners who came within thirty yards of a bathing machine were fined five shillings for each offence. (Sir George Head, who witnessed the bathing in 1835, said that in the circumstances the fine 'cannot be called exorbitant.')

Blackpool had its critics, too, and in August 1828 a correspondent of the *Preston Chronicle*, complaining about the 'want of order and decorum at our fashionable watering places,' described an incident which occurred there when he and 'fifty or a hundred visitors of both sexes were inhaling the breeze from the fine sea.' A gentleman, who turned out to be a county magistrate, was observed running through the assembly on the beach in pursuit of an empty bathing machine which was making its way down to the water. At the water's edge the

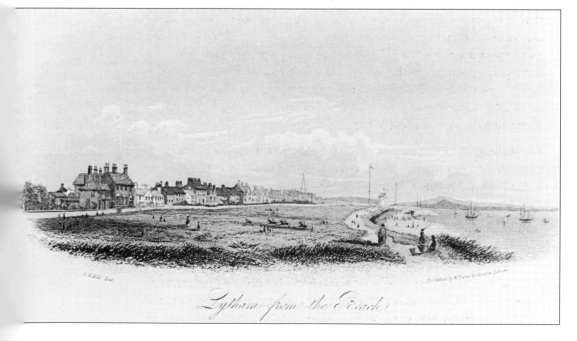

Lytham from the Beach

machine stopped and the magistrate stepped in. 'One would have thought,' the writer goes on, 'that he would have closed the door.' He did not.

With the most perfect nonchalance he began to disrobe with the door of the machine wide open, in the face of the assembled multitude—and it appeared that it was only after hearing a satirical laugh or hum of disapprobation from the people at this novel sight, that he saw the propriety, after thus taking off part of his undress, of disposing of the remainder with a closed door. The debut from the machine of the man's naked person so near the throngest part of the parade, at high water, at ten o'clock on a fine morning, at the very height of the season, did not all accord with my idea of decorum.

The 1830s saw a rapid expansion of the resorts—Lytham, said Catherine Jacson, 'lost all claim to seclusion'—and those who had a high regard for decorum were obliged to seek less frequented spots like Heysham, where 'genteel families' were specially catered for and where in 1836 Edward Baines found the visitors 'more select than numerous.' Countless Lancastrians now regarded sea-bathing as an essential part of their lives, and as William Howitt wrote in 1838:

The better class of operatives in the manufacturing districts consider it as necessary 'to go to the salt water' in the summer as to be clothed and fed for all the rest of the year. From Preston, Blackburn, Bolton, Oldham and all those spinning and weaving towns, you see them turning out by the whole wagon and cart loads, bound for Blackpool and such places; and they who have not seen the swarming loads of these men and women and children, their fast driving and their obstreperous merriment, have not seen one of the most curious scenes of English life.

In the following year A. B. Granville noted:

Manchester people have their favourite sea-bathing at Southport, those of Preston at Blackpool. To Southport the Manchester factor and artisan—the rich and middling comfortable—repair during two months of the year, either for a week of two's residence or a mere frolic. At that period one may see the walls of the smoky city placarded with 'Cheap travelling to Southport', 'Only five hours to Southport', 'Excursion to Southport': and vociferations from a thousand throats to the same effect are to be heard from the top of every species of vehicle in the principal streets.

Granville also recorded an account of a visit to Blackpool, from which it is clear that the sea-bathers had lost none of their appetite since the days of Ayton's tour of the Lancashire coast 26 years earlier:

There are two great rival houses, hotels yclept, in Blackpool, Nixon's and Dickson's—the Capulets and the Montagues—the white and the red rose. The former boasts of a larger and more extended building, conspicuously white from recent painting; the latter of a more projecting cliff over the strand, and a private terrace with greensward and neat rustic seats, quite still and retired, though fronting the sea. This last hotel is frequented chiefly by the higher class of visitors. At Nixon's the company is less select—or rather it is of a lower grade altogether.

Arrived at Nixon's in the very nick of time for dinner and the necessary permission having been obtained in my behalf and that of my travelling companion, we were admitted into a long and lofty apartment having some pretension to the rank of a banqueting-room, in which a long narrow table, groaning under a double line of tin-capped dishes, was awaiting the arrival of the company. A loud-sounding scavenger-like bell soon brought the latter, mob-fashion, into the room; when I took my place at the bottom of the table, near to my coach companion, who having always been a guest at Dickson's, or 'the upper house', sat himself down here to oblige me, not without symptoms of a curling lip and a turned-up nose.

Such a motley of honest-looking people—men, women, and children (for there were some whose chins did not reach the edge of the

Blackpool south beach from *Six Views of Blackpool and Lytham*, n.d.

table)—it has never been my fortune to meet under the like circumstances in such numbers before—fifty or sixty in all—except at
the anniversary dinner at some dispensary.

Methinks the highest in rank here might have been an iron-founder,
from near Bradford or Halifax, or a retired wine-merchant, from
Liverpool, who, in the palmy days of *Port*, found the Orporto trade
a thriving concern. About a dozen chamber-maids acted as waiters,
and there was not a vestige of man-servant, at which I heartily
rejoiced. It fell to my lot to dissect the chicken for the ladies.
Abundance of meat and sauce seemed to be the desirable thing. One
whom I had plentifully supplied with leg and pinion, and no small
portion of the parsley and butter, sent soon after to crave for the
breast, and a little more of the green sauce! The thing was appalling;
and the serious and busy manner in which every hand and mouth
seemed to be at work during the first ten minutes, *sans mot dire*,
plainly showed how palatable was the fare, and how keenly the
sea-air and the sea-bathing of Blackpool, had prepared the company
for it.

At Dickson's the scene is said to be somewhat more decorous and
stately; for there the consuming classes, like the articles to be con-
sumed, are of a different and a better order, although the charge at
each places differs only by sixpence; five shillings being the highest
price for not fewer than five meals daily.

Railways began a new era for the resorts. Lines from Preston to
both Fleetwood and Lancaster were opened in 1840, bringing an
immediate boom to a large stretch of the coast. Visitors to Blackpool,
said the *Bolton Free Press* of 15 August of that year 'are numerous
beyond all precedent.'

The town literally swarms with human beings, and every day fresh
loads roll in covered with dust and crying out for beds. Where all
the people sleep is a mystery, which we will clear up by telling the
reader that last Saturday eight individuals sought a night's rest in
an omnibus and three made the shuttle coach their couch. The
Fleetwood and Wyre railroad seems to have contributed largely to
this extraordinary influx of visitors. The hotels are reaping the
harvest they have had time to dream about through the long months
of winter.

Just a year later the *Lancaster Gazette* reported 'great animation' at
Poulton-le-Sands with 'persons from all parts' taking advantage of the
favourable tide and fine weather. Crowds went from Lancaster and
'returned in all manner of vehicles.' By 1850 the demand for accommodation at Blackpool and Southport had reached saturation point. At
Blackpool, said the *Preston Chronicle* of 20 July, 'railway carriages and

the station were placed at the disposal of persons to sleep in, but in addition to this a great number had to walk the beach all night.' A week later there was not a bed to be had in Southport and 'some parties,' said the *Preston Chronicle*, 'had to go to Lytham to sleep.'

The same edition of the newspaper also described the attractions of Southport:

> The town is enlivened by various groups amongst which are the black serenaders with a harp, etc. About 120 donkeys are kept, but the commissioners are for reducing the number. They wish to dissuade young women from driving these animals as servants are very scarce. The lasses seem to prefer fresh air and exercise and donkey driving to being in servitude. A man has about 20 bows and 100 arrows which he lets out at a cheap rate. Two targets are placed at a distance and the gentlemen seem to be amused by the ancient exercise of archery.

Of Blackpool in the following year it was said:

> None here need complain of lassitude or ennui—there is amusement for all. The horseman, pedestrian, the geologist, the conchologist and zoologist may ever find occupation on the shore and the herbalist on the land . . . The laying out of streets and walks, the erection of handsome houses and shops on every side, the establishment of elegant hotels and billiards, news and coffee rooms, lounges, bazaars, etc . . . and the opening and enlargement of places of worship bespeak the rising importance of the town.

Thanks to cheap rail trips, large numbers of the poorer classes were now visiting the resorts, but holidays, as opposed to day outings, were still a long way off. The Ashworths of Turton and Egerton, who for many years had encouraged their workpeople to take a week's break in summer, remained isolated pioneers. Change, however, was in the air as the following paragraph from the *Blackburn Standard* of 3 July 1850 shows:

> ANNUAL HOLIDAY AT DARWEN—A deputation from the operative classes (appointed at a meeting of delegates from all the friendly societies) waited upon the principal employers to request that the annual holiday in July this year be extended to two days instead of one as heretofore. It has been unanimously agreed by the latter that the holiday this year shall be two days, an indulgence for which the operatives and others have warmly expressed their thanks.

4. Cheap Trips

On a Saturday morning in September 1842, the sound of singing attracted the inhabitants of Poulton-le-Fylde to the village railway station, where, in the words of the *Preston Pilot*, they saw 'a truly impressive scene.' A train taking some 2,364 Sunday school scholars and their teachers on a day's outing from Preston to Fleetwood was drawn up at the platform with each of its twenty seven open carriages 'studded with numerous colours and bearing appropriate mottoes.' During the half hour's stay, 'the whole multitude were engaged in singing hymns,' leaving the villagers in no doubt that a new era had begun. Cheap trips became a prominent feature of Lancashire life as the railway system was extended during the 1840s and '50s; and the excitement they aroused, particularly among working people who had rarely stepped outside their own towns and villages, was immense. 'Cheap trips and pleasure excursions are now all the go and fashion,' said the *Preston Chronicle*, of 10 August 1844, describing a trip to Fleetwood on the previous Sunday.

> The time for starting was advertised for eight o'clock; but in consequence of the great number of passengers and Sunday pleasure-seekers eager to escape from the pent-up town, a delay of more than an hour occurred and it was half past nine before the train departed. It consisted of thirty eight carriages, all of which, with the exception of nine, were of the third class. What will the Bishop of London say regarding such profanity? Thirty eight carriages leaving Preston on a good Sunday morning? Off they went! One thousand seven hundred men, women and children, chiefly of the working classes, on a Sunday excursion. The 'Prince of Wales' and the 'Perseverance' engines were attached to the train and in brief time they reached Fleetwood. Three hundred of the passengers embarked on board the 'Nile' and made a voyage to Piel Harbour, whence several of the party proceeded on a visit to the celebrated ruins of Furness Abbey. A number were also landed on Piel Island, where they explored the ruins of the ancient castle. The excursion however, did not entirely pass without accident. A small boat which was conveying some of the pleasure-seekers (twenty one in number) from Rampside to the steamer, then about to return to Fleetwood was unfortunately capsised through the thoughtlessness of the passengers and the whole party were plunged into the very deep water. They were all, however, rescued from the peril which threatened them and placed in safety on the steamer. On the same day the 'Isabella Napier' took a numerous company to Sunderland [Point] and Glasson. We presume the attractions of these places are very

enticing for a large numbered wandered about exploring their beauties, regardless of time's onward march and were left behind. The train which conveyed the large party to Fleetwood returned to Preston about ten o'clock in the evening.

The poor people of Preston were treated to a day at Fleetwood every August, an event that must have been the highlight of their year. The organisers issued the travellers with printed instructions. Those for 1844 read:

> The steamer will continue to sail during the day round the Light House at twopence each, commencing at 12 o'clock when you will hear a bell ring. The baths at the North Euston Hotel will be open at two o'clock, one for males and the other for females, free. Buns and milk will be given out in the Market House, to commence about one o'clock, indicated by the going off of a balloon. The dance on the lawn (weather permitting) will follow the distribution; the place will be marked out by the Charity banner being fixed in the sand. Bathing in the sea may commence sometime before high water and persons are cautioned not to bathe too near the Public Promenade.

The repeal of the Corn Law in July 1846 was responsible for one of the first factory excursions to the seaside. Richard Cobden, a leading figure in the Anti-Corn Law League and the proprietor of the Crosse Hall calico printing works at Chorley, marked the triumph by giving his workpeople a day's wages and an outing to Fleetwood. Swelled by families and friends, a procession more than 1,000 strong marched from the works to the railway station at 6 a.m., to the music of two brass bands. 'A vast number of beautiful flags and banners' prepared specially at the works were carried by the trippers who filled the thirty nine carriages of the train. The delights of promenading, bathing and eating a huge meal at the Fleetwood Arms put the travellers in excellent good humour, and on their return to Chorley, where 'a vast concourse of persons assembled to witness their arrival,' they marched through the streets with the bands, and 'the festivities were not fully ended until the night was far spent.'

The opening of the railway to Blackpool in 1846 provided an extra stimulus to the cheap trip trade. The resort was chosen for the first mill outing from Swinton, for which large numbers saved up a shilling for the fare and a penny for the band. Few of the trippers had ever seen the sea, and as the great day approached, there was little else talked of in the district. Heavy sleepers, who were afraid of missing the train, which was due to make a very early start from Clifton Junction, grew apprehensive and engaged two old soldiers to go through the village at three o'clock in the morning playing a fife and kettle drum to wake everybody up.

The following report, from the *Blackburn Standard* of 6 June 1849 catches the excitement of the first cheap trip from the Haslingden district:

> On Saturday morning last, soon after daybreak, many of the most active inhabitants of Helmshore and Haslingden were to be seen running backwards and forwards to call their more sleepy neighbours up, in order that they might not be late for the train which was to convey them to Liverpool and back. At five o'clock, both the Helmshore and Haslingden stations were thronged with lads and lasses in their 'very best', and there appeared to be a good sprinkling also of men and women of more sober age. The book-keeper at the Haslingden station, who, unfortunately for him, slept in the office during the night, was 'rattled up' at half past three o'clock in the morning by eager people wanting tickets. The Helmshore party consisted of a large number of workpeople in the employ of Messrs. W. & R. Turner, the extensive merchants at Helmshore, who came up to Haslingden in a long train of carriages drawn by three splendid engines at about seven o'clock. They had an excellent band of music with them, the performers being workmen in the employ of Messrs. Turner. At the Haslingden station, the workpeople of Messrs. Dean and Cronkshaw were in attendance and anxiously awaiting the Helmshore train; and when it was descried in the distance, a general cry of 'It's coming lads' was raised, and the train shortly after reached the station, where a truly busy scene ensued. A number of empty carriages had been attached to the train for the Haslingden party. These were very soon filled without the least accident, and, after some hearty cheers at starting, the train conveying the merry expectant parties was soon out of sight. Not a single accident happened during the day. On the return of the party, the police were in attendance to facilitate the careful emptying of the carriages.

One of the passengers, then a boy of fourteen, recalled in later life:

> There were many stoppages on the way, but the novelty of the experience afforded compensation for a slow journey. At Ormskirk there was a stoppage of over an hour and some of the trippers left

Lancashire & Yorkshire Railway poster (L.R.O. DDPr 35/23, reproduced by kind permission of the County Archivist). By encouraging cheap excursions, to promote business, the railway companies came into conflict not only with those who wanted to maintain the select quality of the resorts but, in the case of Sunday excursions, sabbatarians

the trucks, climbed the sloping embankment and went prospecting for drinks, the train restarting in their absence.

The 'carriages,' he said, were open to wind and weather and the seats were far from comfortable by the end of the six-hour journey. One of the trippers declared that he could have reached Liverpool more quickly on a donkey.

In August 1848, some 1,200 workpeople employed by Hopwood and Sons of Blackburn went to Blackpool. Many 'had never seen a sea-bathing place, been on a railway or passed through a tunnel.'

> Fares [said the *Blackburn Standard*] were 1s. 8d. there and back; and to those in worse circumstances tickets were given or sold at reduced prices. A band was provided by Messrs. Hopwood; and about two hundred loaves and from two to three hundredweight of cheese were stowed in a horse box for those who were unable to comply with the injunction to 'provide themselves with refreshments.'

The trippers flocked to the beach, where their foot, hop, blind and donkey races 'afforded great amusement and attracted a good number of the visitors staying in Blackpool.' The prizes were hats, caps and ladies' dresses.

During Whit week 1848, some 116,000 people left Manchester on cheap trips; in the following year the figure rose to 150,000 and in 1850 to 202,543. The railway companies, hard pressed to meet the growing demand from the excursionists, brought ballast wagons into service. They certainly made few efforts to remove the hazards and discomforts of cheap travelling as a workman from L. Charnley's mill at Lower Darwen found as he headed in an open carriage for Blackpool in July 1851.

> His hat [said the *Blackburn Standard*] was either knocked or blown from his head, and he was advised to jump out of the train after it, an experiment he performed without any serious injury to himself. The man recovered his hat, but lost the train, which was going at a rapid pace.

During the same month, the East Lancashire Railway Company ran a train of ninety eight carriages and five engines from the Preston area to Liverpool. The train, probably the largest ever to run in Lancashire, carried 3,000 workpeople from ten cotton mills in Preston, Bamber Bridge and Lostock.

The poor people's trip from Preston to Fleetwood remained as popular as ever, and the only cause for regret, the organisers reported in 1851, was that many persons 'who are far from being objects of poverty, manage to possess themselves of tickets to the exclusion of others who are really deserving.' The trippers still received their printed instructions and advice, which included the following passage, inserted no doubt at the behest of Joseph Livesey, the teetotal pioneer and one of the organisers of the treat:

> The committee hopes all will enjoy themselves rationally and avoid the public houses and beer shops . . . There are houses in most of the principal streets where you can get hot water and the use of cups and saucers, etc., at a small charge, and where you can be supplied with eatables at prices quite as cheap if not cheaper than at public houses. Persons intoxicated will not be allowed to return by the trains.

ALTHAMS
POPULAR DAY TRIP TO
BLACKPOOL
On Saturday, August 2nd, 1879.

The cheap trips changed the character of the Lancashire resorts, with Blackpool quickly becoming the great favourite of the working classes. It was a transition that was not without its opponents. In August 1851, the *Preston Pilot* declared:

> Unless immediate steps are taken, Blackpool as a resort for respectable visitors will be ruined. The sights and scenes on Sunday last were disgraceful in the extreme, and they together with the inconveniently crowded state of the beach rendered it compulsory for all persons having any regard for decency to remain in the house . . . Unless the cheap trains are discontinued or some more effective regulations made for the management of the thousands who visit the place, Blackpool property will be depreciated past recovery.

This was one of the most erroneous prophecies of the nineteenth century. Most journals took a different view; and as early as 1845, the *Manchester Guardian* had 'rejoiced' in the extension of cheap travelling 'as a great moral agent':

> Those who go from home to see new scenes of towns and country have an interest excited in what lies beyond their daily view; their minds are enlarged . . . they become sober and economical that they may often enjoy this purer source of excitement and recreation.

Six years later, *The Economist* described the railway as the Magna Carta of poor people's motive freedom. 'How few among the last generation,' it asked, 'ever stirred beyond their own village? How few among the present will die without visiting London?' If one substitutes Blackpool for London, then the answer was a very small number of Lancastrians indeed.

This advertisement characterises the many thousands which were posted on stations and public places throughout Lancashire, offering 'the masses' the possibility of cheap trips to the seaside— though in the 1870s and 1880s the emphasis was still on day visits rather than holidays.

Morecambe and Southport joined in the railway boom during the 1850s. The North Western Railway opened the line to Morecambe in June 1848, and soon met a brisk demand, particularly from the West Riding of Yorkshire. Long and well-filled excursion trains were arriving almost daily, said the *Lancaster Gazette*, of 2 August, and many people were unable to find beds.

The Manchester and Southport line, opened at Whitsuntide 1855, prompted the following report by the local paper:

> Never before within memory has the town witnessed so busy and bustling a scene as its streets presented during Whit-week. The railways from the manufacturing districts poured in their thousands daily, who flowed through the streets in one vast living stream and swarmed on the wide expanse of shore like a newly-disturbed ant-hill . . . The donkeys and donkey carriages had a rare time of it and seemed to afford rare amusement to the excursionists . . . The Churchtown bus was crowded every journey from roof to steps, and every other species of conveyance was in continuous request.

The new line began a great battle for the cheap trip traffic, which brought an outburst in the leader columns of the *Blackburn Standard* of 15 August:

> The Lancashire and Yorkshire and the East Lancashire Railway are now running at an insane rate of competition which cannot end to the advantage of either company and which cannot much longer continue without entailing some unpleasant consequences on the public. The traffic competed for, is that between Manchester and intermediate stations of both lines, and Liverpool and Southport. To both these destinations passengers are conveyed at fabulously low prices and in number which call into exercise all the available locomotive power of both companies. On Saturday last this absurd competition was brought to its culminating point by the conveyance of passengers from Manchester and Southport for one shilling—six miles for 1*d*. on one line and ten miles for 1*d*. on the other. Some 9,000 or 10,000 are said to have left Manchester on Saturday. Rough youths, frequently with tobacco pipes in their pockets, are thrust unceremoniously into first-class carriages. The effect of their occupancy of these vehicles may easily be conjectured. These cheap trips show the locomotive propensities of the masses.

In his book, *Eccles and its Wesleyan Sunday Schools*, Edward Moss describes an excursion to Southport from Patricroft in 1856. The journey over the East Lancashire Company's line through Bury, Accrington and Blackburn took four to five hours, an insufferably long time for the party from Eccles, Barton and Davyhulme, who sat on hard seats in carriages which were half open at the sides. The passengers had to endure a tearing wind, but the boys tied their coloured handkerchiefs to the bars that supported the roofs, and the train 'ran fluttering through the country like a travelling fair or an itinerant clothes-drying ground.'

> Near Accrington [the account continues] a notice cautioning the driver to run slowly round a dangerously sharp curve was disregarded by the already half-intoxicated driver with the result that the train was very nearly overturned, the passengers being thrown into promiscuous heaps and immediately thrown back again with much violence as the carriages righted themselves.

The train was halted by the stoker, the driver was removed, and 'all went well thereafter.'

5. *Pleasure Gardens*

After the seaside resorts, the most popular recreational centres in Lancashire were the pleasure gardens of Manchester and Liverpool. The first—23 acres in the Irk Valley, Manchester—was opened by Robert Tinker in 1796 and for more than half a century enabled great crowds to escape from the industrial city into a totally new and often exciting world. To dance to the music of a brass band, to go on roundabouts and swings and then to 'partake of tea and other refreshments at small tables standing under overhanging trees or in alcoves covered with creepers' must have been among the most memorable experiences of many working people. On special occasions Tinker hung the trees with lamps, gave firework displays and sent up balloons. His more prosperous patrons were offered 'good grass for horses on moderate terms.' Tinker died in 1836, but the pleasure grounds (known by this time as the Vauxhall Gardens) continued until 1851 when they were found to contain a valuable deposit of foundry sand and were carted away. Thanks mainly to the coming of railways, pleasure gardens were now drawing crowds not only from the two cities, but also from a wide area beyond.

While visiting Liverpool in 1832, Thomas Atkins, the proprietor of a travelling menangerie, obtained the lease of nine acres of land which he laid out with walks, lawns, a theatre, an aviary and a zoo. The Zoological Gardens—they were on the south side of Derby Road—aroused interest even in Manchester; and Sir Benjamin Heywood has described how a party of thirty to forty members of the Mechanics'

Institution went to see them in 1833 'by the early train on the railway' and how 'one of the party read to us descriptive accounts of the animals as we stood round their respective enclosures.' Like Tinker, Atkins kept up public interest by introducing new attractions. Visitors in 1846 were able to see 'four noble lions' and 'the stupendous elephant Rajah who bathes several times during the day.' There were also concerts, firework displays and a centrifugal railway. Three years later ballet was introduced—the first was *Crystalline or the Invisible Maiden*—and by way of contrast there was 'a colossal pictorial representation of Constantinople.' Balloon ascents, archery, rifle shooting and military displays were other innovations. Blondin, the tightrope walker, appeared in 1860 and again in 1863, the year the lease expired. During the 1840s Liverpool also had the Strawberry Gardens, renowned for tea and shrimps and gala nights when there was a band for dancing. At a later date the gardens were run by a prize fighter who introduced boxing matches and 'sparring festivals.'

Meanwhile in Manchester, John Jennison, one-time proprietor of the Stockport Tea Gardens, was using his enormous energy and restless imagination to transform 36 acres of waste land adjoining the Belle Vue public house into the most famous of all Northern pleasure grounds. His zoological collection at first consisted of a number of domestic animals in cages, some parrots, four monkeys and a borrowed pelican, but when a private zoo at Higher Broughton closed in 1840 Jennison bought most of the stock. He also acquired 'The King of Oudh's Fighting Tiger' and a chimpanzee that smoked a pipe, drank tea and enjoyed being dressed as a Victorian swell. The zoo, however, was only one part of Belle Vue; and in 1848, Jennison's achievements during the previous twelve years were set out in the following advertisement:

ZOOLOGICAL GARDENS
Bellevue, Hyde Road, Manchester

These magnificent gardens have for a number of years constituted one of the most fashionable promenades in the vicinity of Manchester, and the proprietor has spared neither trouble nor expense, annually, to add to the comfort and recreation of all who may favour him with their patronage.

The Gardens and Pleasure Grounds cover an area of thirty-six acres, containing a large and choice collection of foreign and British live animals and birds, and a splendid museum of stuffed birds and other natural curiosities. A labyrinth or maze on the same plan as the one at the Royal Gardens, Hampton Court, has in the centre two octagonal Gothic aviaries, one of which is lighted with eight magnificent stained-glass windows, the intermediate spaces being filled with reflecting mirrors, which give a most brilliant appearance.

ZOOLOGICAL GARDENS,
BELLEVUE, HYDE ROAD,
MANCHESTER.

Mr. JENNISON, PROPRIETOR,

Trusts that the Importance of this Place of Public Resort, equal in reference to the Capital expended in bringing the GARDENS to their present State of Perfection—the Novel and Attractive Style in which they are disposed—their Unparalled Extent—the Vast Assemblage of OBJECTS OF INTEREST, Natural and Artificial which they present—the Facility and Cheapness of Access—the Succession of PUBLIC ENTERTAINMENTS, introduced during the Season, and his determination to maintain the Strictest Decorum and Propriety in their Management, may induce many to avail themselves of a means of Recreation, so Cheap, Healthful and Improving, and confirm the resolution still further to render BELLEVUE Worthy the Support of the Community of Manchester and the Neighbourhood by

The Frequent Introduction of Additional Features of Attraction.

Since Last Season, the Improvements and Additions have been on an Extensive and Varied Scale, amongst these may be named the Erection of a

SPACIOUS BUILDING
FOR THE BETTER CONVENIENCE OF THE

MUSEUM OF CURIOSITIES,
STUFFED ANIMALS AND BIRDS,

And other Objects, to which *Great Additions* have recently been made, including Two VERY FINE SPECIMENS of the

LION AND LIONESS,
A NEW MONKEY HOUSE,

Has also been Constructed, in which is placed a MONSTER CAGE, 21 *Feet in Height and Covering an Area of upwards of* 600 *Square Feet.*

A GYMNASIUM,

Complete in every detail, has been introduced for the Healthful Recreation of frequenters to the Gardens. To the previous Extensive ZOOLOGICAL COLLECTION may be mentioned,

The Addition of Remarkably Fine Specimens of the Leopard, Striped Hyæna, Ocelot or Tiger Cat, Wolf, Bear, Zebu Bull, Ostrich, Vulture, and innumerable other varieties.

In the Grounds the Numerous SERPENTINE and other ORNAMENTAL WALKS and PROMENADES have been entirely renovated and a Large Variety of Exotic and other Plants added.

THE EXTENSIVE SHEET OF WATER,

On which Float many Small PLEASURE BOATS for the further Accommodation of the Public, continues to be a source of Great Attraction ; and the

ELIZABETHAN MAZE,

Affords much Amusement, especially to Juveniles.

To the Admirers of HORTICULTURAL and DECORATIVE GARDENING, the Hot Houses and Green Houses, Ornamental Parterres, Fountains, Shaded Walks, Rockeries, Grottoes, Caves, Arbours, &c., present a Pleasing Assemblage of Objects for contemplation. The

SPACIOUS DANCING PLATFORM,

Has been enlarged to an Area of upwards of 15,000 Square Feet, and in the event of Unfavourable Weather, Accommodation is provided in the Gardens for the shelter of thousands. *Three Floral and Horticultural Shows are held Annually in the Gardens, at stated intervals.*

BELLEVUE is Situated Two Miles from MANCHESTER, on the Road to HYDE; it also adjoins the LONDON and NORTH-WESTERN Line, at the Newly-Erected LONGSIGHT STATION, which renders it easy of approach from MANCHESTER, STOCKPORT, MACCLESFIELD, and the STATIONS on the Line to CREWE ; it is also within Half a Mile of the GORTON STATION on the SHEFFIELD and LINCOLNSHIRE Line.

Visiters can be Accommodated with Wines and Spirits of the Finest Qualities, Guiness's Bottled Stout, Breakfasts, Dinners, Tea and other Refreshments, at a Moderate Charge.

A Powerful Brass Band in daily attendance during the Summer Season.

N. B.—The Gardens are open every day throughout the year, as in Winter they are very appropriate for SKATING, the Waters being very extensive and less than three feet in depth, which renders this amusement perfectly Safe.

Belle Vue was perhaps the most famous of all Lancashire 'pleasure grounds'—other than those at seaside resorts—and was also one of the longest-lived. Its name was almost a byword for a day out—'going to Belle Vue' was something to do on an afternoon off. Close to the city (though originally laid out when the surroundings were rural) and later deep within the built-up area, it was easily accessible, cheap and packed with interest. This advertisement dates from 1850.

There is also a fine bowling green; and in a large paddock are a number of deer, which roam at large in their natural condition. Upon an extensive lake float several light and secure pleasure boats by which parties fond of aquatics may enjoy themselves. Gorgeous fountains throw streams of water in various designs. Numerous and extensive flower beds laid out with admirable taste display an endless variety of flowers, plants &c. of the rarest description; while the arbours, bowers, dancing saloon &c., afford shelter from rain for thousands of visitors. From a large tower which rises to the height of forty feet, the panoramic view of the surrounding country is of the most delightful character—interspersed as it is with sequestered villages, the distant spires of churches, the City of Manchester, and the busy towns of Stockport, Oldham, Ashton, &c., together with the hills of Derbyshire, Cheshire and Yorkshire stretching out in broad and massive outline: these with a thousand other distant objects render the view most extensive and magnificent.

Three grand floral and horticultural exhibitions are held annually at the gardens. Wines, spirits and other refreshments may be had: and lunches, dinners and tea on reasonable terms.

Boarding schools and day and Sunday schools accommodated with innocent amusement.

An efficient brass band in attendance daily.

N.B. The gardens are open every day throughout the year, as in winter it is a very appropriate place for skating, the waters being very extensive and less than three feet in depth, which renders this amusement perfectly safe.

Jennison also introduced horse and dog racing, a spectacular annual firework display—the first in 1852 was 'The Bombardment of Algiers'—and the September brass band contest which began in 1853.

The Pomona Gardens at Hulme enjoyed considerable popularity from the 1840s, and the proprietors, by sponsoring regattas on the adjoining and highly-polluted River Irwell provided one of the most unexpected sights of the whole nineteenth century.

6. *Photography*

'Fixing the shadow of the human form and face would almost be considered impossible . . . but such an extraordinary achievement is now to be seen in Liverpool,' the *Bolton Chronicle* told its readers on 19 October 1841. Photography had reached Lancashire. Advertisements informed the 'Nobility, Gentry and Inhabitants' of the county that 'faithful miniature likenesses . . . 'won from the hand of Nature' in the space of a few seconds' were to be obtained complete with frame for only a guinea each.

Lancashire's first photographic studio was 'a neat and elegant building' in the Mount Gardens, St James's Walk, and housed apparatus, 'the discovery of which is ranked among the greatest scientific achievement of the present age.' For their guineas, the sitters received a small portrait on metal, called a daguerreotype, after the Frenchman L. J. M. Daguerre, who introduced his process into England in 1839. On 23 March 1841 Richard Beard, an enterprising Londoner who had begun life as a coal dealer, opened the first professional portrait studio in Britain at the Royal Polytechnic Institution, London, combining Daguerre's technique with the mirror camera of the American Alexander Wolcott. The Liverpool photographers paid £2,500 to the patentees for the right to take portraits in the city and for ten miles around.

Daguerre's photographic plates were of silvered copper, highly polished and sensitised with iodine and bromide. After being exposed in the camera, the plates were held over a cup of mercury heated to 75°C. The image was then fixed with a solution of thiosulphate of soda and toned by treating with gold chloride.

The early photographic studios had roofs of blue glass, beneath which on a platform the patrons sat as immovably as possible until their likenesses had been captured. On sunny days this took only a few seconds, but when it was wet and gloomy the sitting might take a minute or more. A reporter of *The Times* was much impressed by the new wonder.

> The likenesses which we saw were admirable and closely true to nature, beauties and deformities being alike exhibited. The appearance of the miniature . . . is that of a mezzotint engraving, the likeness being no question of opinion, but plain matter of fact, for nature . . . makes 'no mistake'. There is such subtlety of touch and tone in the likeness as might fill a Vandyke or a Lawrence at once with delight and despair . . . Those who are fond of being flattered will certainly not patronise the photographic method of taking likenesses; but on the other hand, they who really want to know, and we presume that to be the majority, will unquestionably spend a guinea with great willingness in the production of a miniature portrait which their fathers and mothers, wives, sisters and brothers may 'swear to'.

Beard opened a studio in Ducie Place, Manchester, on 18 November 1841, warning the public that 'Dense fog is the only state of the

Taking a daguerreotype photograph in the early 1840s. By the 1850s photography was well established and later in the century it became an almost obligatory part of trips to the seaside or recording family events, even for the relatively poor. The albums of Lancashire families (and now the museum and library collections of the county) are full of countless such pictures, with people in their finery in stiff formal poses.

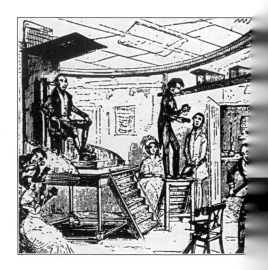

atmosphere which will interfere with the success of the extraordinary discovery.' John Dalton was among the first to be photographed.

7. Music

'In the densely-populated manufacturing districts . . . music is cultivated among the working classes to an extent unparalleled in any other part of the country,' wrote George Hogarth in his *Musical History* of 1835. The parishes of Eccles, Leigh and Deane alone had enough musicians for a 120-page collection of 'sketches'. The author William Millington, a Worsley millwright, was born in 1809 and in 1884 wrote his book 'to show what a high state of efficiency was attained in the study and practice of vocal and instrumental music in the early part of the nineteenth century.' He tells the story of a group of men from the Eccles district who were engaged to sing at a festival in Newcastle upon Tyne. The stagecoach on which they planned to travel was full, so they immediately set out to walk the 135 miles. They began their journey on a Sunday night and arrived on Wednesday afternoon in time to take part in a performance of Handel's *Israel in Egypt*. Millington's account of Ellenbrook Chapel choir with 'its excellent small band' would have applied equally to scores of similar groups throughout the county. Many of the Ellenbrook members were hand-loom weavers who made tremendous sacrifices to become proficient musicians.

In 1862, when the Cotton Famine brought terrible distress to Lancashire, Edwin Waugh (1817–1890) wrote of the 'swarms of strange, shy, sad-looking singers and instrumental performers in the work-worn clothing of factory operatives,' who went about Manchester, 'pleading for help in touching wails of simple song like so many wild birds driven by hard weather to the haunts of man.'

> I believe [Waugh goes on] there is no part of England in which the practice of sacred music is so widely and lovingly pursued amongst the working class as in the counties of Lancashire and Yorkshire. There is no part of England, where, until recently, there have been so many poor men's pianos, which have been purchased by a long course of careful saving . . . The great works of Handel, Haydn, Beethoven and Mozart have solaced the toil of thousands of the poorest workpeople of Lancashire . . . It is not uncommon to meet working men wandering over the hills with their musical instruments to take part in some village oratorio many miles away.

Waugh then recalls a meeting, some years earlier, with the 'Larks

of Dean' ('Th' Deighn Layrocks') a group of musicians from Rossendale, whose society had flourished from the middle of the eighteenth
century.

> In the twilight of a glorious Sunday evening I was roaming over
> the heathery waste of Swinshaw towards Dean in company with a
> musical friend of mine, who lived in a neighbouring clough, when
> we saw a little crowd of people coming down a moorland slope
> far away in front of us. As they drew nearer, we found that many
> of them had musical instruments and when we met, my friend
> recognised them as working people living in the district and mostly
> well known to him. He inquired where they had been and they
> told him they had 'bin to a bit ov a sing deawn i' th' Deighn.'
> 'Well,' he said, 'can we have a tune here?' 'Sure yo con, wi' o'
> th' pleasure i' th' world,' replied he who acted as spokesman; and
> a low buzz of delighted consent went through the rest of the
> company. Then they ranged themselves in a circle around their
> conductor and they played and sang several fine pieces of psalmody
> upon the heather-scented mountain top. The scene . . . made an
> impression upon me which I shall not easily forget. Long after we
> parted from them, we could hear their voices softening in sound
> as the distance grew, chanting their way down the echoing glen
> and the effect was wonderfully fine.

In his autobiography, the cotton spinner Moses Heap tells of the
intense fervour with which Rossendale people pursued their music-
making. Many houses 'were both workshops and music shops' in which
the hand-loom weavers sang as they toiled. To give himself more time
for music, one weaver 'contrived to couple four looms together with
strings, levers and pulleys so that he could produce four pieces of cloth
at one time.' He also made a cello which he played in chapel on
Sundays. Another man walked to Manchester and back, a round trip
of 40 miles, to see a score of Handel's *Solomon* and a group of young
men broke into a chapel at Crawshawbooth because they were impatient
to copy a new tune. On another occasion a youth of 16 carried his
blind and crippled father for three quarters of a mile to a performance
of *Messiah* at Dean; the father sang the tenor solos. Heap knew people
who tramped over the hills in all weathers to join friends in cottage
concerts lasting long into the night. He recounts the story of a young
man, who, after a day's work, walked from the village of Dean to
Haslingden Grane—six miles over two ranges of hills—for an evening's
practice.

> Midnight passed and as 2 a.m. approached, he ventured to say he
> thought he should be getting home as he 'had to be up middlin'
> soon i' th' morning.' An old man, who also had several ranges of

Besses o' th' Barn Band, 1860, from J. N. Hampson's *Origin, History and Achievements of Besses o' th' Barn Band* (n.d.).

The strong tradition of local music-making, which was shared by Lancashire and Yorkshire, was a major element in the cultural life of many communities. Some groups of musicians achieved a wider renown—in the case of the Besses o' th' Barn Band a national fame which has lasted to the present day.

hills to cross, reprovingly said, 'Young chap, if tha'rt allus i' such a hurry, tha'll never mak a musician as long as ever tha lives.'

Heap knew the 'Layrocks' well. Handel gave them unfailing delight, but they played and sang any music 'going at a fine tilting speed.' Their own compositions were largely hymns and anthems and 'if their tunes were often more florid than refined and their renderings more robust than elegant, the faults were not greater than the too-common opposite one of tame and spiritless singing and playing by some choirs and congregations today [1904].'

One might have expected the factory system to retard the musical activities of the working classes, but in Rossendale there is no evidence that this occurred. Heap first took singing lessons at Goodshaw when he was 15 and working more than 70 hours a week in a mill. Forty others attended the class in the tiny hamlet. Heap was also a frequent visitor to a farmhouse near Loveclough where 'I could hear two pianos played at the same time and also one or two violins.' In 1845 a choral society was formed at Crawshawbooth. The members practised in the village school and on Good Friday of the following year gave their first public concert with a choir of 60. It is remarkable enough that a group of working people, most of whom spent 12 hours or more each day in a cotton mill, met regularly in the evenings to study music. It is even more remarkable that their concert, for which they engaged soloists from as far afield as Manchester and Liverpool, consisted entirely of works by Handel, Haydn, Mozart and Beethoven.

Many similar stories could be told. Works by the same four composers were chosen by members of the Darwen Choral Society for a concert on Christmas Day, 1844, to mark the opening of a new organ at the William Street Sunday and Day School. The standard of the performance led a correspondent of the *Bolton Free Press* to remark:

> A stranger hearing these Lancashire chorus singers for the first time would have been delighted and surprised at their wonderful capabilities in the management of these sublime compositions.

'Bands of music' paraded the streets of Lancashire towns and villages upon the least excuse and their number was legion. But not until 1852 did anyone think seriously of promoting a contest. Then the proprietor of the Belle Vue Zoological Gardens in Manchester invited fife and drum bands to compete for a prize. The event was well received and

Music script of the Deighn Layrocks song, *Maid of the Mill* (Lancashire Record Office, with thanks to Rawtenstall Library).

Music and song were closely associated with the preservation and fostering of interest in Lancashire dialect and verse, and many of the nineteenth-century dialect writers also wrote the words of songs.

in the following year he staged the first brass band contest. Eight bands competed and there was an audience of 16,000. The championship, won in 1853 by Mossley Temperance Band, became a much-sought prize and aroused the first stirrings of civic pride in the manufacturing towns, which, through the prowess of their bands, at last had something to boast about.

J. H. Elliott, in his history of the brass band movement, tells how the Mossley bandsmen used to get up at 4 a.m. to practise the test piece before starting work, and how the euphonium player appointed himself knocker-up and rattled the bedroom windows of his colleagues with a clothes prop. There was a memorable occasion when the drummer acquired a new instrument and was overcome during the night with a desire to give it a trial.

> Neighbouring cottagers, who were roused from their sleep by the unwonted disturbance, were compensated, on peeping through their curtains, by the spectacle of a night-shirted bandsman drumming himself up and down the road in the moonlight.

By the 1850s 'banding' had taken a tremendous hold on Lancashire. Brass bands sprang up everywhere and were numerously supported at contests with the fanatical zeal that was later accorded to football teams. When Bacup Old Band competed at Belle Vue in 1864 the whole town became passionately involved, and in the words of Isaac Leach, the band's historian:

he interior of the
entlemen's Concert
all, Manchester
om *Manchester Old
d New*, volume 3).

The excitement in the neighbourhood was intense, and for days before the contest the fate of the band at Belle Vue was almost the sole topic of conversation. The rehearsals in the yard of Broadclough Mill on the Sunday before the contest were attended by thousands. On the morning of the contest special excursion trains were run from Bacup and the mills had to stop.

Words are too weak to describe the scene inside the large hall at Belle Vue when the Bacup board was hoisted as the winner of the first prize. The excursionists from Bacup were frantic with joy and could not tell how to express their feelings. It was after midnight when the band reached Bacup where the whole of the inhabitants were out awaiting their arrival. Along Newchurch Road the band played *John Brown's Body* and the crowds, thousands in number, joined in the strains.

In the following year the band, supported by even greater numbers, again won the Belle Vue championship and the enthusiasm as they walked through the streets from the railway station at midnight 'could not have been surpassed,' says Leach, 'if they had been a victorious army returning from the wars.'

Among the supports at the 1864 contest were six enthusiasts from Weir, who decided on the way home that they would form a band in the village. The result was the celebrated Irwell Springs Band, which held its first practice in a bedroom with a bedstead serving as a bandstand. The spirit of the pioneers may be judged from the laconic entry that was made in the minute book when players were being recruited:

NAME: *L. Hey*
CHOICE OF INSTRUMENT: *Aught*

Not to be outdone by their neighbours at Weir, a group of working men in the village of Goodshawfold collected enough money to buy some old instruments, which were put in working order by a local tinsmith. The men practised for some months in a cellar and at length decided they were competent enough to perform a march through the streets:

Every inhabitant turned out to discover what the funny noise was [one of the players recalled later] and when they found it was the band there was such jubilation as never occurred in the fold before. Home-brewed ale was brought out and this seemed to put courage into the bandsmen. A few weeks later, the band went on Hameldon Moor for the next attempt to play a march. All the fold residents went with them. On striking up, horses, cattle, sheep and wild animals flew in terror. I never could tell which made the most noise—the band or the animals.

From inauspicious beginnings such as this scores of Lancashire bands became town and village institutions and many attained a standard of proficiency that was outstandingly high.

Each summer the industrial towns of Lancashire staged their brass band contests on splendid Saturdays of intense excitement and carnival gaiety when even the cotton masters were known to close their factories. The early visitor to Bacup on 15 August 1868 would have seen sixteen boys 'dressed in fantastic colours' drawing a rushcart adorned with musical instruments and kitchen utensils. These were the doffers from Shepherd's mill, who were to keen to outshine their opposite numbers from the mill of Smith and Sons. Rushcart No 2, when it made its appearance later in the morning, was a good match for its rival. It was covered with a profusion of evergreens and copper kettles and carried a placard: 'May the best band win the first prize'. Its young attendants 'wore long white stockings with knickerbocker trousers secured at the knee by coloured ribbons' and had on crowns made of coloured paper. Throughout the morning special trains, each crowded with supporters, arrived at the station, from which the bands marched to their quarters playing lively airs. Promptly at one o'clock, to the cheers of 10,000 followers, the eight competing bands paraded up Market Street to the contest ground overlooking the town. There the instruments to be given as prizes were suspended from a cross beam and were much admired. Throughout the sunny afternoon and until seven in the evening the bands played selections arranged from well-known operas, after which individual players competed for a four-valve euphonium, a tenor horn and a soprano cornet. The winning band, Matlock, received £30 and a bass drum (new skeleton model) worth fourteen guineas, and ended the contest 'by playing their prize air amidst great cheering.'

Listening to orchestral music and opera was the privilege of the well-to-do, though it was a privilege often abused by some of those who supported the societies that kept the flame of the culture alight. The managers of the Manchester Gentlemen's Concerts complained in 1803 of their 'great repugnance in being obliged to animadvert upon the loud conversation with which preceding performances have been embarrassed,' and Sir Charles Hallé, when he came to England nearly half a century later, was warned that loud piano playing at concerts prevented the ladies from talking. It was not until Hallé began his own concerts in Manchester in 1858 that the custom finally disappeared. Programmes were long and varied with symphonies and popular songs often appearing next to one another. For a full-dress concert in 1845, the Liverpool Philharmonic Society (then in its sixth season) engaged a comic singer and a silver saxhorn band to share the stage with the great violinist, Vieuxtemps, but it was an experiment that was not repeated. Some pertinent remarks about concerts and concert-goers were made by the critic of the *Manchester Examiner* in August 1850:

> The concert of Wednesday evening was what is generally termed 'undress', which means that people who have a love for music, and who attend a concert for the musical enjoyment it affords, rather than the opportunity for gossip and personal exhibition, are permitted to make their appearance in such costume as their taste may dictate without being limited to the peculiar cut of a coat or the form of head-dress. Formerly on such occasions the performance was little better than a rehearsal, but the 'march of intellect' having reached our aristocratic circles, good sense has prompted something better. The 'undress' concerts are putting forth legitimate attraction, and the result is found in the very large and increasing audiences. It is on these occasions that the directors venture upon the performance of a symphony in its completeness, and the forty minutes bestowed upon a production of this order on Wednesday, along with the improved attention by which it was received, show the judicious courage of those in authority as well as the increasing taste of the subscribers. An occasional indication of *ennui* or a light effort at a word or two touching matters not exactly in accordance with the subject can be generously overlooked when we observe such a predisposition to be pleased: the true enjoyment will follow upon the right education of the feelings and taste which such opportunities present. It will come if those who direct have only the energy and courage to persevere in the right direction.

An advertisement promoting the first visit to Manchester of the celebrated soprano, Jenny Lind—the 'Swedish nightingale'.

The concert began with a symphony by Haydn and a song, 'I love the merry sunshine', after which came several movements from Beethoven's Septet. The next item was another song, 'Rose softly blooming' and the first half ended with Weber's overture *Preciosa*. The works in the second half were Beethoven's Seventh Symphony, 'The Mermaids Song' from *Oberon*, a fantasia for oboe on themes from *La Sonnambula*, a ballad, 'I love and I am happy', and the Grand March from Mendelssohn's *Athalie*.

The Manchester Gentlemen's Concerts were started in 1770 by 24 amateur flautists and the Concert Hall opened in 1777, was probably the first in the provinces. The members paid four guineas for twelve concerts and were entitled to take 'ladies and strangers'. In the early years of the century the society introduced much new music, but when Hallé arrived in the city in 1848 standards were not so high, though distinguished soloists (among them Chopin, who was paid £60) were often engaged. Business brought many German families to Manchester and to them the city owes much for the revitalising of its musical life. When the great Art Treasures Exhibition was held at Old Trafford from May to October 1857, an orchestra of 150 was engaged and placed under Hallé's direction. Its success prompted Hallé to form an orchestra of his own.

Of the famous musicians who performed in Lancashire, two—the violinist Paganini and the singer Jenny Lind—deserve special mention if only because they left the voluble journalists of the county utterly at a loss for adequate words. Paganini visited several towns in 1832 and achieved the singular distinction of having public houses at Blackburn, Bolton and Manchester named after him. The *Liverpool Mercury* said of him: 'He combines the energy of a giant with the delicacy of a fairy; and if Orpheus or Amphion equalled him (which they most assuredly did not), we should almost cease to regard their recorded exploits as mere fables.'

Music lovers in Manchester and for many miles around became tremendously excited when it was learned that Jenny Lind had been engaged to sing at the Theatre Royal in 1847. 'In preparation for the visit . . . the theatre has undergone a thorough cleansing,' said the *Manchester Guardian*, of 28 August. The building was painted and coconut matting was put down in the entrance hall. Extra lights were fitted, the saloons were carpeted, the seats were refurbished and new scenes were painted. Regulations drawn up by the mayor to prevent carriages causing obstructions were displayed outside the theatre well before the opening night and the East Lancashire Railway Company announced that 'a special train of first-class carriages will leave Salford for Bury, Rawtenstall and all intermediate stations twenty minutes after the close of each performance.' Mlle. Lind sang Maria in Donizetti's *The Daughter of the Regiment* and Amina in Bellini's *La Sonnambula*. The prices ranged from 5s. for a seat in the gallery to £1 11s. 6d. for one in the dress circle. The visit was enormously successful and one city shopekeeper took the opportunity of displaying in his window the bed occupied by Mlle. Lind in *La Sonnambula*. His claim that it was 'an immense attraction' was probably correct.

8. *Sports and Wagers*

After the passing of the Ten Hours Act in 1847, the Rossendale cotton spinner Moses Heap noted in his diary: 'For a while we did not know how to pass our time away. Before, it had been all bed and work; now, in place of 70 hours a week we had 55½ hours. It became a practice, mostly on Saturdays, to play games, especially football and cricket, which had never been done before.' The Act hastened the movement away from traditional amusements towards the organised sports of modern times; and many Lancashire men who watched league football and cricket in old age remembered the barbarities of the kind seen at Halshaw Moor Wakes, Farnworth, first held in 1827, and described by Simeon Dyson as:

> . . . a saturnalia with bull-baiting, badger-baiting, dog fighting, foot racing in almost a state of nudity, grinning through a horse collar, eating a dishful of scalding porridge with bare hands, and often the more disgusting exhibition of eating a pound of tallow candles and stripping the wicks through the teeth for wagers.

Though sports and pastimes changed dramatically during the nineteenth century there was no decline in wagering. The Oldham diarist William Rowbottom records that in June 1808 the church bellringers of the town won twenty guineas in a contest against their opposite number from Ashton-under-Lyne, and that in August 1811, Colonel John Lees of the Oldham Militia and William Clegg, Esq, ran in a field near the Pack Horse, Failsworth, 'for a certain quantity of dinners and a certain amount of wine.' The colonel won. Near Liverpool in 1822, John Townshend won a £30 bet by walking backwards thirty eight miles in twelve hours, 'an arduous task', said the *Preston Chronicle* of 11 May, 'which he won in great style amidst the acclamations of a great number of spectators.' Another noted pedestrian was Jack Isherwood, the itinerant Bolton orange merchant, who seems to have lost more wagers than he won. In May 1835, Jack, who had a wooden leg, was watched by 'some thousands of spectators' as he tried to walk four miles an hour. He failed by six minutes and was so distressed that 'he required two persons to assist him home.' In October of the same year, Jack took part in what the *Bolton Chronicle* called 'The wooden-legged pedestrian match.'

> The much-talked-of match between 'Peg-leg' Jack, the noted orange merchant of this town, and Joe Whittle of Tottington, who also rejoices in a wooden understanding, to walk four miles for £10 a side on the Chorley New-road came off on Tuesday forenoon. Notwithstanding the unfavourable state of the weather there

was a considerable number to witness the novel match. Of no less than 3,000 who brazed the 'piling of the pitiless storm' were upwards of 30 of the 'timber-toed' fraternity, the majority of whom had thrown a leg at the enemies of old England. At ten minutes to eleven o'clock the competitors for pedestrian honours started with betting at 2 to 1 in favour of the Tottington cove, he being only in his 28th year, while Jack had the snows of 51 winters on his head. The youngster covered the first mile in 16 minutes ten second, being 80 yards in advance of his antagonist. The second mile he performed in 16 minutes 20 seconds, the third in 16 minutes 35 seconds and the last mile in 16 minutes 55 seconds, completing the four miles in one hour six minutes. Jack persevered to the end, but was one hour and ten minutes in covering the ground and was beaten by nearly a quarter of a mile.

Bolton people saw another curious incident in September 1841 when Thomas Horsefall, a young man from Ashton, undertook for a wager to gather 50 peas one yard apart, run a mile with a hoop, run half a mile in a sack, walk a mile and run a mile within an hour. He completed his task in a field near Deane Church in only 35¾ minutes.

We have referred elsewhere to the fights and kicking matches that were once so common in Lancashire. Hardly less revolting were the frequent feats of gormandising for which Haslingden gained the un–doubted supremacy. What other town could have found a man to match the appetite (or the stomach) of James Isherwood, a publican, who in 1827, accepted a challenge to eat twenty raw hen eggs and their shells in a quarter of an hour? 'The terms of the wager,' said the *Blackburn Mail*, 'were, that if he won, the company were to pay for the eggs and a quart of ale for himself; if he lost he was to pay for the eggs and a gallon of ale for the Company.' To the dismay of the watchers, Isherwood finished in seven minutes. The account adds, 'The eggs were to have been duck eggs, but none could be produced.' Four years later an astonishing news item reached the editor of the *Bolton Chronicle*, but, as he observed later, 'it appeared so extraordinary that we could not place any belief on it.' Inquiries, however, showed that another gormandiser was at large in Haslingden, 'For a trifling wager,' said the report,

> The man ate three pounds of thick porridge, one quart of water, one pint of milk, one quart of small drink, two oat cakes; next nine pounds of cowhead without bone, four quarts of water, one quart of ale and three oat cakes very cleverly. After this he said he would like a dozen penny pies, of which he ate seven, when he gave it up. He is a pauper in a Haslingden workhouse, and when he rose the following morning he wanted to repeat the dose. It is computed that the whole weighed 32 or 33 pounds.

No one quite equalled this intake, but Haslingden men continued to back their appetites. In 1866, a resident of the Grane district accepted a challenge to devour two pounds of mutton suet and adjourned to a public house to make the attempt. Unfortunately he bit off more than he could chew, and a newspaper report says, 'On demolishing about three-quarters of a pound the undertaking was abandoned.' But it adds, 'We understand that if it had been beef suet the feat would have been accomplished.' The following week the Haslingden eaters were in the news again. At the Wellington Inn, Grane, says a report, 'a volunteer undertook to eat a 4lb pudding composed of one pound of flour, one pound of suet, a 'quartern' of currants and one and three quarters pounds of milk and *aqua pura* absorbed in kneading and boiling. an eye witness informs us that the operator's jaws were brought to a dead lock on eating three quarters of the pudding.'

The opening of the railway in 1848 brought new opportunities for the Haslingden gamblers. Soon they were gathering on the bridges over the line to make wagers on the number of carriages each train would have; and when a leaping match was held in the town in 1852, large numbers came by rail to see a young man from Blackburn beat a rival from Radcliffe Bridge by 'clearing 25 yards in six rises.'

Though a cricket club was formed at Manchester in 1818, it was not until the 1830s that the game gained wide popularity in

GORTON WAKES

Will commence on SUNDAY the 5th of September, 1824, and continue the Five following Days.

AT THE SIGN OF THE

THE PLOUGH,

At Four Lane Ends, centre of Gorton, which commands a pleasant View of the Townships, the Public are respectfully informed, that they will meet with the best of Spirits, Beer and Porter, and where there will also be the greatest Variety of Entertainment and Diversion.

The Sport will commence on Monday, and continue on Tuesday and Wednesday, with

COCK FIGHTING,

Between HEAP and MARLAND, Esqrs. There will be 11 Battles on Monday, 9 on Tuesday and 7 on Wednesday, for 5 Guineas a Battle, £100 the Main ; to commence fighting each day at 10 o'clock.—Pit Money 6d. each. GILLIVER and RALING, Feeders.

Also on MONDAY a good

SILVER CUP

Value Twenty Pounds, or thereabouts, to be Run for, by Horses of all Descriptions, Three to start or no Race. Entrance Money to be paid to Stewards, between one and two o'clock, to be heats.

Tuesday's Diversion.

A TROTTING MATCH

For a PURSE of GOLD—No Mare or Gelding barred out.

Also a good fat PIG to be Run for.

Persons of all descriptions are entitled to run—the Pig weighs no more than 20 score—Heats.

And a Purse of Silver to be Run for

By Boys under 14 years of Age—Heats—To be Run for between the Horse Heats.

WEDNESDAY.

A Capital Pig to be Run for by Persons same as Tuesday,

But it shall be put to the Stewards whether the full blood animals be discharged or not from this Race at the time of running.

Also a QUOITING MATCH for a good Leg of Mutton ; DUMPLING EATING for a Purse of Silver ; APPLE DIVING by Boys, for a Purse of Silver ; WHEELBARROW RACE ; DUCK SWIMMING, &c. &c.

THURSDAY.

PRISON BAR PLAY for a Hogshead of Good Old Beer. A Purse of Silver is given by the Mayor of the Township to the best Fiddler that attends the Wakes.

Also a RACE by Ladies of description, for a good Holland Smock. Three to start or no Race—the second is entitled to a sash, given by the Stewards.

On FRIDAY

A general TEA DRINKING.

To commence Tea Drinking at Four o'clock in the Evening. After the Tea Drinking, the first Dance will be Widow and Widower, for a handsome sash ; Second Dance by Youths, for a Gold Ring, for Matrimony. Prizes for every Dance afterwards, such as Ribbons, White Gloves, &c.

Music will attend at the Plough during the Wakes.

Gentlemen are desired to keep their Dogs at home. No person allowed to run without Drawers

All disputes to be decided by the Stewards. Plays, &c. every evening as usual.

JAMES KNOTT, Esqrs. } Stewards
JOHN CHORLTON, Esqrs.
THOMAS BARNS, Clerk of the Course.

Printed by W. D. VAREY, corner of St Ann's square Manchester

Lancashire. Thereafter it provided a source of pleasure that increased steadily throughout the century. When Burnley played Preston on Burnley's new ground in July 1833, the *Blackburn Alfred* noted:

> The novelty of a cricket match in this neighbourhood drew together a large concourse of spectators, and the day proving auspicious, gave the fair sex the opportunity of observing this manly game.

The rules of the Preston New Cricket Club, founded in 1837, laid down that the uniform 'shall be blue cap, white flannel jacket trimmed with blue, belt of naval blue leather 2¼ inches wide, and white trousers.' Any player who failed to turn out in this way was fined 1s., and if the club lost, all the members paid 6d. each into the club funds.

The first cricket match at Bolton, in June 1839, was played for a new ball in a field at Tonge, where 'a numerous party of ladies and gentlemen' saw the Independent Club beat Bolton CC 'with eight men to spare.' 'The contest,' says one account, 'was well sustained, though it is stated that several members of the Bolton Club appeared to be deficient in muscular energy.' Another paper reported that 'The only 'bars' to the hilarity of the day were three black eyes produced by three stray balls.'

Enthusiasm for cricket was very great at Blackburn and on one occasion was manifested in the middle of winter. The *Blackburn Standard* of 2 February 1848, carried the following item:

> On Friday afternoon last a very novel cricket match was played upon the ice at Rishton Reservoir, near this town, by two elevens of the Blackburn club—all the players wearing skates. Mr Wardle and Mr P. Heavyside having chosen each a side and the wickets being pitched upon the best piece of ground, or rather the most slippery piece of ice that could be found, the game commenced and was closely contested, one side gaining their victory by only six runs. The players being in skates, it was a matter of no little difficulty for the best of them to keep upon their feet through every stage of the game and no small amusement was afforded to the bystanders by some of the unlucky ones, ever and anon, suddenly exchanging the perpendicular for the horizontal position. The playing, however, on the whole, was remarkably good (especially the batting), and the approach of night alone put an end to the game. Mr Wardle and party scored 102 runs and Mr Heavyside and party 96 runs.

The rules of the Haslingden Cricket Club, which was founded in 1853, forbade wagering, 'however trivial,' and said the players should restrict themselves 'to the honour got.' By another rule, a fielder lying down or smoking during a game was fined 6d. Club cricket was still very much a game for gentlemen and at Haslingden it was some time before members of the working class were selected to play, though they were permitted to field and bowl during practice. As a boy, in the 1860s, the Lancashire and England player R. G. Barlow used to earn 2d. or 3d. for fielding out at Tong Moor for the 'Bolton Gents,' whose professional 'often bowled in clogs.'

The year 1868 was particularly memorable for Lancashire cricket. The All-England XI visited several towns to take on twenty two local players at a time and there was a tour by the Australian Aboriginals, who made up for what they lacked in cricketing ability by a dazzling display of native sports. The team was captained by Charles Lawrence, the Surrey all-rounder, who went to Australia with the first English team in 1862 and stayed to coach in Sydney. The Aboriginals, who were known by such nick names as Tiger, Red Cap and Two Penny, undertook a long and arduous tour that went on until late October. Seven games were played in Lancashire—versus Longsight (twice), versus Bootle at Liverpool (twice), versus East Lancashire at Blackburn, versus the Bury and Vulcan United Clubs at Bury and versus Rochdale. 'The coloured handlers of the willow,' as the *Rochdale Observer* called them, made a favourable impression, though most of the bowling and run-scoring was left to Lawrence and three or four others. The rest came into their own when they exchanged their white flannels and red shirts for the possum skins in which they demonstrated Aboriginal skills. Spear-throwing was usually the first item and sometimes brought an unexpected touch of drama. At Blackburn 'Charley, much to the suspense of the spectators, threw one of the spears out of the grounds of the club and a considerable distance over the wall.' After a sham fight with spears, the Aboriginals showed their skill with boomerangs, some of which, said the *Blackburn Standard*, were thrown so high 'as to be scarcely visible.' On a windy day at Liverpool a boomerang sliced a spectator's hat and cut his face, and at Rochdale a small boy was injured when a man in the crowd imprudently tried his hand, but these seem to have been the only mishaps. The native sports always ended with Dick-a-Dick 'dodging the cricket balls.'

> This [said the *Blackburn Standard*] consisted in the gentlemen allowing himself to be pelted with cricket balls by any thrower and the 'dodging' was accomplished in keeping them off by means of a boomerang in one hand and a rude wooden shield in the other. Several gentlemen tried very hard to hit Dick-a-Dick, sometimes standing very near to him, but were in every case unsuccessful, the quick eye and ready hand of 'the dark-skinned brother' being always equal to the occasion.

Working men were now beginning to form clubs of their own, often in the face of considerable difficulties. The dyers, finishers and bleachers

The County cricket ground, Old Trafford, by H. E. Tidmarsh, from *Manchester Old and New*, volume 3.

who started the Thornham Club at Middleton in 1868, played their first games on a 'ground' twenty six yards by twelve yards which had a brook flowing along one side. The captain who won the toss decided not only which team batted first, but also where the wickets were pitched. One final incident from the 1868 season will serve to illustrate this evolutionary period of the game. In September, the Bacup First XI using broomsticks beat the Second XI using bats by 25 runs to 19. Between the innings the players gave a gymnastic display for which a brass band provided a musical background. In the 1870s, a group of Rochdale tradesmen formed the Early Risers' Club. Matches began at 5 or 5.30 a.m. and were played over two mornings before work.

The 1860s saw the birth of a number of Lancashire athletics clubs, which cultivated many old sports and sponsored several new ones. At the open day of the Haslingden club in 1869, some 8,000 people, including 'a number of fashionably-dressed ladies and gentlemen,' watched pole leaping, running, performances on the horizontal bars, trotting matches and bicycle and velocipede racing. Great interest was taken in the velocipedes, which a reporter described as 'novel machines of various builds.' Most of the 'jockeys,' he added, 'managed their iron steeds with great skill and the pace at which they travelled over the grass, notwithstanding the inequalities of the ground, seemed to surprise most people.' Among the entries were two four-wheel machines with two riders each. The introduction of these pioneer machines was greeted with wonder and admiration by young and old alike, and the Haslingden historian Major David Halstead has described how scores of tacklers, wheelwrights, engineers and others, many of whom had spent years in

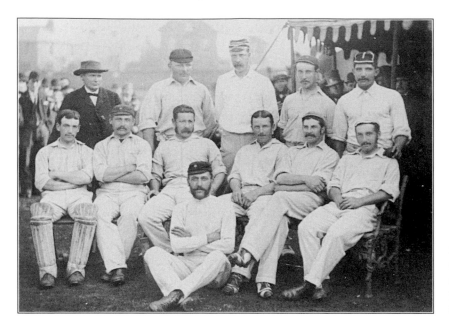

East Lancashire
cricket team, 1860
(Blackburn Library
Local Studies
Collection).

the pursuit of perpetual motion, tried their hands at making them. Two
ambitious brothers named Patterson constructed a tricycle with a front
wheel 7ft. 6in. in diameter and the rear wheels about a foot less. The
machine, known as Pattersons' Elephant, accommodated eight passengers seated in two rows, one above the other behind the steerer. It
got out of control while descending the hill into Accrington, ran into
a house and was not repaired. Another inventor, Richard Barnes ('Dicky
Brush') built a four-wheeler:

> The wheels [said Major Halstead] were of wood, both felloes and
> spokes, and they would be about 45 inches in diameter. There were
> two crank shafts, and the machine carried four passengers, two pairs
> facing each other; and I think all four took part in producing the
> power to push wooden levers backwards and forwards about eight
> or nine inches. How the steering was done was a mystery to me.

One day the machine ran into a sand hole at Baxenden, and though
Barnes managed to extricate it and push it homewards, it disintegrated
at Acre, 'spokes, felloes, hoops and ironwork lying all over the roadway.'
A monocycle was constructed by a workman at a Haslingden saw-mill,
but its inventor was unable to avoid steering it into an eight-foot pit
in the wood yard.

The Haslingden inventors were not alone in their misfortune; and
no account of cycling in Lancashire would be complete without the
sad story of the tricycle made by a Mr Parkinson and a Mr Matthews
of Clitheroe. For more than a year they worked on their machine
until it finally emerged from their workshop on the evening of 5

November 1860. The tricycle had long been the talk of the town, and in the words of the local historian Stephen Clarke, 'hundreds, if not thousands, turned out to see this new-fangled machine' which was propelled by an arrangement of cranks and levers. The two men, who mounted the tricycle at the Castle gates, announced that they would travel through Chatburn to Sawley and because darkness had come on, they attached lamps with candles to the framework. All went well for a hundred yards or so, they on the steep gradient of Castle Street the inventors realised too late that they had overlooked the need for a brake.

> The machine [says Clarke] rushed madly down the Market Place and with battering ram-like force collided with the Dun Horse corner . . . Amid cheers and merry laughter, the inventors picked up their machine and pushed it back to their quarters. After several years it was dismantled and the wheels were used for a fishmonger's hand cart.

9. Sam Scott and 'Steeple Jack'

Two of the most extraordinary entertainers of the nineteenth century made the industrial landmarks of Lancashire their stage and performed feats of daring that have never been repeated. The American Sam Scott jumped from tall warehouses and 'Steeple Jack' gave 'high-wire' displays from factory chimneys. Scott arrived in Manchester in December 1837 and announced that he would jump into the Irwell from the highest building on its banks. He decided on a five-storey warehouse opposite the New Bailey, and watched by an immense crowd appeared on the roof 'attired in lace drawers and a red flannel shirt and a bladder drawn over the scalp.'

> He ran over the slates with surprising intrepidity and after making a short address to the spectators expressing of his hope that he should be encouraged with their liberal pecuniary contributions when he came out of the water, he made a spring into the river below. He presented an erect position during the time that he was in the air, waving his arms as if to break the fall and with his legs and arms slightly separated from each other. In a few moments he entered the water with a terrific force and almost immediately emerged with several small stones in his hands which he had grasped from the bottom, and swam to the opposite beach without having suffered any apparent inconvenience. The river was much swollen by recent rains, but the water could not have been more than 12

feet deep. A considerable sum was collected on his behalf and a second descent was announced for half past two o'clock. At that time the crowd was even greater than before, and after some preliminaries Scott again fulfilled his pledge, causing them greater astonishment by diving head foremost into the water. He ascended to the surface as quickly as on the former occasion and again swam over admist the cheers of the assembled multitude.

From Manchester, Sam went to Bolton, where another huge crowd gathered to see him jump into the canal from the warehouse of the Old Quay Company.

Just as he was preparing himself for the leap [said the *Bolton Chronicle* of 13 January] the police arrived and desired him to come down. Sam replied, 'Oh, yes, I'm coming,' and suiting the occasion to the words, leapt into the water, but was not allowed to ascend again. Sam's principal feat, collecting money, did not take as it appears to have done elsewhere.

A month later, the *Chronicle* reported that 'Sam has now made his most extraordinary jump—from the house of Mr Jones at Warrington to the treadmill at Kirkdale,' but his offence was not stated. Scott was accidentally hanged on Waterloo Bridge, London in January 1841.

'Steeple Jack', the fastest man of his day, probably drew larger crowds than any other entertainer of the nineteenth century. The following

Swainson and Birley's factory, Preston. The scene of Steeple Jack's remarkable demonstrations in April 1853, this great mill was one of the most modern of its time—a huge factory built on a greenfield site on the edge of Preston.

account from the *Preston Chronicle* of 20 April 1853, was written when he was at the height of his powers:

Last evening, the most startling and extraordinary performance of daring feats that has been given in this part of the country during our recollection took place at the 'Big Factory' chimney, Fishwick, in the presence of a larger concourse of gratified spectators than ever assembled in the neighbourhood before. The performer was James Duncan Wright, the renowed 'Steeple Jack', the scene of whose unique exhibition was Common Bank Valley, his stage a rope fastened to the top of Messrs. Swainson and Birley's lofty chimney, and stretching out to the extent of 500 yards in the vale below, and his audience 15,000 inhabitants of Preston and the neighbourhood. A colour was waving from the factory, while on the summit of the chimney another flag flaunted in the passing breeze, and on the ground were two bands of music and two pieces of cannon; so that the *ensemble* of the affair bore a truly dramatic and novel aspect. Jack, who was attired as a sailor, seemed in excellent spirits; and as soon as the signal was given by the discharge of the guns, he swiftly ascended the chimney, and very soon landed at the top. He there speedily affixed a pulley to the rope with which was connected a sort of handle, which acts, when pressed to the cord, with the same effect as a brake to a railway train, and to which, moreover, was attached the seat in which Jack makes all his aerial flights. Having firmly ensconced himself in the seat, our hero fearlessly commenced the terrible descent amid the cheers of the dense and serried mass of spectators. As swiftly as the arrow did he traverse the rope, which is some hundreds of yards high, and coolly stopped midway, where he fired one barrel of a revolver pistol. He then quietly resumed his mid-air journey, suspended over a dread abyss, but 'bating not a jot of heart or hope', he left the chimney looming in the distance behind, and soon rejoined the cheering crowd on firm earth. The next feat was one which surpasses all power of description, but must be seen to be properly comprehended. Jack actually traversed the rope in the manner above detailed in the marvellously short space of time of ten seconds! He fixed the cord in a more perpendicular positon, the signal was given, off went his airy car, a 'whirr' was heard as the pulley revolved with lightning velocity upon the rope, all was intense and breathless excitement among the people—Jack has travelled 500 yards in ten seconds, and arrived safe and sound amid the heartly applause of those assembled! Jack afterwards re-ascended the chimney, where he sent up some fireworks, and stood amid a blaze of fire of dazzling splendour.

New Men

AY 7 1868, was one of the most re-markable days in the history of Lanca-shire. It was a Thursday when the shops and mills of Darwen were closed and when the whole town turned out to see the Marquis of Hartington open an art exhibition in a cotton mill. 'The inauguration of such an exhibition in one of our energetic and industrious East Lancashire towns,' said the *Blackburn Times*, 'is like the turning over of a new leaf and the commencement of a new era in its social history.' The very idea of whole trainloads of people flocking to a mill—even the magnificent India Mill—to look at some of the world's best paintings would have seemed preposterous twenty years earlier and would have been pure fantasy to the grandparents of many who visited the exhibition. Change had been rapid, however, and as early as 1846, John Graham had noted in his history of calico printing:

> Darwen is the most improved place I have visited. In 1812 the village consisted of one short, crooked, narrow street, set without rule or order, and was supported by the then flourishing print works and weaving calico by hand. The inhabitants were the most filthy, drunken blackguards in Lancashire. Now there are flourishing cotton mills and some hundreds of cottages far superior to the old, and a clean, orderly and, I believe, intelligent people. There formerly used to be one small old church and a chapel without a school. There are now two churches and other places of worship.

The transformation epitomised in the above passage left Lancashire poised and determined to enlarge and add to the achievements of the turbulent half century; and by 1868, W.A. Abram, the East Lancashire journalist and historian, was able to write in the *Fortnightly Review*:

> Socially, the condition of the factory labourers has been vastly ameliorated within the last quarter of a century. My first recollections of the factory people of Lancashire date from the year 1843, when I was resident in a manufacturing village on the eastern border of the county. I have often watched the factories 'loosing', to use a local phrase, towards eight o'clock in the evening and noticed how

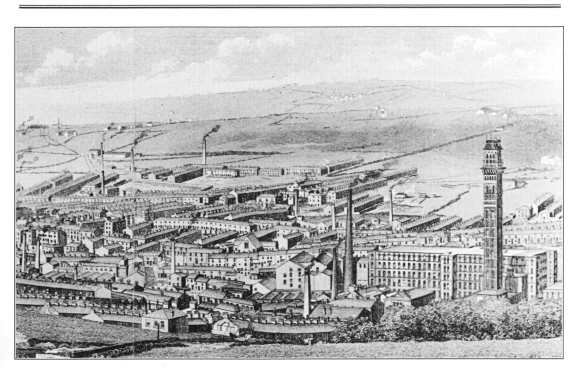

The centre of Darwen, with the India Mill on the right, from J. G. Shaw, *Darwen and its People* (1889). This view of the town, nestling in its valley between moorland ridges, typifies the Pennine industrial community—at least eighteen tall chimneys are visible, even in this picture, and these, with the great bulk of the mill buildings and the long rows of terraced housing, summarise so many the key ingredients of a landscape now largely gone.

the poor jaded wretches—men, women and children, who had been kept incessantly at work, with the briefest intervals for meals devoured hastily in the rooms, from five o'clock in the morning—dragged their limbs wearily up the steep hill to their homes. These miserable objects, many of them grievously deformed in frame, their skins and clothing smeared with oil and grime, the young among them sickly and wan, the middle-aged prematurely broken down and decrepit, and all so evidently dejected in spirit, seemed to my young eyes the very embodiments of hopelessness . . . It was no wonder if these disagreeable impressions led one to consider the old factory system as a system of galling and grinding slavery. The Hours of Labour in Factories Act, passed in 1844, and materially amended in 1847 and 1856, worked a thorough reform. Its beneficial effects upon the population cannot be exaggerated. The excessive hours of labour (twelve to thirteen hours daily for adults and children alike) have been legally reduced to ten hours per day, and females and young persons of both sexes are protected against the pernicious encroachments upon their meal-times which were formerly so flagrant. The Saturday half holiday is now universal. Wages, so far from being diminished by the shortening of the period of labour, have—thanks mainly to accelerated machinery and improved working—largely increased. Moreover, the short-time system of juvenile labour guarantees a certain elementary education to the operative's child. In many other directions marked progress has been made. The low, dark, noisome rooms in which the manufacturing processes were formerly carried on, have been replaced by vast sheds, lighted from the roof, for the weaving branch, and by lofty, large, and well-ventilated chambers for spinning and preparatory processes. A new cotton mill of the first class is a model of spaciousness and convenience. Outside the mill, too, the operative is not uncared for. The lavish provision of public parks, pleasure grounds, baths and free libraries in all the larger Lancashire towns, testifies that the corporate authorities are not unmindful of their obligations to promote the health, happiness and culture of the industrial orders.

The effect of these changes upon both the moral and physical condition of the operatives is most apparent. Far seldomer than of yore do we hear the murmur of popular discontent. Sickness and mortality have been reduced to an extent that is almost incredible . . . The young men and maidens employed in the mills are now as robust as the families of the indolent classes.

Abram was editor of the *Blackburn Times* in 1868 and almost certainly wrote the account of the Darwen Exhibition. In it he said: 'No one can charge us hereabouts with mental sluggishness and physical lassitude, [but] in our eager application to industrial pursuits we have left the nobler half of our natures uncared for. What we are most deficient in is culture.' The exhibition, which was organised to raise money for a new school, showed a true Lancashire resolve to make good the deficiency, and it may also be seen as symbolising the ideal of intellectual progress which came increasingly to inspire the new generation. Darwen on that superbly beautiful May morning would have impressed an Athenian from the time of Pericles. The day was observed as a general holiday. Flags and banners fluttered from mills, shops and houses; the bands of the Local Volunteers and the Temperance Society paraded the streets from an early hour; the great crowds of people gave the town a festive air.

The appointed hour for the inauguration was twelve o'clock, but from ten o'clock a continuous stream of visitors poured into the building and many of them began to take their seats in the nave. Outside the exhibition building the scene was one of much animation. Thousands of persons had gathered in the vicinity of the edifice to watch the arrival of the visitors. These spectators were mostly congregated on the steep slope between the Bolton Road and the India Mill, which overlooks the winding drive to the entrance corridors, and the spacious terrace to the left. This terrace was fringed with evergreens for the occasion, and upon it the visitors paraded and the local corps of the Volunteer Rifles performed its evolutions. The throngs of spectators, the succession of carriages, the radiant countenances and costumes of the lady visitors and the groups of scarlet-coated volunteers made up a pretty and harmonious picture. And in the centre of the scene the glorious campanile shot up grandly 300 feet into the air, dwarfing with its magnitude and shaming with its architectural beauty and fair proportions the by no means contemptible chimney shafts of ordinary construction surrounding it.

Three floors of the mill, some 27,000 square feet, were used for the exhibition which included almost 1,000 pictures and numerous *objets d'art* from private collections. Oil paintings by Van Dyke, Claude, Dürer, Teniers and other old masters were among the works on view and there was a collection of watercolours considered by the *Manchester Guardian* the equal of any displayed at the Royal Academy.

Thousands of people visited the exhibition during the succeeding weeks, and as one pictures the crowds moving through the great mill, one is reminded of Karl Marx's description of the industrial workers as 'new-fangled men who are as much the invention of modern times as the machinery itself.' In the hundred years which followed the introduction of the spinning jenny, Lancashire had changed its ways, its outlook and its appearance almost beyond recognition. It had also changed the course of history.

Index